A MAN CALLED HARRIS

A MAN CALLED HARRIS

THE LIFE OF RICHARD HARRIS

Michael Sheridan and Anthony Galvin

The History Press

2013 is the 50th anniversary of *This Sporting Life* in which Richard Harris arguably played his greatest role. His portrayal of rugby league player Frank Machin got a BAFTA nomination for Best Actor, won the Cannes Film Festival Award for Best Actor and got an Academy Award nomination for Best Actor.

But thy eternal summer shall not fade,
Nor lose possession of that fair thou ow'st,
Nor shall death brag thou wander'st in his shade
When in eternal lines to time thou grow'st:
So long as men can breathe or eyes can see,
So long lives this, and this gives life to thee.

Shakespeare, *Sonnet 18*

First published 2013

The History Press
The Mill, Brimscombe Port
Stroud, Gloucestershire, GL5 2QG
www.thehistorypress.co.uk

© Michael Sheridan and Anthony Galvin, 2013

The right of Michael Sheridan and Anthony Galvin to be identified as the Authors of this work has been asserted in accordance with the Copyright, Designs and Patents Act 1988.

British Library Cataloguing in Publication Data.
A catalogue record for this book is available from the British Library.

ISBN 978 0 7524 8898 1

Typesetting and origination by The History Press
Printed in Great Britain

CONTENTS

PROLOGUE

As the years passed, Richard Harris looked back on his childhood with a special fondness. Nowhere was as special for him as Kilkee, County Clare, where he had passed so many happy summer days. It was his Mecca, his Eden, and the place from where he set out on his journey to conquer Hollywood. It was no surprise that he kept returning there.

He came back most summers in his early days, and when he began to do well, he decided to buy a house in the resort. He purchased a place on his beloved West End, a big old Victorian terraced house called The Billows. It was a spectacular end-of-terrace two-storey building, one of the most elegant on the seafront. The house had an unusual side-by-side pair of double bay windows, with spectacular beach and bay views. It retained many of its period features, including high ceilings, and had six rooms.

Harris made the purchase in 1969, at the peak of his fame. Money was rolling in and he could afford to splash out on his new indulgence. He refurbished the house to the highest specifications, making it one of the most desirable residences in Kilkee.

His friend Manuel Di Lucia, an auctioneer and restaurateur, remembers the purchase well: 'He bought the house for £7,000, then spent £22,000 on doing it up.' That was a staggering amount in the late 1960s, the equivalent today of spending perhaps half a million on renovations alone. Although Harris was in the process of divorcing his first wife, Elizabeth, she had a big say in the design of the new home. He also consulted his sister, Harmay. Little did he suspect that she would be dead within a year, and would never see the project to completion.

Much of the furniture and fittings were brought over to Ireland from London, and only the best was considered. 'It was done up by his wife Elizabeth and his sister Harmay,' recalled Di Lucia. 'It was a mansion. It was the first house I ever saw with gold taps and bathroom fittings.'

Limerick man Vincent Finucane, who had played rugby with Harris at Crescent College, got the job of doing the electrical refitting of the old house. 'I got a contract below in Kilkee to do up his house for him. He had electric storage heating before anyone else. He had all the fancy things.' Finucane also remembers something else Harris had back then: 'He had this fancy piece there with him.'

This would have been in 1970, as his marriage with Elizabeth finally imploded, leaving Harris a free agent. He began dating a 17-year-old actress, Linda Hayden. She was with him for the première of *Bloomfield* in Limerick late that year, and also visited Kilkee, where the renovation work was nearing completion.

The house was eventually finished to a very high standard, and should have proved a haven for Harris from the shallowness and falsity of Hollywood, which he rebelled against. But it didn't turn out that way. The idea of buying the getaway had come to him near the end of his marriage. Perhaps he thought of it as a way of saving his family from the looming divorce. It would allow him and his wife and three sons to get away from everything and spend time together. But when the divorce papers were served, that dream was gone. And the other woman in his life, his beloved sister Harmay, fell ill in 1970. She underwent emergency surgery but never recovered.

It was a triple blow – his wife and family had left him, his only remaining sister had died, and his directorial début, *Bloomfield*, had flopped. Harris had dreamed of filming *Hamlet*, with himself in the title role. For a while that looked possible. Then it was unlikely. After *Bloomfield*, it was impossible. As blow followed blow, it was enough to throw Harris into a deep depression. He hit the bottle hard, and moved from shallow relationship to shallow relationship. Life was one long party; it was a vain attempt to block out the pain.

Perhaps this is the reason why Harris never actually occupied the house in Kilkee. The house was part of a dream, and once the dream died his interest in the house died with it. He only ever spent a single night under its roof. He continued to visit Kilkee, but chose to stay in the Hydro Hotel.

'He actually only slept one night in the house,' Di Lucia said. 'That's all. He used to give the house to a children's orphanage in Limerick, a charity, for them to come on holidays to Kilkee.'

Harris had gone off the house. But he had not abandoned the seaside resort. He spent a few weeks in Kilkee in the summer of 1970, staying in the Hydro Hotel. This was a few months before Harmay's death, and before *Bloomfield* opened, so he was still in remarkably good spirits, despite his divorce. He threw himself into life in the small town, as he had in his teens.

'The Tivoli Cup [for racquetball] was playing at that time,' said Di Lucia. 'Dickie was 40 then, and I was 30. He was here for that week. I said that we wanted a bit of an attraction for the tournament, and would he enter? "Ah Jesus," he said, "I'd never be fit enough for that." So we worked it that he wouldn't meet anyone too strong at the beginning. It was manipulated so that he would meet me in the quarter finals.'

That was a clash that would draw out the crowds. Di Lucia was a very popular local man, involved in everything in the small town. Harris was Hollywood royalty – and a four-time previous winner of the racquetball competition.

'We set it up as a personality type of game,' recalls Di Lucia who, being a bit larger than life himself, decided he would upstage Harris.

> There was a pony and trap down on the beach and I got on that with a big towel around me, and a helmet with horns, and I had my racquet up in the air. Here I was, driving across the beach like a warrior coming to battle. Harris was standing by the alleys waiting for me, and he was bursting his sides laughing. He said: 'You would make a grand entrance and upstage me.' I said it wasn't often people managed to do it!

The grand entrance proved to be the best part of Di Lucia's game. Harris was paired with Mary O'Connor, while Di Lucia's partner was a Limerick woman, Ms Kennedy. The beach was thronged for the encounter, and the crowd got what they wanted. It was a very close game, with both sides going point for point and neither managing to dominate. But eventually Hollywood won out.

'He beat me by one point,' grinned Di Lucia. 'He genuinely beat me. Even at that age he was very good. But then he was beaten in the next round, the semi-final.'

It was a great run for a man of 40, who had lived such a hard life.

Victory in the bag, Harris continued to delight the crowd. He had a few A-listers with him on the holiday, but decided to celebrate with the townspeople instead of retiring to his ivory tower.

> When that game was over that day he took us all up to the Hydro. He took us all there, because all these film stars who were with him were there. He had us all on the lawn in front, and he ordered tea, coffees, cakes, biscuits, minerals for the kids, drinks for the adults. There must have been two or three hundred people there. It all went on his bill.

It was typical of Harris's generosity, the sort of big gesture he enjoyed. Only a few years previously, he had done something similar for a crowd outside the town's cinema. 'He came back to Kilkee a few months after he made *This Sporting Life*, and the film was showing in the cinema here,' said Di Lucia. 'There was a big crowd going to it, because it came in the summertime. I was with Dickie, walking down the street, and he saw all the people standing outside the cinema. And he shouted: "I wouldn't go and see that film, it's rubbish, rubbish."

'But what did he do then? He went into the box office and he hired out the entire cinema. He said: "Go in now everybody. It's all on me."'

When there was a crowd, Harris loved to play it up. But on his own, the slings and arrows of outrageous fortune were constantly buffeting him down.

When Harris gave up on his Kilkee home, he asked his lifelong friend Di Lucia to look after the building, as a sort of live-in caretaker.

Dickie came over with a whole lot of people, like Lulu, Maurice Gibb and Honor Blackman. There were a load of other people whom I can't remember. He came to my apartment. Myself and my wife had one kid at the time. And he just walked straight in, opened the door, and sat down and had a cup of tea. We were having breakfast at the time. He asked what we were doing there. I said I had bought a site outside Kilkee, up the hill, and I intended building a house on it. I was waiting for planning permission.

'I'll show you my house and you can move in there while you're waiting,' he said. 'You look after my house, and when I come over you can look after me.'

Harris paid all the bills, and Di Lucia made sure the house was well maintained. Two years later, their arrangement changed.

'Dickie just walked in as usual. We were sitting in the kitchen having lunch, with a fellow diver from the North. We had a load of crawfish and lobsters and crab on the table that we had caught that morning. We were having a feast. "Oh Jesus," he said, "that's fantastic."'

Harris was not on his own that afternoon. Di Lucia invited him and his companion to draw up chairs and dig in.

I said 'sit down there and grab yourself a plate'. He was with a very nice lady – he was separated from Elizabeth at this stage. He was with a woman called Barbara Lord. She was a dancer with Pan's People in London. She since married Robert Powell, the actor, and they have a couple of kids and are very happy.

What Harris said that afternoon changed Di Lucia's life.

'He turned around to me and he said I should open a restaurant.'

He suggested that Di Lucia should take over the bills for the house, and open his restaurant in the beautiful terraced property. For the next few years, that is exactly what Di Lucia did. Eventually, in 1975, Harris sold the house to an Englishman. Di Lucia moved his restaurant to the house he had been building and it remained a Kilkee institution for the next three decades.

Di Lucia is now an auctioneer, and he handled the subsequent sale of Harris's Kilkee dream home. He remained close to the actor, teaching his kids how to swim and snorkel in the Pollock Holes in Kilkee. He also sponsored a trophy for an annual swimming race across the big bay, the swim he had done so often as a teenager. The race is still held every August.

Di Lucia said:

I had great times with him, and enjoyed his company. I loved when he came to Kilkee. With most film stars like that they would walk past you on the street. But if he knew you, he wouldn't. Anybody, it didn't matter who you were. He would stop and talk to you. That's the kind of man he was. He had a lot of fans in Kilkee. But people never bothered him in Kilkee.

Near the end of his life, Harris made one final visit.

'He wasn't in great form because of the Hodgkin's Disease. But he was never tetchy. He was over with his personal assistant, a Danish woman called Danke,' said Di Lucia.

We were drinking down in Scott's Bar. Then he beckoned us out and we jumped into his limousine. He said he wanted to show Danke his Kilkee. We drove around the seafront, and back to the Pollock Holes. We got out of the car there, and he looked out and said: 'This is my favourite place in the world.' And that is why I put up a statue to him back at the Pollock Holes.

The statue commemorating Dickie Harris in his native Limerick is an uninspired image of the actor in the robes of King Arthur. The statue in Kilkee captures the man in the fullness of his physical energy, stretching for the ball during the annual racquets tournament. To unveil it, they managed to get an actor who has inherited Harris's hellraising mantle, his friend and fellow troublemaker Russell Crowe.

Dickie would have appreciated that.

THE MAN/ARTIST

Richard Harris was a giant in stature, personality and presence both on and off the screen. The contradictions of his nature served only to increase his allure. A man who was pursued by the demons of drink, carousing and brawling in public in his early years, he was also an artist of great sensitivity, highly intelligent, a voracious reader and with breathtaking talents that spanned the disciplines of sport, theatre, music, film and writing. In the broad sense he was a warrior capable of plumbing the depths of human behaviour and yet he had an ability to reinvent himself all through his life and career.

Whatever the extent of his human fallibility, through the medium of hard work and vision he was capable of rising above it and defeating his demons. In spite of his achievements and the dubious mantle of fame, he possessed the common touch that endeared him not only to his peers but to ordinary people. There are few whom the authors encountered on this journey that had a bad word to say about Richard Harris.

He had a fierce sense of self-belief and ambition, but with a facility to view success and failure with equal disdain. He never forgot his roots and never neglected them. The same could be said of his family.

All his life, from an early age, he was imbued with a passion for anything he chose to do and a gargantuan appetite for the more dangerous temptations. He possessed a classic Irish artistic temperament – nothing was worth doing in small shovels, only in spades. Quite apart from his acting career, his myriad talents included singer, poet, theatre director and producer. The sport of rugby was an abiding passion all through his life. And at one time he stared a financial abyss in the face and emerged a multi-millionaire.

In any culture he would be considered a Renaissance man, the true depth of his intellect masked by the public face of a carousing clown. Doubtless he had an inclination for reaching the lower depths of behaviour, but that was a curse in his formative acting years that was shared by his contemporaries, among them

Richard Burton, Peter O'Toole and Oliver Reed. For some, the impulse to success is accompanied by the urge to self-destruct – a phenomenon not exclusive to any generation of the creative world.

His early career coincided with a period in both theatre and film that saw the changing of the old guard: the onset of the Swinging Sixties and the less heady but nonetheless indulgent 1970s, in which the icons of the entertainment business were almost expected to indulge in excess of all kinds – sex, drugs, and rock and roll. A hedonistic lifestyle, in fact, may well have been a convention of the times.

Yet it is not exclusive to those times, nor is such a dubious lifestyle exclusive to the theatre and film world. Scott Fitzgerald and Ernest Hemingway were spectacular drunks, as was, on occasion, the genius James Joyce. History proves it is universal.

It was, however, an aspect of Harris's character that inspired neither apologies nor regrets: 'I had the happiest days of my life as a drinker. If I had my life again I'd make all the same mistakes. I would sleep with as many women and drink as much vodka. My regrets would make me seem ungrateful.'

Be that as it may, this statement likely contains disingenuous sentiment, as there are few, if any, great people in any walk of life who could stand over their worst failures. Richard Harris is possibly no different in that regard. What he was able to do with apparent ease, however, was not to dwell on the past or allow negative episodes to get him down.

'The trick is to keep moving. Don't let them get you and don't let them get you down,' he said in relation to the vicissitudes of life. He put it in more metaphorical and philosophical terms during an interview for *Profile* magazine in 1968:

> Keep switching the lights on and off in all the rooms until you find the one where you belong. But for God's sake shake the shackles from your feet and find your pride and dignity. The world owes no one anything and all we owe it is a death.

If this view was rendered meaningless by the offering of a theory, as opposed to practice, it would amount to just another ephemeral quotation, but the evidence of the rollercoaster nature of Harris's career proves that on more than one occasion the actor and the man actually took his own advice.

The question remains to this day: who was he? What formative influences combined to make him who he was? Are the answers provided by his many statements on the subject, or the assessments by others who claimed to have known him well during his life, or by the many people who have encountered him on his relatively long journey?

The one thing that can be said of him is that in the hundreds of interviews that he gave in print and on television he was generally open and honest. He rarely tried to hide anything that would reflect badly on him in terms of behaviour or artistic shortcomings. That in itself is unusual in a profession that has traditionally – and to this day – been firmly rooted in public-relations spin: the snake-like practice of saying something that means nothing. Harris consistently outed himself without any sense of inhibition or apology, even if his memory of his excesses could at times be faulty.

To a great degree he could have been accused of underestimating, in a public sense at least, the true sum of his achievements. In the tradition of his countryman W.B. Yeats, he cast a cold eye on life, and on death. Even his large ego did not demand such obvious supplication. He was too honest at times, but then he could afford to take that position. In his youth he had been his own man, and time and success would not change him.

Harris was the quintessential Limerickman, always an icon and in death a legend. There is a story about the actor in the folklore of the town for every location, street and pub. He is as identifiable with his native place as Joyce was with Dublin. He played with his reputation. He told local reporter Gerry Hannan that he didn't want to go back to Limerick, 'because they hate me there'. When he was assured this was far from the case he went on: 'Okay, they don't hate me. They don't know what to make of me.' This was, of course, a disingenuous statement and somewhat typical of the man. He wanted to be told that he was liked, even though this was beyond argument. He could also be ambivalent about his birthplace, as was many an Irish artist who ended up in exile with a love–hate relationship with their native town and country. Long before James Joyce experienced the cosmopolitan culture of Paris, Rome and Trieste, he found Dublin suffocating and inducing a form of paralysis to a person of artistic temperament.

He had an uneasy but constant relationship with his native city, veering from love to hate and back again. This adversarial relationship with Limerick probably stemmed in part from his lifestyle. Limerick was one of the most conservative cities in Europe. Home for years of the arch-confraternity, a worldwide Catholic organisation run along almost military lines, the religion was deeply rooted in the city. Drink might be tolerated, but little else. Sexual urges were to be (preferably) sublimated in sport, or drowned in alcohol. No wonder rugby was so popular. When the Jesuit order told interviewers that they would rather not be mentioned in connection with the actor, this was what motivated them. Nonetheless, Harris had a personal charm that won over the people of Limerick. During the mid to late 1960s, as his fame grew, he threw himself heavily into a few selected public affairs, including a campaign to get a university for the city.

In 1970 Harris brought *Bloomfield* to Limerick for a charity première in aid of disabled children, which raised £3,500, a very big sum for the time. For some strange reason he got the impression that his home town was not satisfied with the result. In an interview he vented his ire:

> I will never again appear in Ireland. The local newspaper wouldn't cover it, didn't even mention my world premiere – simply because I hadn't got down on my knees

and knelt at the institutional shrine. My sin was simple: I refused to give the newspaper's proprietor the four free seats she wanted. In my book, for charity, nobody gets free seats. That is the mind-set of Limerick. It's either go the way of the pack, or no way at all. I am not and never will be, a pack animal.

Despite his disappointment, it was around this time that he told Hannan he would lecture or fundraise in Limerick if anyone asked him:

There is no understanding and no forgiveness. Ireland is changing all the time. It is merging itself with Europe and reversing from cowed emigration to proud immigration. The theocratic bullying is over. The people are becoming Europeans. There is education, money, freedom. But Limerick still wants to dwell in the nineteenth century. It is stubborn and that's its problem. It can't welcome me, it can't understand me – because it won't give in.

Shortly after this it was proposed in the city council that Harris should be made a Freeman of Limerick. Unfortunately, the proposal was narrowly defeated. One of the chief opponents was from the Fine Gael Party. Seen as the party of the farmers and the wealthy merchants, Fine Gael were staunch conservatives. In spite of Harris's great artistic achievements, he was paying the price for his hellraising image. Ironically, the councillor who spoke so vehemently in the 1970s against Harris being honoured proclaimed himself a great friend of the actor on his death, and heaped glowing praises on him!

When Harris's brother and manager Dermot died in 1986, he complained to Len Dineen about the poor funeral turnout and the absence of the Old Crescent and Garryowen players in particular. Dineen rightly put him in his place, 'Look around you. All the old faces are here. They respect and admire you. It is you who forgets them, not the other way around.'

Despite the strained relationship, Harris overcame his falling out with his native city. He returned regularly, both to see family and old friends, and to catch up with his favourite rugby team. When he was home he was never slow to lend a hand to good causes.

In October 1979, aged almost 50, he was willing to put his life in danger for a good cause, when the Limerick Variety Club persuaded him to take part in a charity horse race. This was the Madhatters Race, and each rider had to pay £100 to compete, with the proceeds going to charity. Many celebrities had been invited, including Angela Rippon, Eamonn Andrews and Terry Wogan. Harris had the guts to take up the challenge and, at a large race meeting in Greenpark, the traditional home of the sport in the county, he saddled up for the final race of the card. He finished well down the field of twenty riders, but thoroughly enjoyed the adulation of the crowd.

Whenever Limerick felt it needed to trot out a famous son, only two men were considered: Harris or Terry Wogan. Wogan was the BBC's top chat-show host and their most popular radio presenter. Like Harris, he had been educated at Crescent College. Unlike Harris, he was a clean-living man, unlikely to provoke controversy. But Harris was always considered the more quintessentially Limerick man, and he lived up to the image abroad of the hard-drinking, fighting Irish.

During the late 1980s a brief trend emerged within the tourism industry of celebrating anniversaries of dubious significance. It began in 1988, when Dublin declared itself 1,000 years old. The Dublin Millennium was a huge commercial success, and encouraged other towns to cash in on the idea. Ennis was next, with a celebration of 800 years in 1990. In 1991 Limerick jumped on the bandwagon. In 1691 the forces of William of Orange had laid siege to the city, bringing to an end the Williamite War in Ireland. The Jacobite supporters were vanquished and the war ended with a treaty, signed in Limerick. The stone on which the treaty was signed is still on prominent display on the riverbank. Limerick decided to celebrate the 300th anniversary of the treaty. The year was called Treaty 300, and everyone who was anyone was pressed to get involved. Richard Harris was an obvious target, but at that time his relationship with Limerick was rocky. Nevertheless, an approach was made.

Gerry Lowe worked for Shannon Development, a government agency tasked with promoting the mid-west region of Ireland, which included Limerick. He was put in charge of the Treaty 300 project. One of his most difficult tasks would be to bring back the irascible actor to the city. He did his best – he fired off faxes, made phone calls, left messages – but soon realised he was getting nowhere.

'It was almost impossible to track him down because he had four home bases – the Regent in New York, the Savoy in London, his residence in the Bahamas, and the Berkeley Court when he was in Ireland,' Lowe told the *Limerick Leader*.

After weeks of failure, Lowe decided to ambush Harris in London, where he was performing in (and directing) Pirandello's *Henry IV*. He waited in the Savoy Hotel for Harris to return there late in the evening. During the subsequent chat, Harris admitted that the great ambition of his life was to become a member of Young Munster Rugby Club. This gave Lowe an idea, and he persuaded the club to offer life membership to Harris in return for his involvement in the Treaty 300 project. 'Getting life membership of Young Munster was the carrot that lured him back,' Lowe confessed.

A date was fixed for the ceremony, but Lowe was taking no chances. He didn't want Harris to go off on one of his legendary skites, so he drove to Dublin and picked the actor up at the Berkeley Court Hotel. His own car was not good enough for such an important mission, so he got a top-of-the-range Toyota from local dealer Tony O'Mara. He arrived at 9 a.m.

When I arrived at the suite, Harris was with his brother-in-law Jackie Donnelly and I was invited to have breakfast while Richard had a shower. But after the shower, he told Jackie that he had no toilet bag for his toiletries. So Jackie suggested that they ring down to the hotel shop for a toilet bag. Up came a young porter with a carrier bag from the shop and in it a selection of toilet bags. Harris picked out each one and asked the prices. The porter listed off £45, £60 and £70 for the range of Gucci bags. Winking over at me and Jackie, Harris stunned the porter by taking the carrier bag and sending back the expensive toilet bags.

On the road to Limerick, conversation was stilted. But as they drove through Portlaoise, about halfway there, they spotted a young woman with her thumb out, hitchhiking.

'Pull over,' said Harris.

The woman was from Castleconnell, just outside Limerick, and once she joined the two men, the conversation flowed. They stopped in Nenagh, about 20 miles from Limerick, and Harris got out of the car. He went into a local chipper and bought three fish and chips, chicken and three Coca-Colas.

They made it to the Young Munster grounds at Greenfields with an hour to spare, and Harris was in his element. He was lionised as Young Munster welcomed him into their fold and their inner sanctums. He was presented with life membership and a club tie. Then it was on to important business – the senior team were playing Greystones, a County Wicklow club.

Harris was given a special seat for the day, a chair in the box honouring legendary player Tom Clifford. It gave him a perfect view of the game, but Harris needed the roar of the crowd and was not happy to be boxed in with the elite. He stepped out among the rugby crowd and was immediately mobbed. He emerged with a big grin on his face.

'Everything went just right, except the result of the game,' Lowe said. Young Munster suffered a shock defeat by Greystones.

In earlier years Harris would have remained until closing time at the clubhouse, drowning his sorrows. But by 1990 he was off the drink; he wasn't even taking an occasional pint. His discipline did not waver. He gave Lowe the nod, and Lowe brought the car around: it was time to retire for the evening. But instead of taking Harris back to Jurys Hotel by Sarsfield Bridge, Harris decided to take a nostalgic tour of the city. Lowe told the *Limerick Leader*:

He first asked to be taken to Cruise's Hotel, which was in its final year before being replaced by the Cruise's Street development. He even peeked into the hotel, where he was recognised immediately by one of the staff. It turned out that Harris knew her mother. Then he asked to go up past his old Crescent College school and when we reached there he decided to go into the Jesuit church. The church was empty, so we knelt in the front pews to say a prayer and Harris looked around the names over the confession boxes and saw the name of a priest who was his boyhood confessor.

Lowe thought they were on the last leg of the journey into the past when they headed for the Ennis Road and Jurys Hotel, but Harris again asked for a detour, this time to his old family home.

When we got there he had a look and then got out and walked up to the door and rang the bell. A woman answered the door and was stunned to see Richard Harris on her doorstep. He explained to the woman and her husband that it had been his home and was invited in. He recognised the changes that had been made, but also familiar things like the fireplace, which was still there. The hosts asked if he would like to look over the rest of the house and it was upstairs that he showed us the back bedroom where he used to sleep. He also showed us the galvanised roof that he used to climb onto from his bedroom window and the tree he would shimmy down for clandestine night-time dates.

There was one final stop: *The Field* was playing in the Savoy, and the two men slipped into the back row. Inevitably the actor was recognised. Local politician Alderman Frank Prendergast was there with his wife. An old friend of Harris's, they spent some time reminiscing. All in all, it had been a very successful day.

The following day Harris had one task left. The organisers had persuaded him to film a brief television commercial for the Treaty 300 celebration. He delivered his piece to camera by the Treaty Stone, then looked at the camera and grinned.

'Tell them Richard Harris sent you,' he told viewers.

Age had softened old enmities, and past grievances were laid to rest. For the remainder of his life – despite not getting the freedom of the city – Harris was a staunch defender of Limerick. However, as the years progressed his visits became less frequent, as his old cronies died off. Only one brother – Ivan – had remained in the city, so family ties no longer drew him home. He did visit Dromoland Castle occasionally, especially around Christmas time, and he came home occasionally for the bigger rugby games.

But he was staunch in his defence of his native place, even becoming embroiled in a very public spat with best-selling Limerick author Frank McCourt, whose book *Angela's Ashes* was seen to be an attack on the city.

The city did eventually try to honour Harris, when the University of Limerick offered him an honorary doctorate. He considered it carefully but decided not to go ahead with the ceremony. He didn't want his name linked to lesser lights, such as McCourt.

He even overcame the antipathy he had always felt towards the *Limerick Leader*, giving an interview to the newspaper in 2001, a year before his death. The reporter,

Iain Dempsey, met him at the Curraghower Bar, overlooking the falls on the river near the centre of town. It was not far from where Harris had first trod the boards in front of actor-manager Anew McMaster in the house of his friend Mick English, and a two-minute walk from where he had lost his virginity.

'The actor, notorious for his hellraising days, was wearing a long, black overcoat, a pair of dirty runners, and ill-fitting baggy trousers, his wild, white mane blowing in the breeze,' Dempsey reported. 'He looked like a dishevelled tramp, sitting on the wall downing a pint of Guinness.'

News editor Eugene Phelan – who had found that Harris could be difficult – had warned Dempsey to be prepared for the worst: 'He'll either invite you to go drinking with him, or he'll tell you to get lost.'

That day, however, Harris was open and affable. He was in town for two days to shoot a documentary for the high-profile American *60 Minutes*. When the topic turned to rugby he became animated, giving out about a recent result. Munster had lost to Stade Français in the semi-final of the Heineken Cup, and he felt they had been robbed by English officials. He also complained about the lack of Munster men on the Lions team. After venting his spleen, he smiled, and invited the reporter and the photographer who was with him to join him for lunch. The monster had been tamed.

Harris was obsessed and driven, both in a personal and professional sense. He had a notoriously short fuse and valued his independence, especially in the film industry, whose controlling moguls demanded obedience from the artists they employed – on the simple basis of paying top dollar. He despised cant, hated poor workmanship and possessed an overwhelming competitive spirit. He did not like the cult of celebrity: 'Actors are not important. Not like Beethoven, or Van Gogh or Francis Bacon.'

At 6ft 2in, broad chested, manly and extremely handsome, Harris was attractive to the opposite sex. His machismo was combined with the sensitivity of a poet, which added to his allure. He was hugely intelligent and oozed charisma.

In his teens Harris was already over 6ft and weighed 14st. He was completely bewitched by rugby, a passion that would last a lifetime. His great ambition was to play for and captain the national team. In 1947, Crescent College, Limerick, met Presentation Cork in the final of the Munster Schools Senior Cup. Harris was on the subs bench for the game, which ended in a draw. Before the replay, one of the pack left school to start a job, and Harris, still only 16, was called in as a replacement. His brother Ivan was also on the side.

The Cork side had a talented fly-half, and Harris and his back-row teammates practised ways to put the lynchpin of that side out of action. When the coach, Fr Guinane, spotted what was going on he called Harris to the sideline. Puffing on a cigarette he said: 'I am utterly appalled; we will win this game by fair means or not at all.' On match day when Presentation Cork came on the pitch the coach had a quiet word with Harris: 'You may continue with your plan,' he said.

For the first time, Crescent won the Munster Schools Senior Cup. Already Harris had made his mark, even in a modest manner, on Irish rugby history.

It is certain that he could have attained great success as a rugby player had he not contracted tuberculosis as a teenager. The ambition to play for his country as expressed in his childhood fantasy, combined with his talent for the game, would have translated dream to reality. But it is equally certain that had that happened then he would not have reached the heights he did in the acting profession.

There is some debate as to just how good a rugby player he was, but it is also true that other players of indifferent talent managed to play for their country. What is not at issue is his passion for the game, which is obvious from his poetry from a very early age. He entered the acting profession relatively late, at 24, and had it been delayed further by an international rugby career it is likely that it would have been beyond his reach.

The young aspiring rugby international's great-grandfather, James Harris, was an entrepreneur whose business empire had grown by 1864 to include Limerick's largest flour mill, a company dock and warehouse at Steamboat Quay and a bakery in Henry Street. James was the tenth child of Richard Harris and his wife Eleanor, born in Wexford. He moved to Limerick and broke the Protestant family tradition by marrying a Catholic, Anne Meehan. The couple had six children, one of them Richard, the grandfather of the actor.

The family home, Hartstonge House, was rambling and richly furnished with its own chapel. James Harris, a fiercely loyal man, remained a lifelong friend with colourful Scots-born textile magnate and ship owner Sir Peter Tait, who was Limerick mayor three times, and in three decades went from rags to riches and back again.

James Harris was a political liberal and, since his marriage, a staunch and devoted Catholic. During the last quarter of the nineteenth century he was elected secretary of the Harbour Board and became a markets trustee and a shareholder of the Limerick Race Company. He was a stakeholder in the Catholic-funded citizens' tugboat *Commodore*, which was in competition with *Privateer*, owned by the Protestant families of Bannatyne, Spaight and Russell. He died in 1895 at 70 years of age.

By the time he died, James had built up a booming business and the family was one of the wealthiest in the town, yet retained the respect of the citizens because of their warmth and decency, which did not set them apart from the less well-off people of the community. When James's son Richard retired in his eighties, his sons Ivan and Billy took over, the former the mills and bakery and the latter the property assets.

But the considerable family inheritance was put under pressure in the late 1920s with the economic effects of the post-war depression and increased competition. Ivan worked very hard, and was involved in the sports of hockey and tennis. He met and fell in love with Mildred Harty, a local beauty from a distinctly unmonied background, or so it appeared. Her fortunes changed when her mother inherited a substantial sum from an aunt.

The couple got married and set up home in a large house with extensive grounds, on the North Circular Road. They had four children, but by the time the fifth, Richard, was born on 1 October 1930, cracks had appeared in the foundation of the business. Up to that point, there were servants in the household, nannies for the children and gardeners. Ivan had extended the empire zealously and there was a chain of flour mills in addition to more than twenty town bakeries.

Ivan could have been accused of over-expansion, but he could not have known that the biggest British flour merchant, Rank, was planning an all-out assault on its competitors – and, in Ireland, the Harris business was a prime target. The deadly weapon to be used was simple cost undercutting. It was a time long before competition and monopoly regulation and there was nothing to stop big businesses destroying weaker competitors, by whatever means.

Prices charged by the Harris business were severely undercut by Rank and the suppliers were enticed away by under-the-counter incentives and higher prices for their produce. Rank could take the hit over the long term but Ivan Harris could not. The threat was somewhat reduced by Ivan's easy-going and unflappable personality and the fact that the Limerick mill and wholesale business continued to thrive for quite a while. While the commercial storm clouds were thickening, the somewhat privileged and idyllic life at Overdale continued apace. But by the end of his life, Ivan Harris had seen his business empire decimated.

It was clear that the Harris clan, whose origins stretched back to Norman times, were not without ambition. Richard Harris would later develop an interest in his genealogy and claim that his behaviour was genetic and his future had been cast five centuries before his birth.

His achievements as an artist on stage, in film, in song and in poem are quite extraordinary and have long been overshadowed by his fondness for social activity, often to extremes, of which he was not always proud but accepted as part of his persona. The latter have been long and boringly documented and the former somewhat consigned to the shadows of his life. It is one of the objectives of this book to redress that balance and take a more detailed look at the formative years of his life in his beloved Limerick and Kilkee.

His personal life has also been minutely documented in print and is only of concern to this book as a thread in the narrative. It is to a large extent a celebration as opposed to a denigration. There have been a host of contributors to the latter position, one that they are quite entitled to adopt in some cases but not all with a degree of justification.

Richard Harris, despite the faults attributed to him – which he was the first to recognise – was a loving and generous man. He loved the family he was born into and the family he had and the women he married. He took his responsibilities in that regard very seriously and strived to maintain good relations with them during his lifetime.

His driven nature was not conducive to a rooted family ethos and he recognised his own failures in this. By his own admission he had great difficulty in his relationships with women, most graphically expressed in his two marriages.

In a superb, wide-ranging interview conducted by Dublin journalist Joe Jackson and published by music magazine *Hot Press* in 1987, Harris talked openly about his two marriages, first to Elizabeth Rees-Williams, with whom he had three children, and later to actress Ann Turkel. (See Appendix.)

I broke up my first marriage because I was totally selfish. The second broke up because I was totally selfless. I did everything, I was like a nurse-maid. I was father, uncle, lover, doctor, psychiatrist, occasional husband, father-confessor in her eyes. It broke up because I couldn't take that any more. I gave too much because the first one was an absolute catastrophic fuck-up because of my behaviour and I tried to overcompensate in the second.

He admitted that there was a dark, potentially unpleasant and violent side to his nature that did not only manifest itself in bar-room brawling but also during his first marriage: 'Elizabeth writes about it in her book. I think she says I beat her once or twice. I probably did give her a smack across the face. I remember once I did. It was horrendous.' He believed that it was better to end a poisonous relationship and create a healthier one at a distance, especially when there were children involved.

He subsequently established friendly relations with Elizabeth: 'You couldn't get a stronger family than me and my divorced wife. We are not married, don't live together but by Christ we are a family. We are unlike most divorced families because we were not torn apart by the law. You could think Elizabeth and I were still married.'

The failure of his marriages, he said, did not make him bitter and angry; he was a romantic at heart but the practicalities of love were too prohibitive. He did not agree with the French assessment of the difference between men and women, and his views on the subject were quite cynical: 'They use us, we use them and having used them we put them aside and they do the very same.' Such a glib statement from a man of such intelligence does not fit, and is a total contradiction to his lifetime of respect for the mother of his children. It was clearly given for effect.

Nor did this statement reflect the example of his own parents, which he said was a truly devoted union, apart from the usual tiffs, but then theirs was an arranged marriage. It may have resulted from a family introduction but did not take place in the usual sense of arranged marriages.

Perhaps Harris's relationships with women resonated more with his inability to control his passion, a force that, given the nature of relationships, fades in the face of more pragmatic considerations. After all, he would find no difficulty in such investment and commitment to the fleeting exigencies of film and theatre, consigned with equal brevity to history.

One thing Harris was adept at was wearing a mask. After all, it was the essence of his profession. He could present an attitude or an opinion that was consistent with his feeling at the time but not necessarily definitive – and often contradictory. Like any good actor he would appreciate the value of the subtext. He would say that he didn't get on with people on a permanent basis. Well, then, who does? Of his claim that he wasn't gregarious, there is a host of evidence to disprove that, just as there is to his contention that he did not have any friends. He posited the theory that with friendship came responsibility for maintenance and expectations, which was too much to bear.

Gregarious and forthright in his opinions, he was wild and unpredictable, with a large and charismatic presence but nevertheless sensitive, emotional and deeply attached to his origins and family. His collection of poems, I, In the Membership of My Days, is deeply redolent of the latter aspect of his nature.

In spite of his love of male camaraderie and drinking, he was a highly intelligent man with a breathtaking range of talent in acting and singing and, as his poetry proves, a facility for writing that could have blossomed, had his life path been different.

Without obviously drawing any gratuitous or unjustified comparison, and bearing in mind that times were different, James Joyce could often be a destructive drinker as well, as chronicled by his brother Stanislaus, and W.B. Yeats was an inveterate womaniser. Yet unlike Harris, they were lucky not to have the dubious attentions of star-obsessed media.

As for Harris's drinking, he did not fit easily into the category of the 'till death do us part' brigade of drunkards and party animals such as the playwright Brendan Behan, the poet Dylan Thomas or indeed Harris's later contemporaries Richard Burton and Oliver Reed. Harris was able to pull back when the stark consequences of his drinking were put to him. He gave up his two-bottles-of-vodka-a-day habit after being diagnosed with hyperglycaemia (abnormally large sugar content in the blood) and told that if he continued he would have but months to live. He said: 'There must be other things in life besides drinking, though I haven't discovered what they are. Drinking is really a man's occupation. What I loved was the male camaraderie of it.'

Stopping drinking was no easy task: 'I knew it had to or it would kill me. It was only when I crossed the line from sanity to madness that I realised it was all over.' While playing the role of Cromwell he saw a picture of Alec Guinness in the role of Charles I and informed his secretary that the execution should be stopped. She was aghast and immediately rang a doctor.

To strengthen his resolve, he placed alcohol in every room of the house to provide a temptation that he would not give in to, an interesting psychological exercise as opposed to the 'out of sight, out of mind' tactic. He also dabbled in drugs and once flushed a load of cocaine down the toilet after nearly expiring from its effects: 'For a one-month period in the 1970s I was into the drug and nearly died. I was anointed twice. I had no idea how dangerous it was and ended up in the intensive care unit of Cedars-Sinai.'

He won $75,000 from a small syndicate who laid bets that he would not reach his fortieth birthday.

In dealing with his drink and drug problem he eschewed both the established twelve-step route and the popular road of psychotherapy to discover the why as opposed to the what. If he was going to do it, then it would involve a simple stop decision on his own part, as he told Joe Jackson:

I studied pyschotherapy in America for years. I became part of a school and found that one of the most fantastically damaging things about modern thinking is: 'Let us discover why, why, why.' America is saturated with psychoanalysts. It is good for people who are damaged, seriously mentally deranged. It can be useful medical therapy, but in America it is just a fad. Self-analysis is dangerous to unravel – to be so self-interested that you need to know why you do this and that and why you are here.

I loved my mother, hated my father, hated my mother, loved my father, boom, boom. It goes on forever. Ah – that's why, you say, I am that way – but that doesn't change what you are. So Americans start feeling it's wrong to get out of bed on the left side. 'Why do I do that?' Then they spend $150 an hour in therapy five days a week and finally work out why they get out on the left side – and are told to try the right side.

Tennessee Williams was a wreck, I knew him and all the therapy he did was of no help to him, not one bit. He should have accepted what he was and made the best of it. He stopped writing those wonderful plays after he went into therapy. The same with Brando as an actor. I said to him: 'It's a real tragedy all your great performances are lying in a psychotherapist's file in New York.'

Harris was avoiding the basic problem of why the playwright was such a wreck, which had to do with his excessive drinking, which, like Truman Capote, had a huge impact on his personal and professional life. To say that Williams should have accepted such a state was as stark a judgement as Harris would have to make when he himself would face it: to live or die. People in extremity usually, but not always, hang on to anything to survive. Or they will experience a life-changing episode that will prompt a different form of thinking.

It could be viewed as a less appealing aspect of the actor's character – the hard-man stance that belies the sensitivity that lurked beneath. Whatever the provenance of Tennessee Williams's problems, Brando's were much chronicled – an absent father and an alcoholic mother who neglected him to such an extent that when he arrived home from school there was nothing in the fridge, and then there would be a phone call from the local bartender to take the drunken woman home.

There was nothing in Harris's childhood that could match that – nothing near it. He would later come to reflect on a loss that would affect him deeply, as all family losses do. He told Joe Jackson:

My brother Dermot died last year (1986), there is no doubt from excessive drinking – a heart attack. I walked around saying, 'If I'd only known he had a pain in his chest I could have got him into hospital and he could have had a quadruple bypass.' All his friends laughed at me and said that if you told Dermot he was going to die on 15 November 1986 if he didn't stop drinking, smoking and sitting around in bars – he would have replied, 'Ok I'll go then.' He probably had more guts than me. I don't want to go. I am enjoying my life. But then I don't need to drink any more. I can find the excess in theatre or film.

When someone said to me, 'You'll be dead in six months, if you don't stop drinking', I stopped drinking overnight. Same with regards to the four packs of cigarettes I smoked every day. I stopped because I found myself out of breath onstage.

I didn't finally stop drinking until 1981.

He was nonetheless a much-loved man. His so-called elevation to stardom never allowed him to lose the common touch. Ordinary people who met him still speak fondly of their encounters with a man of wit, humour, sentiment, impressive intellect and passion for any subject, most particularly in the arenas of sport and creative pursuit. All recall a powerful presence and seductive charisma.

That is not to say that Richard Harris did not alienate some people along his dramatic journey, but that is something that could be said of all humans, particularly those who inhabit the perfidious world of the entertainment business and the world of Hollywood. That cauldron of ambition, monetary imperative, betrayal and manufactured fame and fantasy has always had, and will always have, a negative impact on some of its most accomplished participants.

His movie career was that of a jobbing actor, and there was naturally going to be celluloid wheat and chaff. That other fabulous actor, Michael Caine, who like Harris experienced an Indian summer in his career, was just as lax in his acceptance of screen roles. When confronted on the subject on the Michael Parkinson show, Caine replied: 'My art is on my walls. I have made so much money out of terrible films, that the only way I can justify them is by putting the money to good use. I have discovered that there is more to life than driving a Rolls-Royce.'

In Harris's home on Paradise Island in the Bahamas he sometimes spent days writing poetry and reading. While he never had to work again, he retained his Hollywood agent and continued to read scripts. He said that he tried to avoid going to Limerick:

Limerick is a dangerous place, going there and not having a drink is like going into a church and not saying a prayer [...]

I remember sitting down in the dust with Richard Burton when we were making *The Wild Geese* together. We were like two old men – once the greatest hellraisers in the world – we were too tired to stand up and pee. After two hours of philosophical discussion, we came to the conclusion that the tragedy of our lives was the amount of it we don't remember because of being drunk.

I always remember what Burt Lancaster once told me: 'There comes a time in your life when you can't get the girl in the film anymore.' What the group of actors of my age – Finney, O'Toole, Burton – had was a fine madness and it was transmitted to our work. So we were always dangerous, dangerous to meet in the street, in a restaurant and dangerous to see on stage or film. We weren't afraid to be different.

Many people who Harris behaved badly towards tended to forgive, blaming the drink rather than Harris himself. Others, less tolerant, pointed to his personality make-up, which was (in their book) full of contradiction. He could be charming, generous and witty, yet he could also be brutally blunt, rude and aggressive.

Harris was proud of his own durability, the fact that his instinct for self-preservation had won against all the odds: 'I once went to see my old friend Peter O'Toole after a play to congratulate him and he looked at me over his glasses and said: "Harris, we should be dead. Think of the lives we have led – fifty lives in fifty years."'

The mighty often fall from great heights to the gutter from such excess of alcoholic indulgence as Harris. He had beaten his demons and become a multi-millionaire. He had a house in the Bahamas and could stay at top-class suites in any of the top hotels in any part of the world. He never gave a damn what people thought of him, and whatever faults are attributed to him, vanity is rarely mentioned.

But it could also be said that Richard Harris emerged from that world more whole and with more integrity than most – and that he survived to his end with those qualities intact. His capacity for reinventing his career has rarely been matched in any celluloid era. In the twilight of his life, from his towering performance as Bull McCabe in *The Field*, for which he got his second Academy Award nomination for Best Actor, to gunfighter English Bob in *Unforgiven*, to Marcus Aurelius in Ridley Scott's *Gladiator* and to Albus Dumbledore in the first two Harry Potter films, he proved that he would never be a man down or an actor easily forgotten.

He delivered brilliant performances in all of them, which not only commanded the respect of both critics and audiences but also of film-makers of the highest order and fellow cast members.

He blazed a trail to Hollywood that other accomplished Irish actors followed, and made it possible by his example – and he would be the last to claim any debt of gratitude. His peripatetic existence was one that others might not have aspired to but it was his own and was stamped with his individuality. 'This is my life and I will live it on my own terms' might be the correct phrase – and he did it without compromise. There was one of him and no other.

Like the character he played in *Cromwell*, he had warts, but when, if ever, did the wart make the face?

This is the Richard Harris, man and artist, whom the authors wish to recognise and portray.

ORIGINS

The lights flickered rhythmically, ticking off the floors as the elevator dropped. They had to use the service elevator rather than the regular one near the reception, because they were manoeuvring a stretcher.

The ambulance men brought the stretcher through the swinging double door of the kitchen, through the busy food preparation area and into the dining room. As they carefully picked their path through the tables, the frail old man on the stretcher – the inhabitant of room 758 for the past ten years – stirred. He raised his head slightly, and his blue eyes twinkled.

'It was the food!' he boomed, his rasping Irish brogue reaching the furthest corners of the dining room of the Savoy. 'It was the food.'

Then he let his head fall back, and he laughed.

A few days later Richard Harris, legendary screen icon and one of the most notorious hellraisers of the 1960s and '70s, was dead. It was 25 October 2002, and the 72-year-old actor, poet and singer had survived alcoholism, drug addiction and bar-room brawls. But a combination of Parkinson's and Lymphoma had finally brought the curtain down. The cancer had festered in his body unnoticed, until a bout of pneumonia in August had hospitalised him and it was discovered. By then it was too late to treat.

In life he had been trouble, and even in death he caused controversy. The headline in the *Sunday Times* was: 'Limerick snubbed in Harris's final scene'.

Noel Harris, his brother, immediately announced that there would be a memorial service in Limerick, after the cremation in London. Harris, an eccentric to the end, was not laid to rest in his best suit, as Irish tradition dictates. Instead he was dressed in the pale-blue jersey of his beloved Young Munster Rugby Club. It was the common touch so typical of the man.

Harris had a huge fan base, and part of the reason was that he was a very accessible star. He had time for everyone. When he went to a rugby game – and he often did – he did not sit in the corporate box, sipping champagne and munching sardine sandwiches. He stood shoulder to shoulder with the real fans in the terraces, and sang as raucously as any of them.

Limerick loved him, and the city was plunged into mourning when he passed. A book of condolences was opened in Griffin's Funeral Home, and people queued up to sign. Alongside the names of friends, former colleagues and city dignitaries were childish scrawls from youngsters who only knew the firebrand from his role as the affable Professor Dumbledore in the first two Harry Potter movies. It was a role he had wanted to turn down, until his granddaughter Ella threatened not to talk to him again if he did.

The entries in the book of condolences showed how deeply fans had been touched by Dickie Harris. One tribute read: 'From a nine year old girl who fell in love with Albus Dumbledore and her mother who fell in love with King Arthur. Thank you for that "One Brief Shining Moment".' Another, perhaps referring to his hellraising reputation, just wrote: 'Rock on Richard'.

Many of the mourners spoke to reporters as they queued. Colette Simms was typical. She recalled how, on her first week working behind the bar at the Corner Flag, a city pub, she served Richard Harris her first pint of Guinness: 'He came into the bar for a quick drink because he was supposed to be leaving at three o'clock that day. But he didn't leave until three the following day. He was a great storyteller, a great character, he had a great presence and he was a great man.'

One of the first people to sign the book was Mayor John Cronin, who said: 'I am delighted that the people of Limerick have got a chance to mourn this great Limerick man. I would encourage the people of Limerick to sign the book to show what Richard Harris meant to Limerick.'

And Limerick meant as much to Harris as he meant to Limerick. To understand the man, we need to travel back in time and understand the place that shaped him.

Richard Harris once described himself as an excessive compulsive. Though the phrase had yet to be hijacked by psychologists, it was a perfect description of one of cinema's most iconic stars. Harris was compulsively excessive in everything he did. He drank to excess, and when he quit drinking, he took to drugs with such zeal they nearly killed him. He took his acting equally seriously, clashing with major star Marlon Brando in one of his first screen roles (*Mutiny on the Bounty*) when he should have been sitting awestruck at the feet of the master. He sported to excess, dominating on the rugby field until illness struck him down. He loved excess, and when he fell out with the current love of his life he was a voracious womaniser. 'I should be in jail for life for sexual harassment. I would never get out of jail. I harassed every female I saw. I made passes at them. And if I didn't they would be wondering why I didn't,' he joked.

Harris never did anything by halves, and cheerfully accepted the consequences – the lost years, the lack of quality roles during key portions of his career, the broken marriages, the bar-room brawls ... Life was lived large and it was a constant drama.

'I had this strange or fatalistic sort of an idea that I was going to die young,' he told one interviewer, Patricia O'Connor, in 1993. 'I thought I would die young, and I wanted to go out and maybe not so much encourage death, but at least in the interim between life and death I would live an exciting life.'

Even that interview, broadcast on RTÉ, the Irish national television station, was a drama. Harris was not meant to be in Dublin, but his plane touched down there while in transit from London to the Bahamas, where he had a house. During the brief stopover, Harris managed to lose his luggage – passport, credit cards, money, and the rough draft of an autobiography he was working on. He had to stay in Dublin to sort the mess out, and RTÉ took the opportunity to interview him. Eventually he got to the Bahamas, but the autobiography never saw the light of day.

Nevertheless, the stories of his life gained wide circulation. The actor used to joke that if he couldn't remember what he had done the previous evening, all he had to do was pick up one of the tabloids and he would be able to get all the details.

He had a devil-may-care attitude that endeared him to the public, and a generosity of spirit that allowed him to make friends wherever he went. On one famous occasion he knocked on the window of a strange house late at night demanding drink, and spent the next three days there. His reputation as a hellraiser was well earned. Along with his contemporaries – Oliver Reed, Peter O'Toole and Richard Burton – he blazed a trail for British and Irish talent on the silver screen, and tore across the social pages of the newspapers in a whirl of alcohol and beautiful women. The four of them burnt bright like comets and were gone. But Harris continued making quality films into his old age. He won new legions of fans with performances in *Gladiator*, *Harry Potter*, and an Oscar nomination for his lead role in *The Field*.

Unlike the other hellraisers, there was more to Harris. Away from the screen he was a bit of a Renaissance man. He had a very successful career as a singer, with his albums topping the charts. He was a poet of note, and even turned his hand to directing. More important, he was shrewd. After forcing himself into the role of Arthur in *Camelot* (1967) – a role the producer did not want him in – Harris went one step further, and bought the stage rights to the musical. That alone ensured that he died a rich man. And at the tail end of his career he refused payment for his final role, as Professor Albus Dumbledore in the Harry Potter movies. Instead he asked for a percentage of the merchandising. The producers were aghast, but in the end had to give in to his demands. As he said at the time, that move ensured his granddaughter Ella could go to any university in the world. The funds were there.

Excess was the motif of his life. As he put it himself:

I had the most exciting life. No human being could have a more exciting life. I did everything you could think of. I just took a chance and ran with it and did it.

I had the most marvellous love affairs, I met the most fantastic women, and I had the greatest experiences; the greatest drunks, the greatest hangovers, the largest vomits – the best. I have been in jail in six countries. Who else can claim that?

Maybe Oliver Reed, his good drinking buddy.

Excessive drinking is often a sign of hidden unhappiness. Psychological forces drive a person to the solace of alcohol. But there was no unhappiness in Harris's childhood, or in his journey through life. He claimed he drank because he liked it: 'I drank because I loved it. I absolutely adored it. I wasn't running away. I was the happiest drunk in the world,' he boasted.

I used to look forward to waking up the next day with a hangover, and opening the *Daily Express* to find out what I had done. Where did I do it? I spent two nights in jail – I have how many stitches? How did I get those? I loved it. It had nothing to do with problems. I had no problems whatsoever. I had a good family. My mother and my father, I have nothing against them. Eight of us – too many of us maybe! People look and say there is a secret demon there. No, there's none.

However, there was a predilection for drink in the genes. His father Ivan was a heavy drinker, while his brother Dermot died a young man after living a life every bit as hard as Richard's. Drink took its toll.

Yet, despite appearances, Harris had another side: he had intense discipline. He threw himself into roles as only method actors can. He got into world-class shape for *This Sporting Life* (1963), so that he could hold his own with the rough-and-tumble professional rugby players who were extras on the film. When he was told that he would die within months unless he quit drinking, he had the discipline to down one last bottle of champagne and then walk away from the booze. He might have seemed to the world to be a hopeless alcoholic, but he was in control a lot of the time.

Perhaps it is that discipline more than anything else that separated him from the other hellraisers of that golden age of cinema. However much he enjoyed the *craic* (a peculiarly Irish expression, meaning hedonistic fun), he knew that he had to do what was necessary to hold on to what he had earned. The wild excesses never threatened his homes around the world, or the security of his family. And he was still making quality films up to his death.

His discipline was a result of his upbringing. Many of the great actors of his age came from working-class backgrounds. Harris did not. He was born into wealth. His family were rich industrialists. He was raised in a large house, with servants to answer his every beck and call. But through his childhood he saw his parents' empire slowly crumble. By the time he reached his teens his mother was on her knees scrubbing her own floors. His father's flour mills had closed, the bakeries were gone, and the family had slipped in genteel poverty.

Harris was always a family man. His childhood had been happy, and he was close to his parents. He could see at first hand how easy it was to lose what had taken such a long time to build up. Whether he ever articulated it, or even acknowledged it to himself, that lesson in how easily things could fall apart was one of the forces that drove him. It gave him a steely determination. That determination could be seen first on the rugby field. It could also be seen in his acting career. When he first set his mind on a place in an acting college, or later on a role in a film, he would move mountains to achieve that aim.

One of his abiding disappointments was that both his parents were dead before that drive pushed him to the top. He never got the chance to use his growing wealth to help out the parents who had given him such a happy childhood.

To understand Harris as a person, we have to understand the forces that created him. We have to go back to Limerick, his home town.

For only out of solitude or strife are born the sons of valour and delight.

Roy Campbell, *Choosing a Mast*

It is a common cliché that adversity breeds greatness. But the life of actor, poet, director and singer Richard Harris showed that the opposite can also be true: a pampered life of ease and luxury can produce greatness. Harris often used to joke about that. In 1973 he told Michael Parkinson that many working-class actors and entertainers rose to the top – men such as Oliver Reed and Michael Caine. He even included Parkinson in that number. But he said that his own background was completely different, and it didn't stop him getting to the top.

Harris was born into wealth, which had been built up over generations through hard work and diligent trade. The Harris family dominated the mill business in the city, supplying flour and grain. But as Harris reached his teen years the family were experiencing something they had not seen in seventy years: they knew want for the first time, as competition gradually squeezed the life out of their business. The servants were let go, the workers were laid off, and the house was downsized.

Harris grew to maturity through the times of change, and perhaps this is what shaped him. He was an intensely competitive man, first on the rugby field and the racquets court, later on the stage and on screen, insisting on top billing long before he had earned that right. But he was also a man who knew how to spend money like it was going out of fashion. He lived life to the full, indulging every passion to excess. Because he knew that it could all come crashing down on him, he lived in the moment, and is remembered as much for his hellraising as for his towering talent.

It all began in his childhood, but the story of Limerick begins before that ...

Limerick is Ireland's third city, behind Dublin and Cork. Sitting on the broad estuary of the Shannon, the largest river in the British Isles, it dominates the western seaboard. The city has a long history. Humans settled in the area over 5,000 years ago, as the Stone Age remains at nearby Lough Gur demonstrate. But the city itself is a lot more recent.

Around the ninth century, the Vikings stopped raiding and started settling, establishing permanent trading posts in key locations such as Dublin, Waterford and Limerick. The western settlement was on the Shannon, at the point where the river broadens out to an estuary. The initial buildings were constructed around the last fordable section of the river, and that is still the heart of the old city to this day; King John's Castle and the Curraghgower Falls, an area of rapids on the shallow river.

Within a generation the Vikings were mingling with the local population and intermarrying. They established fortifications and settlements away from the main trading centre, and commerce became as important to them as warfare. One of their settlements was at Killaloe, at the end of Lough Derg, 10 miles inland from Limerick.

Eventually, a powerful chieftain arose at Killaloe and became king of all Ireland; Brian Boru was the most powerful man in the country, and all the other tribes and minor kings acknowledged his supremacy. Historians now accept that Brian was at least half Viking, and not a pure Celt. Perhaps it was because he was not a true Viking that the other Vikings did not accept his authority as easily as the native Irish. In 916 Brian and his army marched east across the country to subdue the Norsemen of the Dublin settlement. Brian won the Battle of Clontarf decisively, but lost his life in the struggle. He was the last great High King of Ireland. His descendants still live locally, in Newmarket-on-Fergus, just 10 miles north of Limerick.

Limerick continued to thrive, despite the setback. The Normans built a large castle on the river. King John stayed there on an inspection of Ireland, and the castle still bears his name. But by the time Richard Harris arrived, the castle had fallen into decay, and the courtyard and some of the outbuildings had been converted into council housing for the poor.

The city had its own mayor and corporation by the twelfth century, and was always considered an important asset. The British and the Irish fought over it a number of times, including two key sieges in the 1690s.

The first recorded reference to milling comes in 1485, when a poet, Davis, wrote:

A mighty murrain, numbers of cattle died.
This year for four pence is cow's raw hide.
All other things were cheap, a plenty great,
For twelve pence bought four pecks of finest wheat.

Grain was always vital to the prosperity of the city. The Golden Vale is the rich lowlands around the Shannon, in east Limerick, north Tipperary and Offaly. Grain would be transported down the majestic Shannon to the grain mills of Limerick. The Civil Survey of 1654 records four water-worked mills in the city, as well as several large horse-powered mills. Some of these mills did not survive, but a few flourished, including one at Curraghgower Falls, a small rapid on the river close to the castle. The mill was built by William Joynt, a member of the city corporation, and was still going two centuries later, when Larry Quinlivan presided over a concern described in 1840 as a 'splendid mill with great water-power'. Quinlivan obviously did well from the trade, because he ran successfully for mayor. But the mill was destroyed in a fire in 1850 and never rebuilt.

Several of the riverside mills went out of business in the nineteenth century because the river levels were too low to allow consistent use. Then the famine struck, closing more. Those that thrived did so by supplying the workhouses.

It is not known exactly when the Harris family first came to Ireland. They were outsiders who arrived with the planters (English settlers) in the seventeenth century. Harris may be a Norman name, a corruption of the French Henri. It may also be Welsh, from Ris or Rhys. In any case, the family came from the United Kingdom, and were staunchly Protestant when they settled along the east coast. They gradually spread, arriving in Limerick in the early nineteenth century.

The first Harris to make it to Limerick was James, Richard's great grandfather. He was born in Wexford, from farming stock. When he arrived in Limerick he turned to trade, setting up a flour and milling business. He was a good businessman who turned mercantile ambitions into a thriving concern. He also married – and broke with family tradition by marrying outside his faith. He met and fell for Anne Meehan, and converted to Catholicism to be with her. By 1864 he owned Limerick's largest flour mill, as well as a company dock and warehouse at Steamboat Quay, in the docks area. He also owned a bakery on Henry Street. This runs parallel to the river, and is one of the three main streets in Limerick, alongside O'Connell Street and William Street.

By that time, Limerick had become one of the great Georgian cities. The old quarter – known as Irish Town – was based around the castle and the original settlement. It was a maze of little streets and lanes, lying higgledy-piggledy close to the river. The new quarter – known as English Town, or Newtown – was west of that settlement, and south of the river. It was laid out in an elegant grid of wide streets with little lanes linking them. The houses were three- and four-storey, built of red brick with large windows and imposing doorways, often with a flight of steps up from the pavement. The people who lived on Pery Square, Hartstonge Street and The Crescent were the elite of Limerick.

Sometime in the 1860s James Harris acquired a very desirable property on Hartstonge Street, at the end nearest Pery Square. Hartstonge House, which still stands, is a tall, narrow, detached town house. It is four storeys high and has imposing steps leading to the front door, a red-brick structure that looks like it should be part of an imposing terrace. Although there was no garden (it fronts onto the road, and the rear was for access and stables) it was still the best house on one of the best streets. The Harris family remained there for about twenty years, before moving out to a mansion on Ennis Road. The house was subsequently bought by Stephen O'Mara, and the famous opera singer James O'Mara lived there before the family moved out in 1909. The Society of St Vincent de Paul now occupies the building, which has been renamed Ozaman House.

A description from that time from Pat Lavelle mentions: 'What I saw, the comfort and well-being of Hartstonge House, the crowds of relations, the stables with carriages and horses, had all been achieved by the work and energy of two men, my grandfather Stephen and his father James.' The richly furnished home even had its own private chapel, Littleark, which James built to mark his change in faith.

While James Harris was still in Hartstonge House, in 1868, he achieved some local fame when he provided a base for a French balloonist, Monsieur Chevalier. The French aeronaut had spent two days aloft and covered 700 miles in the balloon, which earned him the Légion d'Honneur. Now he was in Ireland trying to drum up funds by offering pleasure flights in his balloon, which was still very much a novelty.

Harris gave Chevalier the use of the yard at Steamboat Quay, and the aeronaut charged people a shilling to watch the construction of the balloon. The assembly took longer than expected; during an early test flight it was badly damaged and had to undergo extensive repairs, which James Harris patiently endured. Finally, in mid-May, it was ready for flight. Chevalier announced the fact in a letter to the local paper, the *Limerick Chronicle*:

> Allow me to inform the gentry and public of Limerick that the injury sustained during the last inflation is completely repaired, and I intend to perform my promise, weather permitting, by ascending in my balloon on Thursday next, May 21, at three o'clock, from Mr Harris' premises, Steamboat Quay, who was kind enough to give me the use of it, free of any charge.
>
> In this voyage I will be accompanied by a lady and a gentleman. Hoping to be still favoured with the patronage of the gentry and public of Limerick, who have expressed so much sympathy for my unavoidable accident, and returning them my sincere thanks, I remain, your obedient servant, A Chevalier.

The second attempt was a success, with the balloon sailing east and disappearing over the horizon in the direction of the village of Castleconnell.

That was the lifestyle that the Harris family had achieved – servants, a stable full of horses and luxury carriages, and the elegant ease of the gentry. Their move from Hartstonge Street after less than a decade was not a downsizing; their new house was one of the best in Limerick. It was a mansion in its own small estate, on the North Circular Road. There were extensive grounds and enough rooms to get lost in, as well as outhouses and stables. There were butlers, maids and gardeners, as well as their own carriages, with grazing for the horses.

James Harris was a bit of an anomaly among the merchant rulers of Limerick in that, like many converts, he was a committed Catholic. He wasn't the only Catholic of his class. In fact, among his rivals in the milling business was the Harty family, into which his son married. But in many respects Catholics were still second-class citizens, despite forty years of Catholic emancipation. This led to bitter business rivalries with families such as the Russells and Bannatynes, both of whom were also involved in the milling business. Despite this, James Harris's business prospered. He died in 1895 and was buried in the family vault alongside his father, who had died fifteen years earlier. Having a vault as opposed to a standard burial plot was an announcement that – at the end of life – you had arrived. His wife died five years later.

His son Richard, then 31, continued in his footsteps, expanding the business considerably, and his wealth grew. He also invested in new businesses, including setting up a phone company. The cost of a one-minute call to Dublin was half a shilling, making it an indulgence of the rich.

The nationalist movement was gaining a foothold in the country, but the Harris family remained decidedly old school. Richard's son, Ivan John Harris, was born in 1896. Richard's father had helped finance the Jesuit-run Crescent College in the centre of the city (built on the best street), but when it came to his son's education, Richard decided to board Ivan, along with his brother Billy, in a British school.

He chose Downside, a private Catholic school attached to Downside Abbey in Somerset, near Bath. Run by the Benedictine order, it was modelled on such institutions of the empire as Eton and Rugby, and provided a very solid education. But it was very much an enclave of the elite. When Ivan Harris returned to his native Limerick, he would have stood out from those about him. He was also the heir to great wealth. He was a catch.

The young Ivan Harris was a gentle, easy-going man who loved sports such as tennis and hockey. He threw himself enthusiastically into the family business, alongside his brother. While his father had a reputation for being stern and austere, Ivan was known as a gentleman, who got on with everyone. Throughout his life he was also a charitable man, and slow to anger. He is well remembered in his native city.

'The family had plenty of money,' said one of the patrons of Quinlan's Bar, near the railway station. This bar, a haunt of Young Munster supporters, was a favourite watering hold of Richard Harris in the later years of his life. 'They were supposed to be a very charitable family. They gave a lot of money to the poor. Very nice people, they were. Richard's father, Ivan, was an out and out gentleman. They gave a lot to the poor of Limerick.'

A handsome man, with a good education, easy manners, charm and wealth, Ivan attracted the eyes of the ladies. Through his interest in sport he crossed paths with a local beauty, Mildred (Milly) Harty. Slim, with porcelain skin and wild red hair, she turned heads wherever she went. She was no shrinking violet, and knew her own mind. The two were instantly attracted to each other.

And Milly came from the right stock. Many generations ago her family had arrived from Scotland, but now they were as integrated as the Harris family, staunchly nationalist Catholic. And though the Hartys did not have the elevated social status of the Harris family, they were players in the local milling industry. However, they did not have the wealth of the Harrises. That was a serious obstacle to the match, at least in the eyes of the older generation of Harrises. But the problem evaporated when an aunt of Milly's mother died, leaving a large inheritance.

The couple got married and appeared to be madly in love. At least, that is how most people remember it. Richard Harris had a different interpretation of the relationship between his parents. He thought the marriage had more to do with politics and money than romance.

'With my father and mother it was an arranged marriage,' Harris told Joe Jackson in a *Hot Press* interview many years after their deaths. 'My mother was a working-class lady with a lot of money. My father had no money. It was arranged by relatives that they should marry. They had eight children, and they loved each other. They had the odd row now and then, but no more than that – tiffs.'

This is an account that the rest of the family reject. Noel Harris, the only surviving one of Richard's siblings, said:

I was always very offended with Richard over the way he spoke about his mother and father, which was all lies, total lies.

I had it out with him many times when he was alive, and I have also made it known to his three sons. If I ever had a disagreement with their father, it was over this issue of what he said about our parents. My parents were lovely people. They were very warm and never deprived us of anything we wanted in life.

My father was a terribly quiet man. He was known as Limerick's gentleman. You'd very rarely see him lose his temper. My mother ruled the house. She was the boss in that house. And my father adored the ground she walked on, which Dick never said properly in life. He always said it was an arranged marriage, and there was no love in the marriage between my father and mother. What rubbish. My father adored the ground my mother walked on.

Milly and Ivan were a well-matched couple, and very quickly their family began to grow. They continued to live in luxury on the North Circular Road for the first few years of their life together. Ivan ran the mill, bakery and retail business alongside his brother Billy. When their father retired in his 80s, both brothers took over, having different responsibilities. For a couple of years, the business thrived. But they did not have it all their own way. There was fierce competition. Three other major mills were looking for the same business: Russell's and Roche's of Limerick, and Glynn's of Kilrush. Both brothers had to work very hard to stay on top of things.

Ivan was turning into a workaholic as the depression of the 1920s began to affect his business. The problem was made worse when a huge UK company decided to open in Limerick. Rank had the financial muscle to push the smaller operators out of business, and that is what they proceeded to do. They undercut, sold for a loss, and were able to offer suppliers better deals than the local firms. One by one the many mills in the region began to close down. The Harris family finally closed their mill in the late 1920s. They then became agents for Rank. Their wealth was being rapidly eroded.

It didn't help that the family had established more than a dozen town bakeries in various parts of the country. Despite Ivan's best efforts, they had become overextended. In the late 1920s they realised they had to downsize, and one of the first things to go was their mansion off the North Circular Road. The growing family moved into Overdale, a house on Ennis Road. This was a very good part of town. The houses were tall, imposing terraces from the early Victorian era, with red-brick façades and high ceilings. Overdale was three storeys high, with a long narrow front garden, a garden at the back, and a laneway at the rear giving access. It was ten minutes' walk from the city centre, and was an enclave of the wealthy. The property had plenty of room, which was important. The family was growing at a rapid rate, as Noel Harris remembers:

We were very close as a family growing up, because there was only two years between us all. There were two years between Harmay and Audrey, there were two years between Audrey and Jimmy, there were two years between Jimmy and Ivan, there were two years between Ivan and Richard, and there were two years between Richard and myself. Dermot and Jimmy were the last two. We were close. They said that if you hit one Harris, you hit them all!

Richard St John Harris, the fifth child, was born on 1 October 1930.

CHILDHOOD

Timing is the secret of an actor's success. Harris got the timing badly wrong – though he can hardly be blamed! The Wall Street Crash had occurred less than a year before his birth, plunging America into a deep economic depression. That quickly became global. Between 1929 and 1932 the devastation hit Europe, driving inflation through the roof and plunging the continent into the chaos that would eventually lead to the Second World War.

By 1930 Ireland was feeling the pinch. The country was helped by the fact that it was relatively undeveloped and largely self-sufficient. But Ireland's largest trading partner was the United Kingdom, and it was suffering badly. Between 1929 and 1932 industrial production dropped by nearly one-quarter, and wholesale prices by one-third. Foreign trade halved and unemployment more than doubled.

At the time there was huge emigration from Ireland, mainly to the UK and America. But both countries were struggling, and emigrants were not able to send the money home that they traditionally did. As wholesale prices plummeted in the UK, they did the same in Ireland. Suddenly the secure base of the Harris fortune looked less secure.

None of that affected the toddler Richard, known to all his friends and family as Dickie. He had a big house with extensive gardens to play in. There were servants to pick him up when he fell, at least in the early days, and his mother was always there, her beautiful smile a beacon of security in his world. It would be a number of years before the economic crash seeped through the walls of Overdale. His childhood was punctuated by three more confinements, and three new siblings. It was a noisy house, full of laughter and joy.

Irish children are traditionally sent to school at the age of 4. Richard was packed off to St Philomena's Junior School. It was on the other side of the city from his home. Overdale was on Ennis Road, the main road north of the city towards Ennis and Galway; his school was on the South Circular Road. It would have been a 2-mile walk to the school, but young Dickie didn't need to walk. His family were one of the few in the city to have their own car, which brought him to the school, safe from the inclement weather.

There were schools much closer to his home – schools where the local children went. But St Philomena's was a private school, the only private primary school in the entire mid-west region. Established in 1863, it provided small classes and highly qualified teachers for the elite of the city. It was a co-educational school, with boys and girls sitting side by side in the little classrooms. This alone would have made it unusual. Traditionally – aside from tiny rural schools – Irish schools have been segregated. The sexes didn't get to mingle until they reached university. Dickie Harris was exposed to a different ethos. From an early age, girls were not mysterious exotic creatures who played behind convent walls; they were his friends and companions. This probably instilled in him a confidence lacking in many Irish men of his generation. He was never at a loss for words when it came to the opposite sex.

School was a harsh place in the 1930s, with corporal punishment and beatings the norm. But Dickie was a tough nut, and he was rarely put out by the harsh regime of the nuns. He was never overly academic, but he kept up with his studies easily. He also enjoyed the rough-and-tumble in the school yard. Occasionally he got into trouble. Once a nun struck him with a ruler, and he wrestled the wooden implement from her, striking her in return. For that display of free spirit he was suspended.

But those early days were mostly happy ones. At home he never lacked for friends – there were seven brothers and sisters milling around, with plenty of space to lose themselves in. The garden was extensive, with plum and pear trees, gooseberry bushes and lawns to run in. A laneway ran behind, where the children also played. Dickie gathered the wild fruits when they were in season, and climbed the trees when they were not. The family had two garages – one for the car and one for garden equipment and junk. This was in sharp contrast to the rest of Limerick. Most families did not have a car to worry about, and for many households the only outbuilding was an outside lavatory, as indoor plumbing was a long way short of universal in the 1930s. The Harris family did have an outside loo – but they used the inside one.

They also had a dog called Reggie, which officially belonged to Dickie's sister. He wrote about it in a poem when he was 9, when the creative streak was just beginning to break out in him. The poem is simple, humorous, but heartfelt:

> My sister had a dog
> Named Reggie
> She loved Reggie
> She said she loved me too
> She kissed and patted Reggie
> She never kissed and patted me.

In the summer the family were wealthy enough to decamp to the seaside for three months. Their holiday destination never varied; they always went to Kilkee. It was as traditional and immutable as the shamrock on St Patrick's Day. To his dying day, Richard Harris maintained that Kilkee was his favourite spot on earth.

The three most popular costal resorts within easy reach of Limerick are Lahinch and Kilkee in County Clare (north of the city), and Ballybunion in County Kerry (south of the city). Lahinch has never been popular with Limerick people – it was a golf town, with a wide sweeping beach that has now become a Mecca for surfers – but it was always the retreat of Dubliners. Ballybunion was as popular as Kilkee, but a bit more downmarket. Everyone went to Kilkee. Whether you were rich or poor, whether you were spending the day or the month, there was only one place to be during the summer.

The town, to this day, is invaded during July and August, when Limerick people outnumber the locals. The population can swell by 5,000 in the summer. Originally a small fishing village, Kilkee nestles in a horseshoe bay with one of the safest beaches in Ireland. The beach is protected from the Atlantic by a reef, and sheltered from the wind by cliffs. The water is often more like a lake than the sea.

In the early nineteenth century a paddle-steamer service was established from Limerick to Kilrush, a port on the Shannon estuary a few miles from Kilkee. After this the resort began to thrive, being ranked as one of the finest bathing spots in the UK by the *Illustrated London News*. As the town was more accessible to people from Limerick rather than Clare, holidaying in Kilkee became more of a Limerick custom. Gradually the town grew, as wealthy merchants from Limerick wanted holiday homes by the sea, resulting in a building boom in the 1830s. The West End became the place to have a home. The houses were in tall, elegant terraces, with big bay windows facing the sea. It was one of those West End houses that the Harris family rented every summer. But they didn't just rent the house; they rented the owner. Back in the 1930s and '40s renting a house for the summer did not work as it does today. The owner of the house would remain there for the summer. Every morning Milly Harris would have to go out and buy the groceries, and then the landlady would use those groceries to cook for the family. Self-catering was decades away. To the Harris family, who were used to servants, this was how holidays should be lived.

The normal way to get to Kilkee was to take the train to Ennis, then board the West Clare railway service. This was the most famous – and the longest still-surviving – narrow gauge railway line in the country. A steam engine towed the carriages in a meandering loop around the south of the county. Timekeeping could be erratic, but when you are off on your holidays a few hours' delay is part of the adventure. The service was immortalised in a song by Percy French, 'Are You Right There, Michael, Are You Right?'

Kevin O'Connor is a journalist from Limerick who was a few years younger than Dickie Harris but knew him and his family well. He went to the same school and played rugby in the same clubs. His father had a bakery and did business with the

Harris family. He recalled those annual excursions to the seaside, so much a part of the Limerick upbringing: 'We used to use the West Clare railway, and sometimes we used to also go by boat from Limerick to Kilrush, then get a taxi or something to Kilkee. Dickie's favourite spot was Kilkee.'

Noel Harris still remembers the excitement of holiday time:

Every summer we went up there. In the beginning we used to go for three months, June, July and August. Eventually, as we got older, it was just July. But it was a large chunk of our childhood. That was where the love came from. We all acquired a love of Kilkee. I still have it. I absolutely adore the bloody place. It's a fantastic place. Beautiful. Absolutely gorgeous. You couldn't go wrong with Kilkee. It was as safe as houses for young children. Great swimming facilities. Nobody ever locked their front doors. There were never any rows, or stealing. It was fantastic.

We'd stay in different places every year. But we always stayed at the West End.

To this day, the West End of Kilkee is full of imposing Victorian terraces and big houses. It was always the moneyed side of the village, while the East End, with smaller houses, was where everyone else stayed.

'We'd stay in many different houses – whatever was available,' said Noel:

We always stayed in a house that was pretty large, because we had a large family. My father brought us down first of all, those of us who could squeeze into the car. The rest of us would go down by the West Clare, or the bus. There was a bus every day to Kilkee. And families were very united in those days. If there was a spare seat in a car going down they would offer you a seat to Kilkee. This was when we were very young.

One can only imagine the excitement that the young Dickie Harris felt as he boarded the carriage in Ennis, with the *Slieve Callen* – the engine – at the front, belching steam, the smell of the coal and turf permeating the entire train. As they pulled out into the countryside he could have been trundling across the vast prairies. He could look out at the herds of cattle and imagine them as buffalo. The trees and gently rolling hills could have concealed whole tribes of Indians.

The train chugged towards Corofin, then through to Ennistymon, Lahinch and Miltown Malbay before reaching the tiny platform at Moyasta. There was no village here, just the small station. The family would have had to transfer to a branch line that took them the final few miles to Kilkee.

The resort was a paradise for a young boy with plenty of energy to burn. Dickie loved to swim, and he was spoilt for choice. There was the beach, but closer to the grand houses of the West End were the famous Pollock Holes, three natural rock pools a few metres deep and several metres long, which are like tidal swimming pools. The closest to the shore was officially the ladies only pool. In practice, however, everyone used the near hole, and this was where Dickie learnt to swim as a young boy.

The second hole was for men and women, but the third hole, furthest out on the reef, was for men only – and this was strictly observed. Men sunbathed in the nip and swam *au naturel*. In a conservative country such as Ireland, this was enough to keep the ladies away.

The best time to swim in the Pollock Holes is when the tide is out. When the tide is in, the best swimming place is Byrne's Cove, on the east side of the beach. This is a rocky outcrop near the golf course, about half a mile from the edge of the town. Again, it was men only, and was enforced by the nude bathing. From Byrne's Cove it is almost a mile across the bay to the third popular bathing spot, New Found Out. This is on the West End, between the beach and the reef, and consists of a high wall, whitewashed, with diving boards. The highest board is 13m above the surface of the water. Traditionally this was a proving ground for young men. Only the bravest would take the plunge from the high board. Dickie loved posing at New Found Out, and as he got older he was one of the daredevils who caught the girls' eyes with spectacular leaps.

As he became a stronger swimmer, he began to swim across the bay from Byrne's Cove to New Found Out. This is a daunting swim across open water, with a depth of over 60ft for much of the way. The only company was the occasional jellyfish, and the odd curious porpoise or dolphin.

'You'd see them all out at the Pollock Holes. They were all very strong swimmers,' remembers Kevin O'Connor.

Dickie was a strong swimmer rather than a good swimmer; he could stray out into deep water and bring himself home safely, but his stroke lacked finesse and he wasn't fast. 'We all swam in Kilkee,' said Noel Harris. 'He was never a great swimmer. He was a reasonable swimmer, but he never swam seriously.'

Manuel Di Lucia, the son of Italian emigrants, was born and raised in Kilkee. He was ten years younger than Dickie, but remembers him clearly. They ended up lifelong friends. 'He introduced me to swimming the big bay at an early age. He took me across the big bay as a young boy,' said Di Lucia. 'He did it on his own many times. It is one nautical mile exactly, at high tide. And that is the only time to do it.'

Di Lucia took to the swimming with enthusiasm, eventually becoming a diver and a qualified diving coach, as well as setting up a Marine Search & Rescue unit at the resort. He was responsible for turning Kilkee into one of Europe's major and busiest diving centres. He never forgot the role Harris played in that, and in 1970 he started an annual swim race across the bay. The cup for the winner is the Richard Harris Cup, and the actor paid for it.

'His sons were here this year [2012], and some of his grandchildren were here to present the trophy. One of them said they might try it next year. I don't know whether they will or not,' laughed Di Lucia.

Swimming wasn't the only sport on the beach. A version of racquetball, called racquets, was played against the wall of New Found Out every summer when the tide was out. Dickie excelled at this sport, winning the annual tournament on a number of occasions. His brothers were almost equally skilled, and there was always friendly rivalry within the family. The tournament was something Harris continued well into later life, making the semi-final at age 40.

Life in Kilkee was full of fun, and Dickie was at the centre of every bit of trouble, every scrap of action. Di Lucia recalled those carefree years: 'He used to come to Kilkee all the time with his family. All his brothers – they used to all come to Kilkee. They were all interested in beach sports and water sports. And he was a great swimmer. He was a brilliant racquetball player.'

But it wasn't just the sporting prowess that made Dickie stand out. He was a one-man Irish Jackass.

'There were several kinds of stunts he got up to,' said Di Lucia. 'One stunt he was supposed to have done, but I didn't see him do it, was to cycle along the top of the strand-line wall, over where the alleys are. That's about 40ft high. He is supposed to have cycled along that.'

The wall Harris was cycling along was less than 1ft wide. On one side he could have fallen onto the road, but on the other side he would have plunged to the rocks below, and would have been lucky to escape with broken bones. It was a sheer drop of more than 40ft, and was the wall against which the annual racquets tournament was played. Cycling there was a crazy thing to have done. But it was not unusual for him. Others remember even wilder stunts.

Kevin Dineen was a baker from Limerick, who holidayed in Kilkee. He was two decades older than Harris, but knew the family well as he was in the same trade. He remembered seeing a bizarre sight one afternoon. He was on the beach, looking up at the top of the wall, towering the height of a three-storey building above him. Many daredevils walked along the wall as a challenge. There was a big crowd watching in awestruck wonder as a boy of about 12 was doing just that. But what had them all amazed was that the boy was doing the walk on his hands. That was typical Harris.

'Another stunt which I did see him do was this,' said Di Lucia:

He cycled up a plank, up over a wall, back where the Diamond Rocks holiday homes are built. All that was there was bare grass and mounds of earth. There was a natural pathway down by the side of it, and he put a plank up against the wall and it was done as a dare.

He got up on this old bicycle, cycled along the pathway, up the plank, and off and into the sea on the other side. Mad. The bicycle would follow him, but someone got the bright idea that they would tie a bit of rope around the bike, so that when he went off, the bike wouldn't go after him. It would just go down and pull back so that he wouldn't get hurt with the bike landing on top of him.

That is what he did. That was in his teens. Probably one of the last seasons he would have been here. He was around 17 at the time. There was this adventurous, crazy streak in him.

One of the highlights of the summer was the horse races, contested every year on the strand. The races were held over two days in September, the last hurrah of the summer, before Dickie had to board the train for the journey back to Limerick.

When he was 12, Dickie wrote a poem about his childhood. Published in his poetry volume I, *In the Membership of my Days* (Random House, 1973), it is an imaginative eulogy on the joys of growing up carefree. It is a picture of innocence – and full of allusions to the movies that were becoming an important part of his life. He loved losing himself in films, whether they were action, adventure, gangster or even romance.

In the poem he also spoke about rugby, which was as important to him as the fantasy world of the silver screen. In his fantasies he saw himself in the green jersey, leading Ireland out against the old enemy, England, at Lansdowne Road. He was big, fast and strong; there was no reason why it shouldn't happen.

But the poem also foreshadowed the changes that were coming over the large family, of which he was a middle child of eight. Wearing hand-me-downs was the norm, but not for a family of the supposed wealth of the Harrises. By the 1940s the family were in decline, and the signs were becoming obvious. But they were happy.

It was perfect, except for one small problem. With eight siblings it was hard to get the attention of their parents. As a reaction to this, Dickie became the family show-off. His father could be a bit forgetful at times, and would often drop his newspaper, look over the top, and ask: 'What's his name again?'

'Dickie,' an exasperated Milly would reply.

Ivan Harris, by all accounts, could be a bit distant from his kids. That was how things were with Irish fathers. They provided the money, ate the dinner at the table with the family, and disappeared behind the paper. They spent their days out working, and their nights bemoaning their fate in the pub. Their weekends were spent on the golf course, or following the local rugby or hurling team.

Ivan was into hockey and tennis, and these sports gave him an outlet away from the family. He was a figure who was only called in when discipline was needed. Physical contact between an Irish father and his son was more likely to be a slap than a hug. It made Dickie all the more determined to raise hell and be noticed.

But the signs were there that the security of home would not last forever.

'I remember great wealth and opulence when I was small but I also remember it disappearing. My mother, who once had servants coming out of her ears, was, in the end, down on her knees scrubbing floors. That's how I knew it was going,' Dickie recalled years later.

Another way he knew it was going was by the choice of school when he finished in St Philomena's. His father had gone to Downside, near Bath. But the British Benedictine school was not considered when Dickie came of age. At around 9 years old he was transferred from the cosseted environment of the co-ed little primary school near home to the tougher environment of a city-centre school.

True, it was at the start of the war. But the Blitz was more than a year away, and no one could have known the six years of horror that Europe would be plunged into. And anyway, Britain would be expected to escape the worst of it as it was not part of mainland Europe. The city of Bath did escape relatively lightly. There were two terrible nights of bombing in April 1942, because the city manufactured tanks. Over 400 people were killed. But the destruction was small compared to that in London and other cities. The only time the war touched the school was when two RAF pilots were showing off by buzzing the cricket field during a game in May 1943. One clipped a tree and crashed. Ten people were killed and fifteen injured.

The real reason Dickie was kept at home had nothing to do with the war; it was down to money. By the late 1930s the family fortunes had entered the final stages of their terminal decline. It had taken a decade, but the Harrises were no longer a wealthy family.

Ivan Harris and his brother had worked hard to keep the business afloat, and they were shrewd businessmen. But neither man was their grandfather; they were too easy-going, and lacked the killer instinct and drive of the true tycoon. Perhaps they overstretched themselves, but they didn't know how bad the depression would get, or how long it would last. And, as has already been mentioned, the final straw came when the giant British company Rank decided to monopolise the milling business in the UK and Ireland by targeting their successful rivals. In Limerick there was one obvious one: the Harris mills.

By the time Dickie came of age to attend secondary school the strain was beginning to tell on his father, who had already seen the mill and the bakeries close. He was still working around the clock to keep his wholesale and retail outlets open on William Street and Henry Street. In a poem written by Dickie in 1942, a few years later, he asks Santa Claus for a real aeroplane, a horse like Trigger, real guns and a car that won't hit the gate if he arrives home drunk like Daddy.

Seeing his father occasionally arrive home drunk may have desensitised Dickie and his brothers to drink. His father later battled alcoholism and there is no doubt that drink played a part in the early death of his brother Dermot. Children often repeat the mistakes of their parents. And there was a wild streak in the family anyway.

'One half of the family were kind of wild, and the other side were dead sound. Dickie was on the wild side,' said Kevin O'Connor.

For a while the family's local businesses – such as the bakery on Henry Street – continued to turn a profit, but the servants and the gardeners were a thing of the past. Milly Harris washed her own clothes, cooked the family meals and scrubbed the floor. And her younger sons lost out on the chance of a British public school education.

Dickie was sent to a local school, right in the heart of Limerick.

4

SECONDARY SCHOOL

The Sacred Heart College is a Jesuit school. The Jesuits are the intellectual wing of the Catholic Church, and founded a school in Limerick in 1565. Over the centuries the school came and went, according to the political winds of the times, but in 1859 the Jesuits were invited to revive their Limerick school. They chose premises on Hartstonge Street. This was the street on which Dickie's grandfather James bought his house just a few years later.

Within three years, the Jesuits had moved their school to a bigger building on The Crescent, the wide avenue that leads west from the centre of town. It was the best address in the city, its elegant façade rivalling the most elegant streetscapes of Georgian Britain. The order expanded, buying neighbouring buildings and erecting a large church attached to the school, which became known as Crescent College.

The curriculum included classics, mathematics and modern languages, and offered to prepare boys (Dickie was finally in a segregated school) for 'University and the Ecclesiastical Colleges; for the Learned Professions; for the Public Service – Civil and Military; and for the department of Mercantile and Commercial Life'. Dickie was being groomed for the sort of life that his father had been prepared for before him.

The Crescent was a fee-paying school, catering mainly for the city's growing Catholic middle class. It received no government support. By the end of the 1930s the number of pupils remained small, as few could afford education beyond the basics of reading and writing. There were only 130 in the school. But through the 1940s – the years in which Dickie Harris was a pupil – the school began to expand rapidly, with numbers quickly reaching over 300. Part of the reason for the expansion was the appearance of social climbers in the newly independent Ireland.

The Crescent was identified as a bastion of the upper and middle classes. One teacher there, Fr William Hackett, lamented that people who sent their sons to the school were 'making their way into the upper middle class on the back of the Jesuit vow of poverty'.

This elitist viewpoint was very prevalent in the 1940s, but died out a generation later, and The Crescent moved to a greenfields site on the edge of town, where it became a large and democratic comprehensive school. The modern Crescent Comprehensive is a world away from the school Dickie Harris attended.

Legends have grown up about his time in school. One of the most persistent is that Harris was the nucleus of a group of tearaways who underachieved academically and caused disruption in the school. According to the story, repeated in a number of articles and books about Harris's life, the school became so exasperated that they set up a special class for the dullards, and kept them isolated from the general student body. The class was more reformatory than school, and its eleven pupils were not expected to bother themselves with such trivialities as study and exams.

The truth is that Harris created that myth himself. During an interview on the BBC with Michael Parkinson in 1973, he told the story:

> I wasn't extremely successful at school. There was a special class in my school created for eleven boys. I was brought up a Jesuit Catholic, and they were very proud of their academic honours and the students they sent out into the world. There were eleven of us at this particular time in this particular school that they didn't want in the school. But they couldn't kick us out.
>
> So they invented a class for us eleven boys which was totally non-existent. Even today if you go back to the school you will be told that the class did not exist, and these boys did not exist. In fact I remember well an American journalist went over to Limerick to do a story on me. She knocked at the school door and asked to speak to the Dean of Studies, and she said: 'Didn't Dickie Harris go to school here?' He said: 'I'd prefer you didn't mention him in relation to this school.'

The last line may well have been true. Ireland was a very conservative society, and Harris's reputation as a bed-hopping drunk was not something his old alma mater would boast about. By then he had been labelled the most promiscuous man in the world. But he was never in a special class, or excluded from school activities. In fact he was a bright, inquisitive student, and popular in the school because of his prowess on the sports field. He did get into occasional trouble, and despite his love of English and his inquisitive mind, he was no scholar.

Vincent Finucane was a friend of Harris in secondary school, and played rugby with him briefly. He remembers:

> He was born in 1930 and I was born in 1930, and he was in the same class as me in school. I was there five years in the Crescent College. He was in my class for two years. He was a bit of a character. Nothing brainier than the rest of us. But he was no fool.

Although Finucane was a Gaelic Athletics Association (GAA) man (he was later a substitute goalkeeper on the Limerick county hurling team), he played rugby at The Crescent, because of his height and strength. He never took to the game, but kept in contact with Harris throughout their adult life. Finucane ran a successful television and electrical shop on William Street in the city, and when video recorders came on the market he used to tape games, which he posted over to Harris in London. This began in the mid-1980s, when the technology became available, and continued until the time of Harris's death in 2002.

He remembers Harris as wild and full of fun. After rugby games he would go from pub to pub celebrating. But in those schooldays he was not drinking, just enjoying the *craic*. Even then he was a larger-than-life character, full of devilment. But at school he did well, keeping up with his studies. He was an inquisitive boy and liked to ask questions. In those stricter times asking questions was not encouraged, and so Harris stood out. Often he would just ask a question to put the teacher under pressure. Sometimes he would make farting noises, then look around in innocent bewilderment as the class erupted in laughter.

'We had some great teachers,' said Finucane. 'They were the best in Munster, the Jesuits. Harris could come in there and ask a teacher a question. He could ask anything. We would be looking at him, wondering what the answer would have been, grinning to ourselves,' he recalled.

Like many of the people who went to school with Harris, Finucane never knew that the actor was dyslexic. Being intelligent, Harris was able to conceal his difficulty with reading, and he enjoyed writing.

Of course, he didn't know then that he was possibly dyslexic. He said himself that he only realised in his thirties that he suffered from the condition, which makes reading difficult. But the condition was rarely diagnosed in those days, and Harris was never formally diagnosed as dyslexic. His brother Noel said:

He maintained he was dyslexic I couldn't answer to that. I never found him dyslexic at all. He could certainly read, and read poetry very well. I don't know of his classroom work because I was two years behind him in The Crescent. We all went to The Crescent. He was never a scholar. He was never interested in studies. He was good at one language, which was English. And I think he devoted most of his time to learning English. Writing poetry was his pastime in those days.

Harris liked to perpetrate the myth that he was a dunce in school, saying once:

We used to get school reports at the end of every term. I remember a Christmas term, and the report said: 'Mathematics, out of a hundred, two. French, out of a hundred, one. Algebra, out of a hundred, none!' And out of the accumulation of all the numbers, there wasn't a pass, there wasn't a 40%.

My father had to sign the report. He was obliged to sign it and return it to the school. In the end he didn't bother. He wrote to the Dean of Studies: 'Dear Rev Fr McLoughlin, I am very pleased with my son Dickie's progress in the school.'

Harris was no academic, but he did as well as the other boys and, according to Vincent Finucane, he had no difficulty keeping up. Though he enjoyed the *craic*, he was not the class clown.

Harris, in a moment of candour, agreed. He emphatically told one interviewer (Patricia O'Connor, 1993): 'I did not play the clown at school.'

As it was assumed that Richard would enter the family business after school, there was no pressure put on him – or any of his brothers – to do well academically. All they really had to do was attend, not get into too much trouble and do well on the rugby field. Richard was more than capable of living up to those expectations.

'There is a famous rumour of him,' said Noel. 'Apparently – this is only hearsay – one day the teacher asked everyone in the class to keep quiet, Richard was asleep. And it was best to keep him in that humour. Anyway, he was never a great student, and I think he would admit that himself.'

English was the one exception; Richard had a great love of the language, and particularly of poetry and drama. At that stage he was not a recreational reader, but he was scribbling verse, and was memorising verse and bits of plays.

'He could mime and do all kinds of impressions of different actors from when he was quite young,' said Noel. 'He could quote Shakespeare as if he was just reading a book. All of this naturally happened for him, because of his love of English.'

He took part in a few school dramas during his years at The Crescent. At that stage his older brother Noel was considered the performer in the family, and by all accounts had the best singing voice of all the Harrises. But Dickie liked the limelight, and had a reasonable singing voice of his own. He may have got some of his roles on the strength of Noel's performances – if one brother had carried a show, perhaps the other could too. He took roles in a few productions, including the light opera *Martiana*, by William Vincent Wallace, for which he received some praise. But the stage was not his thing at that point in his life.

By now Harris was in his teens, and no longer pampered. He was expected to make his own way to school every day, crossing the river at Sarsfield Bridge and trudging the length of O'Connell Street to The Crescent. The great benefit of this was that it brought him through the heart of the city on his way home after school. This gave him ample time to indulge his real passion in life: the cinema.

Dickie had always lived a rich, imaginative life, as some of his early poems reveal. In the 1940s there was no television. You had to make the effort to go to a cinema if you wanted to see a film. It was the end of the golden age of Hollywood, with the star system still fully in place. Studios put major stars under contract and they built the films around the stars, as opposed to the modern practice of coming up with a story first, then casting it. Often the films were forgettable, but the performances could be sublime. Harris loved them all: Maureen O'Sullivan and Johnny Weissmuller in the Tarzan series, Humphrey Bogart and Jimmy Cagney, Clark Gable, Mickey Rooney and Bette Davis.

It was common for schoolboys to go to the cinema once a week. There would generally be a double feature: two movies with a 'short' in between. There were plenty of cinemas in the city centre to choose from – including the Savoy, the Capital and the Carlton. One might be showing a western, while another had a sweeping family saga or a gritty gangster story. And all the cinemas were on the path home from school. Dickie went to the cinema several times a week, and watched everything.

'Films were his thing. If you wanted him at four o'clock in the afternoon, the cinema was where you would find him, watching all kinds of things,' recalled Vincent Finucane. 'His legs would be up on top of the railing. I often went in and saw him there. We all did. We would all go in, watch a western. But he went to everything. He went twice or three times a week.'

He was a voracious and enthusiastic cinema-goer. Sometimes that enthusiasm could spill over into boisterous behaviour. He loved the westerns, and like many of his friends he would 'shoot up' the lobby on his way into the theatre. Once inside, he would often shout comments at the screen and pass funny remarks. Gangs of teenage boys are the same the world over, but Dickie's enthusiasm, far from being infectious, could sometimes cause problems. At various times he was banned from many of the city cinemas. But the bans were never permanent.

Harris roved the half a dozen or so cinemas that Limerick boasted, often with a few close friends. Sometimes money was short, so they would pool their resources and buy one ticket. Harris would go into the cinema and take his seat, but then as the cinema darkened before the first feature came on, he would slip out and open a fire-exit or a back door, letting his friends in to join him.

There was tremendous excitement about the cinema. The show would begin with a short film, often a comedy, or perhaps Pathé news from around the world. Then there was an intermission, where there could be a speciality act such as a magician or ventriloquist, or a fifteen-minute singalong to the wail of the Wurlitzer organ. Then the main feature would begin, holding the audience spellbound for the next hour and a half.

Legend has it that during a performance of *Julius Caesar* at the Lyric, starring Marlon Brando, Harris began chanting Mark Anthony's famous 'Friends, Romans, countrymen' speech alongside the American actor on screen. He was forcibly removed.

In November 1947 yet another cinema opened its doors in the city. The Royal could sit 600 people, and set out to be the plushest and grandest establishment in town. Staff had to have a knowledge of cinema in order to hold their positions in the new venue. The doorman was a former boxer, Denis Hayes, who was movie mad. He talked about nothing but the silver screen, and the gossip associated with the stars. He also roamed the aisles, keeping order. This was not always easy, with wild teenagers having fun.

Hayes recognised in Harris a fellow enthusiast and came to an agreement: if Dickie helped keep order on the balcony, he could slip in for half-price. The arrangement worked; Harris was a 'big man' among the teenagers, and if he told a fellow teen to shut up and behave, the boy shut up and behaved. Thanks to the arrangement with Hayes, Harris could see any film he wanted at the Royal.

Sometimes Harris would spend an entire day at the cinema, turning up for the matinee, staying for the middle show, and only slipping out after the final evening performance.

He was equally enthusiastic about watching live theatre, which was far more vibrant in Limerick back then than it is today. There were several touring companies, and Limerick was full of local amateur groups. Some put on plays, while others concentrated on light opera and musicals.

The Gate, along with the Abbey, was one of the driving forces behind the revival of Irish theatre. The Abbey was the national theatre, based in Dublin. They nurtured the talents of dramatists such as George Bernard Shaw, John Millington Synge and Sean O'Casey – and ignored writers such as John B. Keane, who would become very important to Dickie Harris later in his career.

The Gate was founded in 1928 by flamboyant actors Hilton Edwards and Micheal MacLiammoir. The company concentrated on emerging Irish writers, and modern European drama. Although they had a permanent base in a beautiful old building in the heart of Dublin, they toured the country with productions. Any time they came to Limerick they drew big crowds. Harris, in contrast to his school friends, made sure he was in attendance.

'Who knows if it all began then? I went to every performance of The Gate that came to Limerick. I was obviously drawn to what was happening on stage as much as the movies,' Harris said.

Di Lucia remembers the teenage Harris as being always very dramatic. There is a spot on the cliffs near Kilkee known as The Amphitheatre, a natural rock formation in a perfect crescent, which looks startlingly like the amphitheatres of the ancient Roman world. Harris loved the spot. Di Lucia recalls:

We would have barbecues, back at a place called the amphitheatre, just up from the Pollock Holes. And he would stand up on a rock stage, a ledge inside the amphitheatre, and recite poetry and Shakespeare and all sorts of things. So that was in the early days, when he was in his teens. He was always interested – that was before he went to London. He was a very dramatic kind of man.

While the world of stage and screen was important to Dickie, all his friends knew this was only one side of his life – and not the most important, at least at that time.

'The rugby was his hobby – films and rugby,' said Vincent Finucane.

As a boy Dickie had fantasised about leading Ireland out against England. When he entered secondary school he got the chance to turn that fantasy into reality. And he was ready. By the time he hit his early teens he was 6ft 2in, and weighed 14st. He was big and strong, and he wanted to be noticed. Crescent College had a strong rugby team; to get his place he would have to be good. It helped that his brothers had broken the ground before him, proving that the talent ran in the family. The rest was up to Dickie.

He quickly mastered the basics of the game, and got onto the various school underage teams. Being tall he played a lock, one of the forward positions. Locks form the second row, and push against the front row during scrums. They provide the power. They are also important during the line-outs because of their height. In the better-disciplined teams the locks are lifted by teammates, allowing them to snatch the high balls and feed them to their own team. They are involved in rucks and mauls. In a nutshell, when rugby gets physical, the locks are called in. An impetuous, temperamental and energetic teen like Harris – never adverse to a fist fight – was a natural for the position. Often, big men lack athleticism, but Harris was athletic. A fast and skilled player, he liked to rove around the field and was a prolific try-scorer.

In many countries, schools are ranked by their exam results, their performance in science fairs and similar criteria. But in Ireland there is only one way to judge a school: its performance on the sports field. Schools are either hurling schools, football schools or, less commonly, rugby schools. The snobbier schools tend to be the rugby ones. Crescent College was an out-and-out rugby school.

'His love at school was rugby. Rugby football was what kept him in school, frankly,' admitted Noel. 'He was very fit. He used to be doing weightlifting and bodybuilding for the rugby, because rugby was his sheer passion.'

By the time he reached age 16 Harris had got the Intermediate Certificate out of the way, the Irish equivalent of the British O Levels. He was now eligible to play for the school's senior team. As summer approached he knew he was close to selection. But a year makes a big difference, and he was a bit on the young side. He was two years younger than some of the young men he was training with every evening after school. That year, Crescent got to the final of the Munster Schools Senior Cup.

The Senior Cup is the premier rugby tournament in the province for schools, and has been contested since 1909. In the 1930s Limerick schools won three years out of ten. In the 1940s they matched that record. But in 1947 Crescent were still looking for their first win in the tournament. It was a huge deal for the school, and the excitement was intense.

Harris was a sub on the team. The school was desperate to ensure that they got the win, so the coaches – all priests – scoured the student body for big, strong teens. That was when Vincent Finucane was asked to temporarily switch from hurling to rugby. Vincent recalls:

> I was born a GAA man. My father and my father's father were GAA men. Inside in the school there was rugby, and after that you could do what you liked. I was at the Crescent College and I wasn't playing rugby. I didn't know anything about it whatsoever. It was a foreign game to me.

Fr Guinane (Gerry Guinane, the coach of the school's senior side) said to me one day: 'Is there any chance you'd do a trial for the school rugby team?' I didn't refuse him. Up beyond the railway there was a pitch, Priory Park. It is still there. We would go up there two or three days a week, and I was practising rugby. All I knew was the line-outs. I was a front row forward. Believe it or believe it not, Gordon Woods was also in the front row. Keith Woods' father.

Keith Woods played for Ireland fifty-eight times in the 1990s and early years of this century, and still holds the world record for the most tries scored by a hooker in international test games (fifteen). Finucane recalled:

And Richard Harris was on the team. I was up there with Fr Guinane, and he would be teaching me how to play rugby, with all the other lads. And I was about 6ft tall. And I was able to jump up and catch the ball and throw it out. Great stuff. Richard Harris was up there in that same field every evening, taking penalties. That was what he was doing, wearing himself out. Every evening. Over the bar.

Finucane had a talent in the line-out and rarely lost a ball, which secured him his place on the team for the final. Harris struggled to get a game as the team already had two good locks.

The school's first final caused great excitement.

'I went to Crescent in 1947, and they won the cup that year under the captaincy of Paddy Berkery, who went on to play for Ireland as a full back,' said Kevin O'Connor:

I was six years behind Dickie, and at that stage I wouldn't have known him that well, except as a brilliant rugby player. He was on the 1947 team that won the Munster Senior Cup. Dickie played in the front row. He then played in the second row in the 1949 team that won the Munster Senior Cup.

The final was played against Cork team Presentation College. It was an indecisive match that ended in a draw, and Harris had to watch from the sidelines in frustration. His older brother Ivan was on the field, which probably added to his anguish.

A few weeks later the final was replayed, and there was now a place for Dickie, alongside his brother, on the field. Dickie could read the game well and Crescent went on to win – their first win in the Senior Cup. They repeated that success on a number of occasions.

Finucane still remembers the successful campaign: 'Eventually I got on the team. The first match we had was against Cork Presentation, down in Cork. Crescent against Cork.'

This was the Cup Final, and one of the few games Finucane played with the team. 'I was terrified going down to Cork, because I could make an awful mess out of it. But in the line-outs I got maybe eight out of ten. At my ease, and no trouble to me. We won the match fifteen to five. The celebrations were mighty.' He played a few games the following year, but wasn't interested in keeping it up, and that year Crescent were knocked out of the tournament in the early stages, ending Finucane's rugby career.

Under the careful supervision of the priests, the boys on the rugby team could not get into too much mischief, but Harris did disappear, touring the pubs of Cork. Finucane maintains that Harris was not drinking at that stage:

> Richard Harris went around Cork that night, going into pubs and shops and everything. Going wild. We were very close on sixteen. Fr Bates, who was with us, went bananas. He kept saying, 'Where is he, where is he?' Dickie wasn't drinking. He was wild, but he was just celebrating. Eventually he turned up, but we had to wait a long time for Richard Harris.

The team had travelled to Cork in a fleet of taxis, and the last taxi to leave for home contained Harris. Two of the priests were there – head coach Fr Guinane and Fr Bates. Finucane was the final passenger. It was well into the night when they left Cork, and 1 a.m. in the morning when they drove through Croom, about 10 miles outside Limerick. Despite the late hour, Fr Bates whispered to the taxi driver to stop outside South's Bar, a few hundred yards from the school. He wanted to have a pint before retiring for the night, to celebrate the famous victory.

'It was about one o'clock in the morning, we were outside Croom, and they all got out for a wee,' said Finucane:

> Richard heard Fr Bates saying that to the taxi driver. So when Fr Bates went out of the taxi to do his wee, Richard says to the taxi man not to mind the priest, and to pull up outside the priest's residence at the school instead.
>
> Anyway, we passed South's Bar, and Fr Bates got all excited about it. We pulled up outside the college itself. Richard got out of the car, and as loud as he could shouted: 'What an unearthly hour of the morning to be coming home.'
>
> This is gospel truth – there were heads outside the window up in the Crescent. The priests were mortified. Don't forget, he was going to school the next day and they were teaching him. But he didn't care. That's what he did.

Once Harris made his mark on the team, he wasn't going to lose his place. He held on to it for the final two years of his schooling. In 1948 the team did not do well, but in 1949 they made the final again, and this time Harris was a regular starter, assured of his place.

O'Connor recalled:

Once, famously, he gathered the ball from a 25m drop ball. He gathered it and kicked a drop goal. That's a hard thing to do. It was probably 40 yards out from the goal. He was very talented. He might have made international status, but he got TB at the age of 19 or 20.

Shortly after this historic second win, Dickie Harris was finished with school. 'I don't think he was good enough to go for the Leaving Cert, but that could be because he was dyslexic,' said Kevin O'Connor. The Leaving Certificate is the final State exam in Ireland, the equivalent of the British A Levels. It is necessary for anyone hoping to enter third-level education. Dickie Harris had no intention of taking his education further.

Noel Harris remembers:

He didn't do his Leaving Cert. That was common. Fathers never gave advice to their children in those days. The Harris family were quite well off. I've always felt Dickie hid from this.

Any time he was interviewed he hid that point, and that upset me. We were always very comfortable. We were a pretty wealthy family. And it would be a natural thing to think in a family like ours that the sons went into their father's business. That was traditional in those days. And there was never any pressure put on us. Our father never put pressure on us to study. I was the only one who sat the Leaving Cert and got it, up to that stage. But Billy, my youngest brother, followed me, and he did it and got it as well. But Jimmy and Ivan and Richard and Dermot never sat the Leaving Cert.

It was time for Dickie to make his mark on the world.

5

A ROMANTIC INTERLUDE

It has been said that Dickie Harris had two passions in his life – rugby and acting. This is not strictly true. He was equally passionate – if not more so – about women. He grew up to be a voracious womaniser, once dubbed the most promiscuous man in the world. Even at the age of 70, two years before his death, he had to discreetly remove a woman from his hotel bedroom before allowing a journalist in for an interview. He wasn't embarrassed about being caught with a woman in his room, he just wanted to preserve her anonymity. He was behaving like a perfect gentleman.

'The women I've been with – they're all grandmothers now. But sexuality between two people is private. You don't capitalise on it, and make money out of it, just to show what a great ladies' man you were. You don't do that,' Harris told an interviewer when publicising one of his final roles, Albus Dumbledore in *Harry Potter*. 'I think people who do that, I hope the money burns in their pocket. I don't need that. I wouldn't do that.'

If Harris had indulged in kiss and tell, he would have had some great stories to relate. He had so many notches on his bedpost that it looked like it had been attacked by woodworm. Some of the names were legendary: Ava Gardner, Princess Margaret, Rita Gam, Merle Oberon, Empress Soraya of Iran, Nina Van Pallandt, Mia Farrow. Ava Gardner was a particular favourite because she was one of the few women who could out-drink and out-smoke him!

But it all began rather innocently. At the age of 6 he sat beside a young girl in St Philomena's, and fell for her. 'I was mad about her. I sat beside her, aged 6, 7, just before I went to the Jesuits,' he said.

Most Irish boys never got the chance to mix with the opposite sex, so the few years in a co-ed school had given Dickie a distinct advantage when he began to develop a serious interest in girls in his teens. Although he was not a pretty boy, he was big and tough, with a raw physicality that attracted the ladies. And he could talk for Ireland.

When Harris hit his teens he felt the normal stirrings of any red-blooded male. But Ireland in the 1940s was a very repressed society. Sex outside marriage was absolutely taboo, and any young woman who found herself pregnant knew her life was over. A chaste kiss was considered very risqué behaviour. Despite this, Harris loved the ladies and pursued them with a passion.

One of his first obsessions was with a local beauty, Grace Lloyd, the sister of a friend of his. But she had no interest in him and the relationship floundered before it began.

'I don't think she had any love for me,' he acknowledged.

As Dickie entered his teenage years, the summer retreat to Kilkee became more and more important. He felt as if the seaside resort was a sort of spiritual second home. He loved the small streets and lanes, the different swimming holes, the walls where teens sat during the day, the dark spots where they gathered by night. Kilkee was an escape. Back home in Limerick you moved in certain circles – school, sports club, neighbourhood, social class. But in Kilkee everyone was thrown together, and you met new people. You were exposed to exciting possibilities. And you were away from the prying eyes of neighbours and parents. Your mother was busy trying to look after eight kids. Your father was home in Limerick working for the week. Supervision was slight.

It was in Kilkee that Harris made his first tentative steps with the opposite sex. There were fumblings in the evenings, inexpert gropings and stolen kisses. It was very exciting. Although he didn't lose his virginity at the seaside, he took the first important steps there.

Harris said later in his life that he had his first pint of Guinness and his first sexual encounter with a woman in Kilkee – but he lost his virginity back home in Limerick. It happened in the grounds of the local maternity hospital on Ennis Road, which was very close to the centre of town and had leafy grounds with plenty of shrubbery.

However, the promiscuity of his later years was not something he indulged in at that early age. Like other young men, he was looking for that someone special – and enjoying the search. He went through a number of romances, but found no one extraordinary. Despite this, many people have their own stories about Richard Harris. You wouldn't be a true Limerick person without your own Harris story. One man recalled:

My mother was the love of his life. She worked in a shop on William Street, and he went in there every day. He was always flirting with her, but she wouldn't go out with him. He had a reputation. Years later he said on a television interview that he left his one true love back in Limerick. That was my mother.

Perhaps. But there are plenty of others with similar stories.

Harris had more to worry about than girls during his teen years. Tragedy struck the family in 1946. Dickie's sister Audrey, whom he was very close to, fell ill. As he was enjoying his first taste of success on the rugby field, his beloved sister was beginning to lose strength, and was complaining of a stomach pain. The problem was eventually diagnosed as intestinal cancer. Treatment was uncertain, with little prospect of success, but the doctors did their best. Audrey underwent a series of operations, none of which improved her condition. The intensive surgery and therapy drained her of strength.

Finally, in February 1946, Audrey passed away at home, in Overdale. She was just 21, and had recently got engaged to a local boy, Donagh O'Malley. He came from a political family and went on to become a very influential Education Minister. The family were devastated. Dickie took it very badly. Although on the surface he appeared full of bluster and machismo, the reality was that he had a sensitive soul. He poured his pain out into his notebooks. Poetry was a release. There was a big age gap between Dickie and Audrey, but she was his older sister and he was very attached to her.

Tragedy followed tragedy. The next blow to hit the family was when Jimmy was diagnosed with tuberculosis. TB was a terrible disease that killed at least half of the people who contracted it. Would the family be burying a second child? Twenty years earlier TB would have been an almost certain death sentence, but in the years following the war, antibiotics were becoming more prevalent. Streptomycin became available after 1946 and people were beginning to survive the disease.

'My eldest brother Jimmy had TB, and he went to hospital with it,' remembers Noel. 'And he was in hospital for quite a long time. I can't put a figure on it, but to me it was over a year he was in hospital, confined.'

Jimmy eventually made a full recovery. But it was not to be the last brush the family had with illness; Dickie himself was diagnosed with TB in the early 1950s.

But that was far in the distance. Dickie had a lot of living to do before that. He went on a number of dates, and embarked on a number of short relationships that went nowhere.

His first serious romance was with a woman from Waterford, who worked for a bank. Elizabeth (Betty) Brennan was just 19 when she moved to the city. Slim, elegant, with deep brown eyes and very short bobbed dark hair, she had a pixie look about her. She was a lively young woman who enjoyed a varied social life. She liked to get out and meet people, and she and Dickie moved in the same circles. Dickie was a freethinker who felt stifled by the conventions of conservative Limerick. Betty was a breath of fresh air.

Dickie met her first when he was out with some friends after celebrating his 21st birthday. He was instantly attracted to her but she was flirting with his older brother, Ivan. It took a few weeks for Dickie to work up the courage, but eventually he made his move and asked her out. Quickly a deep friendship developed between the two.

He remembered those days as happy, tranquil ones. Their social life revolved around the tennis club, and the hotels and ballrooms of Limerick – as well as, inevitably, the cinema. He also took her to the theatre regularly, as his interest in the stage developed.

Cruises Hotel, in the centre of town on the main O'Connell Street, was one of their favourite haunts. The manager there, Jack Donnelly, was from Dublin. Prior to managing Cruises he had managed Hydro Hotel in Kilkee, where he met and fell in love with Harris's sister, Harriet May (Harmay), and they had married. Dick always got on well with Jack, who remained a stabilising influence on his life, and a constant link with home throughout the years. Jack went on to manage more hotels, including the Berkeley Court in Dublin, where Dickie often stayed in later years when he was in the capital. Famously, he was occupying the most luxurious suite in the hotel in May 1989 when Frank Sinatra came to Dublin for a concert in Lansdowne Park. Harris graciously vacated the suite for the American singer. Perhaps he felt he owed him; he had slept with two of Sinatra's wives.

Noel Harris recalled a funny story from those early days:

Dick used to pretend to go to bed early at night-time. He used to have his own room at Overdale, at the back of the house. And he used to say goodnight to his mother and father, and to anyone else who was there, and go up to his bedroom. But he no more went to bed at night than I would.

He used to wait until everybody had gone to bed, and then he used to sneak out the back window of his bedroom. There was a lean-to shed below his bedroom window, leaning down at an angle. That was the store where we kept all our coal and turf. He used to sneak down the sloping roof, and he would go out the back gate. He used to go and spend the evening and the night with his girlfriend. And he would sneak back in at six in the morning and pretend he was never out. He would be called by his father and he would pretend to wake up and they would go off to work.

The girlfriend was Betty Brennan. Noel recalls:

One day my mother was in the garden and she noticed that all the slates on the lean-to shed were out of place, and she was wondering what caused it. She put two and two together, and she knew. So she waited one night for him to go. She pretended she was in bed. And he sneaked out as usual to meet his lovely girlfriend. And my mother went down to his bedroom and locked the window.

So when Richard came in the back gate and went up the sloping roof, he couldn't open the window. So how was he to get back into the house? He waited and slept outside in the front seat in the garden. He waited outside until my mother and father were having their breakfast. And when the door opened he walked in. My father said good morning to Richard, and Richard said to his father, 'Goodnight, dad,' and he went up to bed!

It was funny at the time, but Milly Harris, the matriarch of the clan, was clearly disapproving of Richard's new romance. She did not like Betty Brennan, and made no great attempts to conceal that from her son. His girlfriend was not welcome at Overdale, and got a frosty reception any time they accidently crossed paths.

The amount of time the couple were spending together – especially the amount of time after dark – was considered scandalous. Wind of the affair reached Betty's father in Waterford, and suddenly the young woman got transferred back there – 80 miles from Limerick. Today you can make the journey in under two hours, but back then it would have taken twice that time. And Richard didn't have a car. The transfer put a great strain on the relationship. But the couple didn't break up. They tried to make a long-distance romance work. Richard would go down to Waterford as often as he could; it was on the way to the ferry port at Rosslare so there was a train. But after a few months Betty was transferred again, ending up in Dublin. Dickie continued to visit, borrowing a car occasionally from one of his brothers for the three-hour journey. The couple remained close, but distance and separation were taking their toll. Eventually the relationship just fizzled out, as both of them moved on with their lives.

In parallel with Dickie's love life, he was also experimenting with the joys of alcohol, although there are contradictory accounts of his early relationship with the demon booze. Harris himself said that he was regularly drunk from the age of 17 onwards. This would have been in his final two years at school. He told stories of bingeing, and going on wild adventures. One story he often repeated was of doing a delivery to Dublin for his father at 17. He drove a lorry up to Dublin and made the delivery. He had promised faithfully to be back in Limerick for 7.30 p.m. Instead, he went drinking.

At closing time he staggered out and got into the lorry. He thought that if he stayed on the back roads he would get home fine. But on one road he encountered a bridge. Thinking he could make it, he didn't bother slowing down. There was a sickening crunch as the roof peeled off the lorry, and he got hopelessly stuck under the bridge. Then he saw a swinging light as a garda (policeman) approached.

'No problem here, officer,' he said. 'I am just delivering this bridge to Limerick.'

It was a story regularly trotted out at chat shows and press conferences, but his brother Noel says it never happened. There was not even a grain of truth in the tale.

'No such thing happened,' he said. 'Deliveries in those days were made by horse and cart. There was no such thing as lorries in those days. And certainly we didn't have a lorry in our mill or our bakery. It was all horse-drawn. He never drove a lorry under a bridge, never.'

Noel says that Dickie wasn't much of a drinker back then. He was too obsessed with keeping himself fit for the rugby field:

He wasn't a drinker and he wasn't a smoker in those days. That all started when his acting career started. I don't know how he started smoking. He had the odd drink with us, okay. When he was 19 or 20 he would have a pint or two. But he wasn't a serious drinker. Neither was any of the family a serious drinker at that stage. He liked the lifestyle of pubs, and the fun that went with it. But he never smoked until he joined the acting profession. Then of course he became a notorious smoker.

Noel did say, however, that Dickie's character began to change in his late teens, as the exhibitionist came to the fore:

When he was young he was no different from anyone else, I promise you that faithfully. When he was a young teenager he learnt like everyone else how to grow up. His character – you could see his character changing when he was in his mid-teens. He developed this character where he was an entertainer, a complete showman.

Others agree that he wasn't a heavy drinker in his youth. Manuel Di Lucia recalls his years in Kilkee: 'I never saw him drink as a youth. He might have taken a beer in his early twenties. His favourite drink was a pint of Guinness, and he used to drink in most of the pubs in Kilkee – mainly Scotts and Naughtons.'

Di Lucia said that Harris was well able to hold his drink in later life, and was never, in his company, a fall-down drunk:

As far as I am concerned, as far as my dealings with him, I have never seen him out of his mind drunk. I have seen him merry and in good form, but never have I seen him overnight take too much drink. I couldn't say that about him. He was a very decent man, very honourable. If he said he would do something he would do it. And I had great times with him, and enjoyed his company. I loved when he came to Kilkee, or if I met him anywhere else.

He was always coherent. Not fall-down drunk. He had a kind of a devil-may-care kind of attitude in some cases. He would tell the wife he was off for the paper, and end up in Dublin. He'd be in the pub and then maybe head off for a rugby match and then fly back after that, and maybe then another time say he was going to Kilkee, and end up in the Bahamas.

Harris often told another story of his early days, about hitting a double-decker bus in Dublin so hard he knocked it over, for which he was banned from driving for life. It is a great story, with its implications of drink and devilment. Unlike the bridge story, it has some germ of truth in it. But drink played no part in the accident.

'He did hit a double-decker bus in Dublin, in a hired car,' said Noel Harris:

He was driving down Marlborough Street to go to the Abbey Theatre. He was in a hired car and he had a girlfriend with him. He had met the girl in Kilkee, and he arranged a date in Dublin, to take in the play. He crossed Lower Abbey Street and he hit a bus. He wrote the car off, and he damaged the girl badly, and he was hurt himself. Both of them were injured, and the car was written off.

His life was in acting at that stage, so he must have been in his early twenties. It certainly wasn't from drink, I can tell you. At that stage he used to take a drink, but he wasn't a serious drinker. The crash was due to the fact that he didn't know the geography of Dublin.

Harris's father had to pay for the clean-up – medical bills and the damage to both vehicles. Harris was convicted of dangerous driving, and was banned for a period. But not for life, as he used to enjoy claiming.

'He maintains he was banned for life, which is bullshit,' said his brother. 'That didn't happen. That's just television talk. That accident could have happened to anybody.'

The accident did have one consequence: Richard Harris never drove again.

6

A SPORTING LIFE

Harris was living a double life. For ten months of the year he was a Limerick man, holding down a job in the family grain business that he didn't enjoy, playing rugby for one of the city clubs, and romancing the women. For two months of the year he was a Kilkee man, living a life of leisure and exuberant physicality.

The summer was a respite from the constant rugby training, but that did not mean it was a time of idleness. Kilkee had its own unique summer sport, a game called racquets. This was a very old game, quite similar to modern squash. It was played against a high wall, either singly or in pairs. Harris loved the game.

Racquets began as an eighteenth-century pastime in debtors' prisons in London. The prisoners modified the game of fives (handball) by using racquets to strike the ball instead of their hands. This sped up the game, which was played against the prison wall, sometimes using a corner to add a sidewall to the game. Quickly the game became popular outside of prison, being played in alleys behind pubs, before spreading to British public schools.

In Kilkee, one of the premier beaches of the empire, it was no surprise that the game became popular. At the western end of the sheltered horseshoe bay there are cliffs, and in 1850 a high wall was built there to protect the road at the top of the cliffs. The wall is 40ft high, and was built by a local contractor called McNamara, from Lahinch. West Clare was in the grip of the post-famine poverty and hunger, and the construction of the wall was a famine relief scheme.

With the flat, hard sand of the beach, and a high wall running alongside, it was not long before locals began to play handball against the wall. Handball is a native Irish game, similar to squash except the ball is punched, or fisted, against the wall instead of being struck with a racquet. Visitors, of course, did use racquets, and the game became established as a summer favourite. A large square of the wall was plastered and whitewashed to form the playing surface, and tournaments were arranged. The whitewashing was organised by Captain J. Wallace in 1935. But the most important tournament was the annual Tivoli Cup. The cup was presented by Captain Wallace of Ennis and was contested for the first time in 1935. It was a mixed-doubles tournament played in July.

Ivan Harris was a great lover of racquet sports, and was instrumental in establishing tennis as a popular sport in Limerick. At one point he sponsored the annual tournament. All his sons were enthusiastic players.

Limerick people dominated the event, and it was not until 1945 that a Kilkee local won it. But one family more than any other dominated the sport. James Harris, one of Dickie's older brothers, won in 1943, then repeated the win a year later. He failed to win three in a row, when Brendan McGreen of Kilkee won. In 1946 Ivan Harris was the winner. Young Dickie played well but did not survive to the finals. His chance came in 1948.

Dickie went on to win four in a row, dominating the annual event until 1951. He is the only person to have won four in a row, a record that stands to this day. In 1958 Billy Harris, the youngest of the brood, won the family's final title. The competition continued until the 1990s, when it died out. One man won seven tournaments (Paul Costello of Kilkee, between 1961 and 1974) but no one matched the four consecutive wins.

Harris loved the game, and understood every nuance of it. He kept the strings of his racquet loose, because that gave him far more control over the ball. The whitewashed wall was rough, and he knew every bump and contour of it. When he served he knew where the ball would go.

Di Lucia remembers those days well – he also played in the tournament:

Dickie was a brilliant racquetball player. We used to play a game on the beach called racquets. We used to play that with a tennis racquet and a black air ball, a small black air ball, like an unshaven tennis ball.

He was the only Limerick man ever to win the Tivoli Cup (which was played every July) four times in a row. And that was one of the big attractions in Kilkee back in the 1940s, '50s, '60s and early '70s. It was played on the beach, and everyone watched. There was a local man who won it six or seven times, but he didn't win four in a row. The thing is, Dickie is the only Limerick man ever to win four tournaments.

It was the highlight of most Limerick people's holiday, because it took place in the last two weeks of July, and it was a big attraction. There would have been hundreds and hundreds of people at it, from all walks of life in Limerick.

Noel Harris said: 'He won the racquets tournament four times. I never won it. He beat me in the final. It was played in mixed doubles. Each male had a female partner. It was huge. It was played always in the third week of July and it was called the Tivoli Cup. It was called after Tivoli House in Kilkee, which was owned by the Stokes and the Wallace family in Limerick.' Noel and Dermot were the only two Harris brothers not to put their names on the cup.

The consecutive wins made Dickie a bit of a local hero, year after year. Ever the show-off, he was glad to ham it up, and to exploit any romantic opportunities his status brought him. Many years later, when he was 40, Harris played one final tournament, reaching the semi-finals. But he never managed to put his name on the trophy again. In 1952, although he didn't realise it at the time, he was in the early stage of TB, and some of his youthful vigour was being robbed by the disease. Although he still came to Kilkee, he was slowing down, though imperceptibly.

'TB weakened him,' said Di Lucia:

Swimming would not be as strenuous as running or cycling or anything like that, because you are floating in an element. And you can swim as fast or as slow as you like. And you can take it easy. With running you are pounding all the time. The kind of swimming he did was leisurely swimming. He never went back to the rugby, or won the racquets again.

Along with his romantic and social life, the young Richard Harris also had to cope with the more mundane matters of life after school. He had to work, and he was still obsessed with the game of rugby. The actor in him had not yet begun to emerge.

Once he left school it was time to get a job. But the years after the war were tough, and the Harris business empire was crumbling fast. Kevin O'Connor said that the situation was becoming obvious to everyone.

Their business went into a decline in the 1940s. Ranks had opened up a plant on the Dock Road, not far from the Harris mill. The decline was obvious – they weren't able to provide jobs for all the family. That's an indication. Noel worked as a car salesman for Limerick Motor Works when he left school, then went to Shell and moved to Dublin. Ivan had a very poor job in Limerick. I cannot remember what Jimmy worked at.

This was an exaggeration. The family had lost their mill and closed the bakeries, but they were far from destitute. They had two large retail-wholesale outlets in the city, one on Henry Street and one on William Street. They acted as agents for Rank, and sold animal feed as well as flour and flour products. Dickie left school and went straight to work.

Jimmy was already working alongside their father in the William Street branch, so Dickie was sent to the Henry Street branch, to work under older brother Ivan. He was being groomed to take over the running of it, so he did a bit of everything. In his first few weeks he was the general dogsbody. He monitored deliveries and stock, did odd jobs, and did his best to promote and advertise the business. He was even the chief mouse-catcher!

During his rugby-playing days Dickie had clashed with a Rockwell College player, Mick English. Mick was a few years younger than Dickie, but if anything an even more aggressive and committed player. He made his international debut for Ireland while still in his teens, and was capped sixteen times for Ireland, as well as playing on a Lions side. He was from Limerick, and lived near Sarsfield Bridge, close to the centre of town. The two young men became firm friends. Mick recalls: 'At Rockwell College I was fortunate to be on a Junior Cup-winning team in 1949, and also played against Crescent in the Senior final that same year. We lost eight–nil. Not a good day. Richard Harris played in the second row for Crescent that day. We became good friends.'

Every morning Dickie would walk in from Overdale and meet with English.

'We met on a daily basis on Sarsfield Bridge and walked together to work. I went to my clerical job with the Insurance Corporation of Ireland, and Dickie to his father's flour store in Henry Street where he was the chief mouse-catcher,' English recalled many years later.

Harris used to love looking back on those days and telling tall tales. In 1973 he told Michael Parkinson:

> My family were very rich. My great-grandparents were extremely wealthy. They had flour mills and baking powder mills and bakeries. I wasn't extremely successful at school. When I left school what was I going to do? My father said come into the business.
>
> There wasn't much I could do. They had these huge big barns and lofts, and I spent my day going around with a stick, frightening the mice away from the flour.

He did chase mice; all of the staff had to. Grain was precious, and was of no use if it was infested with rodents. But he didn't patrol with a stick; he had other work to occupy him. And anyway, his preferred weapon was an air rifle. Occasionally, when business was slack, he would stand at the entrance to the grain store, immobile, just waiting. When a flicker of movement would catch his eye he would slowly bring the gun around and let off a shot. Who knows, perhaps he was practising for future iconic roles in westerns such as *A Man Called Horse*, and *Unforgiven*?

Noel Harris said of those early days:

> He went into the business immediately after leaving school. He was doing what anybody else was doing. The mill was gone. The bakery was gone. But we did blend certain products of our own, and he helped there. Ivan and himself, they both worked in Henry Street, which was a retail shop.
>
> Jimmy and my father looked after William Street. William Street was the same as Henry Street. We were agents for Ranks at that stage. Flour and animal feeds. That's where he worked for a couple of years.

But Harris was languishing in the store, and was not fully committed to ending up a minor merchant in a small city. Wholesale and retail animal feed must have felt tame in comparison to his stardom on the rugby field. And Harris felt he did not have the instincts of a businessman. Subsequent events – such as his purchasing of the rights to *Camelot*, and his insistence on a percentage of the merchandising on the Harry Potter movies – showed that he had all the capitalist instincts of his grandfather. But he didn't recognise that in himself at the time. He felt that he was wasting away in the store.

On top of that, the business empire was vastly reduced from when his father had taken over, and he knew that. There is little need for a captain to sail a sinking ship.

However, he stuck with the mill for a couple of years. What else would he do? He took his weekly wages and spent them at the cinema, and in a round of local pubs where he socialised. According to Betty Brennan, the money didn't always last to the end of the week!

Working for a family business had one important advantage: there was no boss looking over your shoulder. Even though he was not in charge when he entered the store, he was the owner's son and was being groomed for management, so his eccentricities were indulged. This gave him more time to concentrate on the important things in life: booze, women, cinema and rugby. Harris lined-out for two of Limerick's famous sides. His first senior club is now well known, but when he joined he was one of the first generation of players. Old Crescent RFC grew out of the team that won the Munster Schools Cup of 1947. The coach of that team, Fr Gerry Guinane, saw great potential in that winning side, and persuaded them to stick together and form a new club. In September 1947 Old Crescent was founded. Membership was initially confined to past pupils of Crescent College, but it later became an open club. However, the school is still a feeder for the club, providing many of their players.

In the 1950/51 season, the new side got to the final of the Munster Junior Cup, losing out to Cork Constitution by five points to three. Richard Harris was one of the stars of that season. He was a prolific scorer and showed huge promise. He also represented his province, Munster, at the under-20 level. He was having a great season.

A report in the local paper, the *Limerick Leader*, in March 1950, eulogised the performance of the rising star on a bleak and wintery St Patrick's Day (17 March). The headline said it all: 'Harris Outstanding as Old Crescent Advance'.

The Limerick side were not expected to do well against the experienced Cork team, but they won sixteen to two, advancing to the Limerick final of the Munster Junior Cup. The report read: 'Harris's Hat-Trick':

> The more fit Crescent eight had more of the loose and line-out play and full credit for their victory must go to their excellent backing up all through. Standing out head and shoulders over all others was Dickie Harris. Rarely have I seen the second-row forward play a better game. He was continually on the ball and led

almost every rush. His line-out play was magnificent and his work in the tight was untiring. Altogether a brilliant display. What more need be said when it is recorded that he scored his sides three tries?

Harris was an animal on the field. Aged just 19, the world was stretched out at his feet. The honours and the international caps were almost within his grasp.

Kevin O'Connor, who played for Old Crescent a few years later, remembers the young star:

There is a lovely story about him playing with Old Crescent. He played a game in Galway for Old Crescent. They were staying in a hotel in Salthill (a district of the city) down by the seaside. They were sitting around, and there were very few staff on. The phone rang, and Harris answered the phone. The man on the other end said he was Doctor Lane. He wanted to come up for a meal. Harris said they had some lovely fillet steak, would he like that?

'Yeah.'

'Would he like chips with that?'

'Yeah.'

'And all the trimmings? Mushrooms?'

'Yeah, I'll have that,' said the doctor.

Harris put down the phone and went straight into the kitchen. He said Dr Lane was coming up and would be there in fifteen minutes. 'Have two boiled eggs and a slice of toast for him.' The mischievous streak in him was deadly. He was always a play actor.

But he was also a skilled player. Being ambitious, he had to move from junior rugby to senior. So he had to make the move from Old Crescent to one of the other clubs in the city. Garryowen and Young Munster were the two most prominent senior clubs. Before the establishment of Old Crescent, most former Crescent College players drifted into Garryowen, so that is where Harris went to play at senior level.

His brother Noel recalled:

He played for Garryowen. But there was a ferocious rivalry. He played for Old Crescent first, which was a junior club in those days. Then he played for Garryowen in 1953, and they won the Munster Senior Cup.

All the good players who came out of Crescent College to Old Crescent ended up playing for Garryowen. If you look at the Garryowen team that won the Munster Senior Cup you'll see seven or eight former Old Crescent players in that team. And Dick was in that team. And so was Gordon Wood, who went on to play for Ireland, and Niall Quaid, and all those fellows. They were all schoolboys who played with Richard and me at school, and who played with us at Old Crescent.

Richard Harris never forgot those glory days. 'Rugby has always been there for me, even if I have occasionally gone AWOL,' he wrote in the *Telegraph* in May 2002, on the eve of the Heineken Cup Final. Munster lost out to the Leicester Tigers in that game. Reflecting fondly on the sport he said:

> I have enjoyed its many pleasures, as a player and spectator. Perhaps it is the sociability or possibly it's just the sheer physical pleasure that appeals. Very little on this earth can beat soaking your body back to life in a warm bath after an afternoon of cold rain, mud and pain with the prospect of pints and high jinks ahead. A warm glow envelopes you.

Harris's new club, Garryowen, was one of the longest established and most famous clubs in the city. They had won the Munster Senior Cup in 1947, while Harris was still a schoolboy, and to date they have won it thirty-eight times, more than any other club in the country. Harris began the season brilliantly, firmly establishing himself on the squad. Although he didn't play in the final that year, he won a Senior Cup medal.

He said of his playing days:

> I was a second-row at school but seriously miscast. I should have been a flanker. I loved roving, snaffling tries, putting in big hits – though we called them tackles in those days. I attended Crescent College, played in two Munster Schools finals and represented Munster Schools and Munster Under-20, before TB struck and I discovered books, women and a hitherto unsuspected, or submerged, desire to act and show off.
>
> God, they were great days. To play rugby and glory in your fitness. To feel invincible. If you could just bottle the moment. Rugby was life in Limerick. It was a love of sport and also a parish thing. The junior teams were based around parishes and local pride was always at stake. We were tribes and you needed visas to move safely between parishes. Intermarriage was almost unthinkable. Garryowen man/ Shannon girl? Scandalous.
>
> The rugby was intense and bloody hard – savage in fact – but, because we were neighbours, people were respectful and forgiving. Sometimes it was 'them' against us – touring sides, the interprovincial champs – and the competing parishes became a tight-knit diocese. We could be quite parochial. The players and supporters in far-flung Cork – the Posh – hated us and the feeling was reciprocated. Deep down – so buried as to not be ordinarily visible – we also respected each other as fellow Munstermen, but such solidarity was only rarely displayed or articulated.

Playing on a Munster Senior Cup winning side would be the highlight of Harris's playing career. He would go no further. Life conspired against him. He always said that he wanted to play for Ireland, or at least for Munster at senior level, but there were forces shaping his life behind the scenes, and his whole world was about to be thrown upside down. What emerged was a new man, with a new direction. But the transition would not be a painless one.

'I would give up all the accolades of my showbiz career to play just once for the senior Munster team. I will never win an Oscar now, but even if I did I would swap it instantly for one sip of champagne from the Heineken Cup,' he wrote, in 2002.

Was he good enough to play at that level? There are mixed views.

'He was very talented. He might have made international status,' said Kevin O'Connor.

Noel Harris was less sure. 'He'd have loved to play for Ireland. Sure, we'd all love to have played for Ireland,' he laughed:

> We would all have loved to play for Munster senior teams as well. But no. I don't want to take from him. He was a forward, and he was quite good. When he played he was very very fit. He devoted his life and his time to training for rugby. Other interests in those days did not count. He wasn't a very serious drinker. He wasn't a smoker. His life was based around rugby football. And he was quite good. A lot of people will admit that he was quite good. But he was a bit fiery on the field. It was easy to upset him.

He had an artistic temperament, restless and easily distracted. One opponent said that he played being a rugby player more than he actually was one. He was great at the macho posturing. He was all show, looking like a talented and dangerous opponent. But he flattered to deceive. There were flashes of brilliance, but he did not live up to his promise consistently enough to reach the top. Perhaps he knew that himself, which may have added to his restlessness.

It is significant that his friend Mick English was on the Irish team in his late teens, and had already toured with the Lions by the age at which Harris had hung up his boots. Harris did manage to make the Munster Schools team in two seasons, 1948 and 1949, but that was not enough to make him stand out, not even within the walls of his own home. Four of his five brothers made the Munster team during their teen years. One, Ivan, even went on to play for a top French club, semi-professionally.

Harris did not retire by choice. In 1952 he began to notice that his energy levels were falling, and his weight was dropping. Sometimes, when climbing up the lean-to in the early hours of the morning, he found himself short of breath.

Noel Harris thinks that part of the problem was his lifestyle catching up with him:

> As I see it, he was very careless with the way he lived over a certain period of time. Sickness did develop, but in my view part of the reason was his lifestyle. Richard

was very wild. That goes without saying. There were certain things in life he used to do. I maintain that brought on the TB, or the spot on his lung.

Late nights and the beginning of an unhealthy relationship with alcohol played their part. And Richard wasn't in a happy place in his life. The collapse of his relationship with Betty Brennan hit him hard. And he was developing a bit of a reputation for public displays of drunkenness, a reputation his parents were not happy about. He felt stifled by the conservatism of Limerick, and wanted to get away. He seriously considered emigrating to Canada. He even filled out the paperwork. But his deteriorating health prevented any move across the Atlantic.

Stress may have been a factor, but whatever the cause he was facing a genuine medical condition. Whether it was full-blown tuberculosis is a question that could be debated. Richard had noticed a certain shortness of breath beginning to affect him. Always a fit man, and a non-smoker at that stage, it was a big concern. In 1949 a spot had been detected on his lung. His brother Jimmy had spent over a year confined to a sanatorium with TB, but had made a full recovery. Was Dickie about to undergo the same ordeal?

Tuberculosis is a terrible disease caused by a bacterium which most commonly affects the lungs. Today it is completely treatable if caught in time, but back in the 1950s it was fatal in roughly half of cases if left untreated. The patient would slowly fade away, losing strength and weight, becoming a shadow of their former selves. That is why it was also called consumption; it consumed the victim from the inside.

Treatment back then was roughly the same as it is today: massive doses of antibiotics, administered over several months. A cocktail of different antibiotics are used, as the body gradually builds up a tolerance to the medication. A minimum of six months' treatment is required, and often treatment can go on far longer.

TB is an infectious disease, carried in the air and on spittle, so the sufferer has to be isolated, at least in the early stages of treatment. In the early 1950s, when Dickie Harris first began to feel listless, about 7,000 cases a year were diagnosed, putting a huge strain on the medical services. Treatment always began the same way. The patient was isolated for a couple of months in a sanatorium. Health Minister Dr Noel Browne, in 1948, had insisted that each county had its own sanatorium.

TB was a silent scourge. There was a stigma attached to the disease, and sufferers became the unmentionables of Irish society. Having a brother or a sister with TB was enough to get you removed from a seminary; your blood was considered tainted, and you were not a suitable candidate for the priesthood. In business, it could blight your promotion prospects. No one wanted to be associated with the disease.

One Limerick man said: 'My father-in-law (now deceased) was sent to the sanatorium in Limerick in the 1950s when he was 8 or 9 on suspicion of having symptoms. He climbed out the back window and went home that evening. Smart boy, he felt he was more likely to catch TB than have it already.'

Sufferers were infectious at the beginning, but after a certain period of treatment they were no longer a danger to others, and were allowed to receive visitors. This was when Harris began to see who his real friends were.

He told Parkinson:

Illness is a great burden on your friends. In the first week or month they all come and say: 'You'll be up in a month, in a week.' You have fifteen friends, and after a couple of months you have six, and then you have three. And then you have one. And then you are on your toddle. They only come at Christmas or birthdays. They are either looking for presents or giving presents, one or the other. And so I was put on my own, thrown on my own resources. I used to invent people and talk to them. The King of England, or the Pope, or whatever – never the Pope!

In an interview with *Hot Press* magazine (Joe Jackson) he said:

I probably did feel abandoned, but that word sounds stupidly romantic. But it is what I felt then. Friendships can cushion you, hold you back. When I had TB I gave up everything I'd thought was important to me. Friends stopped calling: 'Oh fuck it, I don't want to see Dickie Harris, he's still ill in bed, mightn't we catch what he has?' So yes, it was then I started studying theatre and reading books and working out what I wanted to become.

Richard Harris was luckier than most. He did not spend a year or more in a sanatorium. He was confined instead in Overdale, beginning with a number of months' bed rest. He never went to hospital and so it is possible that what Harris was suffering from was a mix of nervous exhaustion and the early stages of TB. If it had been the full-blown disease there is no way he would have been allowed to recuperate at home.

'He was confined in Overdale,' confirmed Noel Harris:

He was diagnosed with a spot on his lung – minor TB. It was treated before it became the full-blown disease. He wasn't confined in the hospital. He was confined at home and treated at home. I believe myself it wasn't quite TB, it was purely a spot he had on his lungs.

TB was quite common in those days. If Richard had had full-blown TB my father would never have allowed him to be confined in his own home. My father would have insisted he go to hospital and be treated properly for TB. But he didn't. My eldest brother Jimmy had TB, and he went to hospital for it. And he was in hospital for quite a long time. I can't put a figure on it, but to me it was over a year he was in hospital. But Richard never went to hospital.

How long he was confined is a matter of conjecture and speculation. Harris himself maintained that he lost almost two years of his life. But this is not possible; there is not a two-year gap in his life. He was playing rugby, then he wasn't. Then he was off to London. However long he was confined, it was a lot less than the twenty-two months he claimed it to be in many interviews in later years.

'I maintain he was confined to home for a couple of months,' said Noel. 'He said two years, but please believe me, I am right. He was wrong. Twenty-two months was not possible. It was six months at the most. But he was most definitely confined to bed. And he was wiped out. He wasn't just resting at home.'

Harris spoke about the loneliness of those days, but he did have some visitors. Not as many or as often as he wanted, but he was not completely abandoned. His rugby buddies did not forget him entirely. Tommy Monahan, a former president of Young Munster, the vicious rivals of Harris's Garryowen, said that some of his colleagues and teammates called on the sick player. But he said that the visits happened while Harris was in hospital, which contradicts the account of Noel.

'One of our players, Christy Horgan, got TB. He was in the bed beside Harris over in the city home,' said Monahan. 'And all the Young Munsters would go out to see Christy, and no one used go over and see Harris.'

He said that Richard fell in with the crowd that were calling on Horgan and, being a sociable man, he enjoyed the *craic* on the visits. Gradually a relationship grew up. The end result was that Harris switched allegiances, becoming a lifelong Young Munster fan.

'He fell in with our crowd. There were no Garryowen guys calling in, and that's how it happened,' said Monahan.

Noel Harris agreed that his brother became a Young Munster man during those days recovering from TB, but he differs in how it happened. He is adamant that Harris was never in the city home. However, it is possible that the actor spent a short time in hospital while the initial diagnosis was made, then was transferred home when it was realised that he did not have the full-blown disease.

'The connection with Young Munster is this,' said Noel:

My mother had Overdale, our house, painted every single year. The contractor who did the work was a man called Willie Allen. And he had a son called Willie Allen junior, who used to help his father. Willie Allen junior played for Young Munster. And of course Dick and he were ferocious rivals on the field. When he came to do the painting of Overdale, Richard was in bed. Willie Junior used to spend his break up in Dick's room talking rugby. It came about that Willie discovered that Dick was a little bit lonely. Not many people came to see him. And it was Willie who brought the Young Munster players that year. All these fellows who played against Dick came out to see him at night time. And this is where it developed.

Kevin O'Connor felt that Dickie would have been drawn to the image of the Young Munster men, who personified rebel manliness. He drank in Charlie St George's on Parnell Street, which was one of their strongholds:

> He respected them as rugby players, and as hard, tough men. These were the guys who were in the War of Independence, and most of them would have been on the republican side. One of them was shot down in a pub by the RIC at the time. Harris felt more at home with them than with the old Garryowen players. He was a republican supporter himself.'

Those days and long nights confined to his bedroom on the second floor of Overdale, above the lean-to he was no longer able to scramble down, forged his lifelong love of the club. But side by side with this devotion to a new club – a club he never played for – was a growing love for literature, and a rich imaginative inner life. In his loneliness Harris began imagining characters in the corners of the room, and talking to those characters. He wrote furiously, and lost himself in books.

Harris had always had a love of the English language, but prior to his confinement it had emerged as an appreciation of cinema and theatre, an ability to ape the speeches of the great actors, and his own poetry, which he wrote from his early teens. He was not a great reader. That changed when he found himself stuck in bed for months on end.

'He really only developed this love of reading when he was ill,' said Noel. It was a love he maintained throughout the rest of his life. He maintained that he came to reading late because he was dyslexic, and perhaps this is true. 'It was while he was ill that he developed the tremendous love of the Shakespearian plays,' his brother recalled.

Gradually, Harris's strength returned. He spent the autumn and winter of 1953/54 in his room, but as the year turned, his health began to turn with it. TB responds reasonably quickly to antibiotics, and the treatment – a single huge pill containing a cocktail of antibiotics that had to be swallowed each morning – was working its magic on his system. Sufferers say that within three months of treatment commencing energy levels return to normal, and the patient begins to regain weight. They remain confined until the condition is completely eradicated, but once they are no longer contagious they are commonly allowed to leave the hospital or sanatorium for the day, returning in the evening.

In Easter 1954 Richard Harris was ready to take his first tentative steps back into the world. Where would he go but to his beloved Kilkee? He spent a number of weeks mooching around the resort that spring, reacquainting himself with friends, revisiting his favourite pubs. But he had quietened down considerably. The vital energy was dimmed. He was no longer doing handstands on the strand wall or ramping bicycles into the sea. He wasn't swimming the big bay. He was gradually allowing his strength to return, and reassessing his life.

There were changes. He never played rugby again. His interest in the sport did not wane, but he never laced a shoe in anger after the successful 1953 season. Aside, that is, from his iconic role in *This Sporting Life*, a decade later. Another change was that he stopped working for the family business. He had been restless and unfulfilled in the job, and would have probably left it in any case, had his brush with TB not speeded up the process.

In later years, Harris joked about his final days on the job. His favourite story was that he led the workers in the mill out in a strike against his father, over pay. In 1973 he told Michael Parkinson:

> I remember when he finally got rid of me. I thought all his workers and millers were underpaid. So I brought them all out on strike against my father. And they all had signs that said: 'Your son said we should all have more money'. So he got rid of me.

The audience loved the story. But that is all it was – a story. Actors are notorious inventors, and he was putting in a performance for Parkinson. It went down brilliantly – except at home. He told the story often, and each time it was like he was driving a nail through his father's heart. It was a continuous source of friction between the two men.

Noel Harris said:

> He told Parkinson that he caused a strike in the mill. That's a rubbish story. The mill was closed twelve years before he ever went into the business. The Harris mill was closed before the war, the main mill that he was talking about, where the first day that he joined the mill he caused a strike because he maintained that the staff weren't being properly paid. That's fucking rubbish. I had to tell his children. Even his children believed him that he did that. The mill closed in the late 1930s. Dick didn't leave school until 1949, so where is the story?

The truth is more mundane, and so not suitable for a prime-time chat show. After recovering from TB, he never returned to the store on Henry Street. He was looking for a new direction in his life:

> I didn't set out, as Olivier did at the age of 6, to be a great actor. I didn't realise I wanted to be an actor until I had TB in my late teens. There had been a sense of desperation before then, wondering what the hell I was going to do, or be. Much of it had to do with establishing an identity, saying I may be just number five in the family, but I must assert an identity above and beyond all that. I wanted my parents to recognise who I was. That probably gave me my energy, my drive.

One thing had become increasingly important to him. He had begun to develop an interest in drama. It was always latent within him. His love of literature and language would have drawn him to the stage if nothing else did. But there were other factors. One was his friendship with Mick English, which survived the TB. Some of his early acting experiences happened in the company of this rugby buddy.

7

THE ACTOR IS BORN

Acting in the early years of the Irish Free State was a wandering and fickle profession. In the rural areas, fit-ups were popular. A troop would arrive and set up a tent, stage shows for a few days, then pull out and fit up in the next town. Sometimes they would use the local parish hall instead of carrying a tent. The productions might feature musicians and singers, a magician, maybe a rickety projector and a movie, and a play. 'Fit-ups' didn't visit the cities, but touring companies would take over a local theatre for a few days, bringing some welcome colour to the lives of the inhabitants.

One of the most famous of the actor/managers who toured Ireland from the 1930s to the 1960s was Anew McMaster, a Monaghan native. A powerful Shakespearian actor with an international reputation, in 1925 he decided to set up his own company and tour the country, presenting the classic plays to schools and theatres. He managed the company, directed the shows and starred in them himself. Limerick was often on his itinerary. He would visit the city once or twice a year.

His business model was simple. He kept the stage spartan, and the cast tight, so that he could tour economically. They would stay with local families in boarding houses, and everything was done to keep the costs down. McMaster used to stay in the home of Mick English. Harris recalled the excitement caused by the annual visit of the strolling Shakespearian company, and the famous actor and his family who stayed at the English home near Sarsfield Bridge.

In an interview in 1998 he told Limerick man Joe Leddin:

Anew McMaster used to stay in Mick English's mother's house. And Mick, myself and Terry Curtain used to go there night after night. There was a big fire in the kitchen, and Anew McMaster would regale us with stories about Shakespeare, and with stories about the theatre, which began to ignite me, to ignite my imagination.'

We did a production of *The Mikado* out in the English's orchard. Mick's mother got a little wicker basket that had fruit in it, and she threw it on the floor. She put the basket on Mick's head as a little cap, and a little white dress. Mick, me, Teddy Curtain, and a group of others, performed in front of Anew McMaster, Mary Rose McMaster and Margery McMaster, in the orchard. That was the beginning of my career as an actor.

That was nothing more than fun, and for Teddy Curtain and Mick English, the end of their thespian ambitions. But Dickie enjoyed the limelight. He loved hanging around the professional actors, and lending a hand. He said:

Anew McMaster gave Mick, me and Teddy Curtain two shillings, and we played the crowd in *Oedipus Rex*. Mick and Teddy and me, along with Patrick Mcgee and the famous Harold Pinter, and all we had to do was say: 'Oedipus save us, Oedipus save us.' They were terrible. I was brilliant.

Mick English remembered the influence of McMaster on the young Harris. He recalled being asked to provide bodies as extras for a stage production of *A Tale of Two Cities*. English provided him with some of his friends, including Harris and Teddy Curtain. Curtain was a classmate of Harris. They were paid half a crown each per performance to do the mob scenes.

'Subsequently Harris was badly bitten by the acting bug, and spent hours talking about acting in my mother's kitchen with McMaster. McMaster persuaded him to go to London and join an acting school,' said English. 'Anew McMaster was a huge influence on him, telling him the best thing he could do was go to London.'

Harris helped out with a few of the productions, but he didn't take things too seriously at that stage. He wasn't the showman in the family. The Harrises were known as good singers, but Richard was not the one with the voice.

Ironically, his two brothers, Noel and Dermot, whose names did not make the Tivoli Cup in Kilkee, were the ones with the reputations for singing. Noel was a star with the local light opera society, the Cecilian's. The Cecilian Musical Society is a Limerick institution. It was founded in 1919 by the Jesuit order, the priests who educated the Harris family. They staged all the classic musicals and light operas – Gilbert and Sullivan, *West Side Story*, *Guys and Dolls* – and put on shows every year, to a very high standard. They were big productions, with large casts. Richard never showed the slightest interest in getting involved – but Noel did and he never had to languish in the chorus. He was the leading man. Noel joked:

They all say the wrong Harris went to Hollywood. I was the one involved in that world as a young man. I was in the Cecilians. I did all the lead parts in their productions. Richard never had a great voice. I had. I was the one God gave a pretty decent voice to, and I had it trained in Limerick for five or six years. I studied under a professor in Limerick on voice production.

I took the lead in all my school operas, and then when I left school I graduated into the Cecilian Musical Society. I was with them for a number of years, until I got married, and work took me to Dublin. Jim had a very good voice as well.

Kevin O'Connor confirmed where the talent lay: 'The best singer in the family was Noel. I was in several shows with him myself, with the Cecilian Musical Society. Noel was a very handsome guy, and a much better singer than Dickie, but Dick sold records all over the world. Ironic, isn't it?'

Dermot, who went on to manage Dickie, was also a good singer.

What really turned Richard into an actor was an encounter with a fit-up troop in Kilkee as he recovered from TB and looked for a new direction in his life.

Harris spent the summer of 1954 in his spiritual home by the sea. But instead of swimming, playing racquets and chasing women, he walked the streets and brooded. He also had a pint or three in the local hostelries every evening. During the holidays, a university drama group arrived in the village to put on a show. Drama has always been popular in West Clare – the Doonbeg Festival, which takes place only a few miles from Kilkee, is one of the most popular stops on the amateur drama circuit. There would be full houses for the show.

The group was led by Lelia Doolin, a young Cork woman. She was a few years younger than Richard, but was already seen as an academic high-flyer. She had studied French and German at University College Dublin, then won a scholarship to study at the Brecht Theatre in Germany. After that she went to University College Galway (UCG) to study for her masters. She went on to work for RTÉ, the Irish national television station, as a producer and presenter. She was also artistic director of the Abbey Theatre, and a film producer.

In 1954 she was the auditor of the DramSoc, the UCG drama society. Along with actress Kate Binchy, and Michael Garvey who went on to be a producer with RTÉ, she set up one of the last of the fit-up companies. Called 'The Guild', they took the company to Kilkee, where they set themselves up in the local hall. Throughout the summer they staged a number of productions. As the place was full of holidaymakers from Limerick crying out for entertainment, the venture was a big success.

The company took two houses for the summer. One was in the East End, and the boys stayed there; the other was in the West End, and that is where the girls stayed. The girls got the better side of town. They shared all the chores evenly. One minute you could be doing the lights, the next minute boiling the potatoes for the communal dinner.

'Dickie's interest in acting started in Kilkee that year,' confirmed Noel:

We were staying in a house overlooking New Found Out in the West End. There were two semi-detached houses, the very last houses on the West End as you go towards the Pollock Holes. They were shaped like a castle. We had one of those houses, and the second house was taken by the college players.

A girl called Lelia Doolin was down in Kilkee doing the summer season. Dick got involved with them. He used to help them with the scenery at different times. He got into the whole atmosphere of acting because of Lelia Doolin.

Dick introduced himself to the group, and asked could he help out backstage. The group was glad of the extra pair of hands. Harris was glad of the diversion.

'He can thank her and her group, that they gave him the taste for acting. He rarely slept in our house that summer. He used to sleep in their house with them. He totally threw himself into it, and this is where he developed his sheer love for acting,' said Noel.

A number of years later, while Harris was performing a one-man show on the West End (of London, not Kilkee), Lelia Doolin was doing an arts documentary, *Broadsheet*, for RTÉ. It was 1963, and Harris was getting good reviews for *Diary of a Madman*, a show he had produced himself based on the short story by Nikolai Gogol. Doolin's documentary was on the Irish invasion of the British stage, and young Harris, along with fellow hellraiser Peter O'Toole, was among the future stars she interviewed. He appeared in a traditional knitted Aran sweater, rather than the more conventional jacket and tie of her other interviewees. On the billboard behind him, his own name appeared above the name of the play – and every bit as big. The ego had landed.

'When Richard was starting to make his name in London, producing his show in the West End, Lelia interviewed him on television. He was a very young man starting out, but she interviewed him because of this love affair or friendship that developed between them in Kilkee,' said Noel.

In fairness there is no evidence that there ever was a love affair between the pair. But there certainly was an affair that summer, and it turned into a lifelong obsession: by the time summer was over, Richard was in love with the stage. When he returned to Limerick he joined the College Players, a local amateur dramatic group. The group had been established in 1926 and held weekly workshops for enthusiastic learners. He claimed that he joined the group on a whim. He said he was walking past a hall and saw their sign, saying 'You can be an actor', and thought, why not?

The truth is that the seeds of an acting obsession had been sown in his early dealings with Anew McMaster, and watered during his summer in Kilkee. So when he noticed the sign, he was ready for it.

He enthusiastically joined in the weekly workshops, learning the basics of his trade. It was quickly apparent that he was a born show-off, with a great deal of stage presence, but no discipline. He knew it all, and wasn't interested in direction. It had to come instinctively, an expression of his soul.

One man who was heavily involved in the group, Kevin Dineen, said that there were no signs of great acting ability. It was all presence and showmanship. Dineen said that Harris at that point had all the makings of a good variety artist – perhaps a magician or a comedian. Harris was not long with the College Players, and never established himself as an actor. Unlike Noel, he did not get the leads. He struggled to make the crowd scenes.

'He was never on stage in Limerick,' said Noel. 'There is no record whatsoever of him ever having appeared in a play in Limerick.'

There was a rumour that he had a minor part in a production of an obscure European play that the group staged. The play was *Easter*, by August Strindberg, a Swedish playwright from the turn of the century. *Easter* was a symbolic religious drama, and heavy-going, but the College Players did not shy away from hard work. Harris took one of the minor roles, just a few lines.

According to Noel he did not begin smoking until he began hanging out with actors. And he began to drink more heavily as well. He maintained his rugby friendships, and continued to drink in the rugby pubs, but he also dropped in for a pint to the more arty pubs in town, such as The White House. He also began to develop more bohemian friendships.

One of the people he hung out with was a young poet with a growing reputation. Desmond O'Grady was destined to become one of the more important – though little-known – figures in Irish literature. He was born in Limerick in 1935, so he was a few years younger than Harris. He was in his late teens when they began to move in the same circles, but they quickly became firm friends.

Is there any significance to the fact that many of Harris's close friendships in those days were with people a little younger than himself? His rugby buddy Mick English was three years younger than him; Des O'Grady almost five. In Kilkee he became a close friend with Manuel Di Lucia, a friendship that lasted his lifetime. There was a large age gap there too.

Actors love to be the centre of attention. It is one of the big draws of the profession, and by all accounts Harris was typical of the trade. Being the fifth of a large family he was always vying for attention. His exploits on the rugby field could also be read in that way: playing the macho sporting hero. His pranks at school, his smart comments in the cinema, his handstands on the strand wall at Kilkee: all were cries for attention, different ways of saying 'Look at me!' Actors need their acolytes. When they become stars, the acolytes follow naturally. But Harris was no star then. So perhaps that is why he gravitated towards younger men, men who would look up to him.

Des O'Grady was a teen with an intense love of literature, and a burning ambition to leave Limerick for more cosmopolitan shores. These were two things he had in common with Harris. It was enough to form the basis of a solid friendship.

O'Grady did achieve his ambition to leave Limerick. A few months before Harris took the plunge and went to London, O'Grady scraped together the fare to Paris. He taught in the 'City of Light' and also began to write seriously. It was the start of a peripatetic career that took him to Rome, the Middle East, America and, finally, to the American University in Cairo and the University of Alexandria, Egypt. He gained his MA and PhD at Harvard, specialising in Celtic languages and comparative literature, and published nineteen volumes of his own poetry, as well as eleven volumes of translated poetry from different cultures.

Funnily enough, he also tried his hand at acting, appearing in Federico Fellini's *La Dolce Vita*. Nobel prize-winner Seamus Heaney said of him: 'Desmond O'Grady is one of the senior figures in Irish literary life, exemplary in the way he has committed himself over the decades to the vocation of poetry and has lived selflessly for the art.'

O'Grady has now retired to Ireland, but is in poor health.

Mixing with O'Grady brought Harris into contact with others in the rather limited Bohemian subculture of Limerick. One of those was a young artist, Jack Donovan. Again, he was four years younger than Harris. Born in 1934, he loved painting, but unlike his two friends, he had no ambition to fly the coop. He was quite happy to remain in Limerick. In 1951, at the age of 17, he had entered the Limerick School of Art and Design, in the centre of town. He eventually became part of the staff of the college, and between 1962 and 1978 he was head of the college. He is one of the most influential artists the city has produced, being responsible for training several painters and sculptors who went on to gain international reputations. He is still in Limerick, living in Croom, a small village just south of the city, and he is still producing art. Although he did not consider himself an intimate friend of Harris, he remembers well the years they moved in the same circles:

I knew him mainly through Des O'Grady, the poet. He was a good friend of Des, but I wouldn't have been bosom buddies with him. I was a student at the time, only 19 or 20. I was living out in Rathkeale and coming in to the art college. But we had a few good sessions together.

Harris and O'Grady and myself, and a small group of us, we drank together several times. We all drank in the White House. We were always a bit wild. It is hard to know how heavily he was drinking at that stage. I wouldn't say he was too heavy a drinker, as far as I could see. He certainly wasn't alcoholic. Most people that age, and particularly in the kind of Limerick we had then, we all drank maybe too much.

He definitely stood out from the crowd. He was taller than the rest of us, and he had broad shoulders, a typical rugby player. He was handsome, I suppose. He was an intelligent man. We were all sceptics at that time, unbelievers. I think, outside of the interest in the arts, that was the attraction. He was definitely a freethinker. Was he a ladies man? He probably was – we all were, after a few pints!

Harris was just one more face in the crowd, but Donovan said that he found the actor an enjoyable companion. But O'Grady was the pin that held them together, and once O'Grady was gone, they drifted apart. They did not remain in contact as adults:

> I remember that occasion, when O'Grady went to Paris. That was before Dickie left for London. We saw O'Grady off on the train, then we had four or five pints together in Charlie St Georges, which was across the road from the railway station. I liked him. He was interested in painting, he was interested in poetry, and in rugby. Rugby was big with him.

Donovan knew that Harris wanted to be an actor, but that he was finding it a struggle. He had been rejected for all the leading roles by the College Players, and he took that hard, blaming one of the more experienced members for the snub.

'I remember him with Kitty Brady,' said Donovan. 'She used to do drama, and she won something at the big All Ireland Amateur Drama festival in Athlone. On one occasion Dickie told me that he was interviewed for the College Players, and he didn't make the cut. I think he blamed Kitty for that.'

But part of the problem may have been that Harris simply wasn't good enough at that stage. 'Full of bluster with no great technique – that would probably sum him up when I knew him,' said Donovan.

Harris might have been taking knocks in his new world, but he was an unbounded optimist and did not let them affect him. He had an inner confidence, and a faith in himself. He belonged in front of the lights, and was never a shrinking violet.

One day, as he was walking down O'Connell Street, he spotted a familiar figure near Roches Stores, a big city-centre department store. He did a double take, confirming that he had indeed spotted Rita Gam, the Hollywood starlet. Why she was in Limerick that May afternoon is not known. But Harris would have known her anywhere. Half French, half Romanian, and fully American, she had sultry dark looks and a great body. She was three years older than him, and had already starred in a number of movies. Her most recent was *The Thief*, where she was paired with Ray Milland. It was an unusual film noir, a black-and-white cold-war spy thriller distinguished for the fact that there was no dialogue in the movie. Some loved the gimmick, while others thought it made for a dull and slow-moving evening. Harris was well aware of the controversy. *The Thief* had played in the Savoy cinema only weeks before.

Never a shrinking violet, Harris approached the beautiful stranger and chatted with her briefly. A friend of his, photographer Dermot Foley, was passing by and Harris got him to take a picture. More than fifty years later Gam still looks beautiful. Harris looks awkward, slightly smug and a little star-struck. He almost looks shy.

The photograph was published in the local *Limerick Leader* a few days later. Gam, who was the chief bridesmaid at the wedding of Grace Kelly to Prince Ranier the following year, went back to her glamorous lifestyle. Little did she know that within a few years she would be another notch on the Harris bedpost.

Many factors were pushing Harris towards the stage. His encounter with Lelia Doolin and her fit-up crew, his annual fun with Anew McMaster, his stumbling efforts to get into the cast of the College Players: all were pushing him in one direction. He still had an obsession with rugby, and his desires on that front were still alive, but he was changing. Now he was drinking more heavily, he had begun smoking, he wasn't lifting weights or taking care of his body the way he had before the touch of TB. He knew his life was coming towards a crisis, and he felt strongly that the crisis would be resolved only by leaving home and searching out new horizons.

Around that time, a few of his rugby buddies suggested he travel to Dublin with them for an international match. He didn't need much persuasion. The plan was simple. They would travel up the night before and then hit the pubs to build up some Dutch courage. Then they would hit the dance halls and show the Dublin girls how Limerick men party. Harris, a self-proclaimed 'horny bastard', was in his element.

It was not an easy journey to Dublin. None of them had a car, so they were hitchhiking. A bunch of guys together is trouble, so they struggled to get a lift. Finally a succession of trucks and lorries got them to the outskirts of the capital, then a car stopped and brought them the final few miles. The friends then proceeded to put their plan into operation. They hit the bars.

There were four friends together, and they were in very high spirits. As they roved down one of the streets, something caught Dickie's eye. He walked over and read the poster. It was for a production of *Henry IV*, but not by his beloved Shakespeare. This was a more modern work, by Italian writer (and Nobel prize-winner) Luigi Pirandello. It was a study of madness, with both comic and tragic overtones. It was heavy-going, and only a real theatre lover would have been enticed to part with the ticket price.

'You go to the dance,' Harris told his shocked friends. 'I'm going to this play.'

That night was when the final pieces fell into place, and the epiphany was complete. His destiny was decided.

Henry IV remained important to him; in 1990 he produced and starred in a very troubled, but successful, run of the play on London's West End.

Harris remembered what Anew McMaster had said to him on his last visit to the city. If he wanted to become a successful actor – and he could – he would have to go to London to do it. That was where opportunity lay. At Harris's age (already 24) he could not let the grass grow under him. He would have to get to one of the drama schools and do a crash course to bring his technique up to standard.

Harris had been sending to London for information, but he knew that he just had to take the plunge. He sat his parents down and explained to them what he wanted to do with his life.

Legend has it that his mother was tearful, but his father was delighted to see the back of him, growling, 'For God's sake, let him go.'

A lovely story, but like many that Harris was to tell over the next five decades, it was pure fiction. His father was surprised, but supportive. His parents were always supportive of Dickie, and the rest of their children. Noel said:

> He got on very well with my father and mother. There was never a row in our family. I can remember it distinctly when he approached my father and said to him: 'I am going to become a professional actor.' And I can remember my father, by Jesus, he couldn't believe it.
>
> Was he upset? Not at all. But he was totally surprised that it happened. He never saw Richard having a desire or a love of acting. I mean, he was never on a stage in Limerick.

Despite this, the family gave their blessing. Richard gathered his meagre savings and took the train for Dublin, from where he would take the boat to his destiny.

LONDON CALLING

Harris left Limerick for London in 1955. It was the lot of most of the Irish emigrants who boarded the boat for Holyhead or Liverpool that they would end up working on the roads. Living in grimy bedsits, the only escape from their dull and desperate lives was alcohol. Harris would have been prepared to put up with the discomfort in order to achieve his ambition, but he assumed that it was only a temporary measure before he went on to greater things.

It was time for him to follow the trail of exile, for there was nothing left for him in Limerick. He had no interest in the family business or conventional employment of any kind. He was known as a young man with some talent as yet undefined, but somewhat feckless; of good and respectable breeding but with no real prospects. There were few actors in Limerick and Ireland at the time. A career in acting was unheard of – and was certainly viewed by his father as little more than a waste of time.

Apart from learning the rudiments of his profession, Harris would also be free of the suffocating, depressing atmosphere of mid-1950s Ireland and the crushing influence of both conformity and the moral imperative of the Catholic Church. He was brash, loud, confident and fun-loving, and out of kilter with the social and religious ethos of his native city and country. He was ready for any opportunity that London would offer. At least in this imagined cosmopolitan atmosphere he felt he had some chance of turning dream to reality, which in his home town would be a virtual impossibility.

In London, he went for an audition to the Central School:

I walked in with all these aristocratic-looking ladies and gentlemen sitting there, looking at me saying, 'What are you going to do for us young man?' I replied, 'Shakespeare.' I did my piece and afterwards they said to me: 'What right do you think you have to enter our profession?' So I looked up and said: 'The same right as you have judging me.' Then a bell rang, a little man came in and they put me out.

He immediately applied to the London Academy of Music and Dramatic Art (LAMDA) and was called for an audition. After performing pieces from *Richard III*, *Cyrano de Bergerac* and improvising, he was told that he was accepted on to the course. At 24, he might have seemed a man to his mainly 17-year-old classmates and, as a self-admitted poor student, he would find it harder to study the texts. But in the Stanislavsky class he found his acting feet, which gave him great confidence as an avid fan of Brando. He was also interested in direction and, in the absence of classes in this discipline, was put in charge of the end-of-term performances, which included extracts from Shaw's *Saint Joan*, Miller's *Death of a Salesman* and Synge's *Playboy of the Western World*.

He also was able to feast on theatre in a manner that would have been impossible in his native country. Limerick largely had to wait for the touring companies and Dublin was dominated by the Gate Theatre and the Abbey, given the witty sobriquet 'Sodom and Begorrah' as a result of the dominance of homosexuals at the Gate under the control of Micheal MacLiammoir and Hilton Edwards, and the devotion to plays of the native tradition at the national theatre. He was in his element in the large social pond of London, away from the claustrophobia of his home town. However much he loved Limerick, as he once said, if you farted everyone in Limerick would know it. His dynamism and energy had an outlet, there were plenty of young and beautiful students around and he was imbued with ambition.

In London, Samuel Beckett's *Waiting For Godot* was playing at the Arts Theatre, directed by Peter Hall, and *Hamlet*, with Paul Scofield, was playing at the Phoenix; the Royal Shakespeare Theatre was in continual repertory at Stratford. Harris also met up with his Limerick friend Desmond O'Grady, who was pursuing the literary path of Joyce in Paris and was in equally tight financial circumstance. The pair resumed their literary discussions from their times in Limerick. They talked about plays and poems and *Finnegans Wake*, and filled their minds even if their stomachs were empty.

It was in the company of O'Grady in a pub that Harris overheard a conversation about a new production of Brendan Behan's *The Quare Fellow*, which was being produced by Joan Littlewood. He told his companion that he would try for it, telephoned the workshop and spoke to the manager, Gerry Raffles, who, when establishing the actor's age, informed him that the role was for a man twice his age. Harris persisted and told him he could play to that age, so the manager said he would see him.

This refusal to give up against the odds was an ingrained characteristic that would stand the fledgling actor in good stead, for it was plainly absurd that a 25-year-old could fit into the ageing skin of a 50-year-old; make-up and greying of hair would only serve to underline the obvious gap. Joan Littlewood thought the same and halfway through the audition interrupted, telling Harris that he was far too young for the part. But there was another small part that he could play for a wage of £10 a week. Had he not insisted on being seen, this opportunity would never have arisen.

There are some men who wait for the tide, Richard Harris was not one of them. It was not simply that a door had opened for him, he had burst through it.

He had taken his first step on the ladder to fame and it was a big boost financially. He had been kept by an income from his aunt's shares, but when everything was taken into account there was very little left to live on.

He was never one to stick with the school curriculum, so next he decided to do his own thing and direct a stage adaptation of a Clifford Odets scripted film *The Country Girl*, which had starred Bing Crosby and Grace Kelly and which he renamed *Winter Journey*. During the gestation of the idea he had based himself at the Troubadour cafe on Old Brompton Road, which became his office with an entourage of six or seven other students of LAMDA. He felt that he could not cast the heroine's part from the college so put an advertisement in *The Stage*, which produced an immediate and voluminous response.

The auditions were held at the cafe and one young actress by the name of Elizabeth Rees-Williams, who was at RADA, so impressed the director that a week later he offered her the part. She had been introduced into the equation by a friend, Peter Prowse, who had been cast in the male lead role. Harris was equally impressed with her stunning good looks, and some of his fellow students felt that this had a bigger influence on his decision than her acting ability, which was not widely admired.

She was in her fifth term at RADA and the head confirmed the general view when he told her that her future as an actress was somewhat limited. In truth, she was having a whale of a time outside classes. She was also from a privileged background, daughter of a Liberal peer, Lord Ogmore, though apparently the director had no idea about that when he cast her.

The play was booked in for a run at the tiny Irving Theatre off Leicester Square and the investment that Harris had managed to scrape together from his own meagre resources was unlikely to be recouped. Harris did not anticipate a success with *Winter Journey*, it was only a case of dipping his foot in the water and satisfying his first creative desire to become a director. He was convinced, as always, that he would go on to greater things. Harris was so absorbed in the rehearsals that he initially showed no interest in his leading lady. There was no question of even a small attraction at this juncture. Elizabeth kept her family background to herself in case it might lead the fiery Irishman to despise her in some way.

She could, however, hardly fail to be intrigued by his handsome features and rugged build and even more so by his personality and enormous energy. One quality that Richard Harris possessed from an early age was charisma, a quality that would last him a lifetime. He had both a powerful and overpowering presence that was matched by a razor-sharp intellect. He was hugely well-read by this stage and had a strong opinion about everything. It would prove an irresistible force for a young woman of an entirely different family background and the pair eventually became romantically involved. This led to the couple visiting his relations in England and ultimately a meeting with her parents, whom she had previously informed of the relationship.

He was hardly an attractive proposition from their point of view. The acting profession was of course notoriously insecure, a game of lottery depending as much on luck as on talent. Right place, right time was the imperative as opposed to the inevitable path of more conventional professional pursuits. But Lord and Lady Ogmore could not have known that this prospective son-in-law was a horse of a different colour when it came to the matter of any profession he chose.

Elizabeth organised a dinner at which her suitor would be introduced to her parents. The young Harris was unfazed and had no problem in explaining the present state of his straitened circumstance. Lord Ogmore enquired of Richard's intentions and if he was saying that he would like or wish to marry his daughter. He received a simple one-line affirmation.

Permission was granted and the engagement was reported in early 1956 by Fleet Street columnists and picked up in the *Limerick Leader*, an even bigger subject for Harris's home town. He had hardly left his place of origin and he was already receiving star attention – a role that obviously he would have to live up to: prospective marriage would not be enough.

In that regard, the production of *The Quare Fellow*, even though Harris's part was small, would put him on the road to success. The show opened on 24 May 1956 in the rambunctious presence of the playwright Brendan Behan, who got up on the stage after the curtain, made a speech to the audience and sang 'The Old Triangle'. Behan's no doubt alcohol-fuelled involvement had no effect on the reviews, which were hugely positive. In fact his antics, in the very staid arena of English theatre, got plenty of coverage and drew attention to the production.

The most influential reviewer, Kenneth Tynan, famous for his withering assessments of plays that did not meet his high standards, said that it was a tremendous new play: 'Joan Littlewood's production was the best advertisement for Theatre Workshop that he had yet seen, a model of restraint, integrity and disciplined naturalism.' It belonged, he added, to 'theatrical history'.

Throughout Harris's career he would always acknowledge the debt he owed to Joan Littlewood, referring to her as a superior woman, a marvellous lady who taught him everything he knew.

Harris was enervated by the impact of what would have been considered, at the time, as alternative theatre to the establishment, which was about to be overtaken by so-called new and lesser actors not schooled from the usual sources, and influences that for the younger participants were more oriented to the films coming out of the changing ethos in both Britain and America.

It was clear, whatever his circumstances of the time, that the Irish actor had an ambition to reach the same heights as the icons of the screen that had obviously inspired him. In his heart it would be only a matter of time. He was one of a group of Irish actors who took the option of pursuing the greater opportunities that London had to offer, including Norman Rodway, T.P. McKenna, Donal Donnelly and Godfrey Quigley among others, some of whom would become fixtures on the capital's stage. All would experience tough times before breaking through, including Donnelly, a superb character actor who was less enamoured of the route than Harris: 'I managed to live on £6 a week by working as a waiter or a post-office sorter, but I was not able to act until I found night work at the Royal Court.' His Limerick counterpart was in a hurry, which may have had something to do with his relatively late start but was also undoubtedly down to his gregarious personality and drive, which in a short space of time had already brought him notice of a high order.

Arthur Miller had been to see *The Quare Fellow* and had been so impressed by Harris's performance that he saw him as perfect for the longshoreman Louis in *A View From the Bridge*, which was due to open in the Comedy Theatre in London.

He would receive even more notice for his upcoming marriage to the debutante daughter of Lord Ogmore. For the press, there would be a fairy-tale element to the unusual union of a relatively unknown Irish actor and a young woman born into a family of privilege. In Elizabeth Rees-Williams's circle of friends there would have been considerable disquiet about what was perceived as a rather impulsive action, most particularly as the choice of her affection had little or no financial prospects.

The 20-year-old Elizabeth was undaunted and accompanied Harris to Limerick to meet the family. The visit was big news and was covered extensively in the *Limerick Leader*. In the normal course of events such a story would fade in future editions, but little did the newsman and the local public anticipate that in the personage of Richard Harris the narrative had just begun.

There was further coverage in the London papers in the run-up to the marriage ceremony, which took place on Saturday 9 February 1957 at the Catholic Church of Notre Dame de France, Leicester Place. The bride wore a fifty-year-old bridal gown of ivory satin that belonged to her great-aunt, the train of which was carried by two pages. A reception for 300 guests was held afterwards at the House of Lords. The grandeur was in stark contrast to the small flat in Paddington that would be the married couple's first home.

In the wake of the public and media attention on the high-profile wedding, it was back to basics for the golden couple. Harris went to the Comedy Theatre to perform in *A View From the Bridge* and Elizabeth secured a role in a repertory company in Blackpool, where Richard joined her at the weekends when he finished his run. He was soon out of work, but not for too long, as Joan Littlewood offered him a part in a modern-dress production of *Macbeth* at Stratford East, with a tiny £4 a week for rehearsals.

He invited family and friends to the performance to see him in a Shakespeare play in which he had all of four lines. When it came to delivering his lines he could not remember them, but heard his mother in the front row saying: 'Isn't he marvellous?' He went on to play a major part in the Workshop's production of Pirandello's *Man, Beast and Virtue* helmed by a director from Czechoslovakia, which got good reviews but did not do well when it was transferred to the Lyric Theatre in Hammersmith.

But there Harris had been noticed by director Cliff Owen, who was looking for cast members for a television play entitled *The Iron Harp*, written by Joseph O'Connor. He was invited to read for the part of a blind man at a casting agent's office. On the day, he was under pressure for time and chronicled what happened afterwards:

> It was ten minutes to four and the reading was at four o'clock. We were living in Earl's Court at the time, right opposite the tube station, but if I was to travel by tube I would not make the appointment and I said to Elizabeth I will have to invest in a taxi fare if I'm not to be late. We broke open the gas meter and I took the money to pay for the taxi fare. I arrived at the agent's office and he kept me waiting for an hour. By then I didn't care whether I got the part or not. I could have travelled by tube for sixpence and I had spent ten shillings on a taxi to get there.

He turned in fury on the agent, reminding him what exactly that money meant – four meals for him and his wife. He read the part and a few days later it was confirmed that he had landed it with a fee of £50, the equivalent of almost five weeks' work with the Workshop. But the step up to television would lead to an even bigger break.

When *The Iron Harp* was aired it was seen by an influential former agent and casting director for Associated British Pictures, Bob Lennard, who had been involved in the career paths of top actors including Richard Todd, Laurence Harvey and Robert Shaw. He was hugely impressed by the performance of the Irish actor, recognising a strong screen presence and acting quality.

He arranged a seven-year contract with Associated British Pictures with a salary of £30 a week for the first year, rising to £90 in the final year. It was a huge boost for the actor, indeed for any actor of the time, to have a guaranteed income of any kind, never mind for seven years. It couldn't have come at a better time, as Elizabeth was pregnant. Thus Richard became a vibrant presence in the pubs frequented by the ex-pat Irish acting community – and was highly popular among them.

He got a part in his first movie, *Alive and Kicking*, and departed to Scotland for the location shoot. On 2 August 1958, at Queen Charlotte's Hospital, Elizabeth gave birth to their first son, Damian, to the utter delight of the father. His next acting job followed, in *Shake Hands With the Devil*, and this time the location was his home country. It was an exciting development as the film starred James Cagney and also an ensemble cast of Irish actors, many from the Abbey Theatre.

One of the National Theatre's most distinguished actors, Cyril Cusack, became friendly with Harris, and the young and beautiful Dana Wynter was also impressed by the Limerick actor when they met on the set at Ardmore Studios where interiors scenes were shot: 'I remember his good humour and boisterous personality. He had a splendid presence on the film set.' Harris, in effect, was feeling his way, gobbling up the experience and whatever lessons he could learn by working in the presence of stars such as Cagney and Michael Redgrave, and listening eagerly to the advice of Cyril Cusack.

It was of no concern to him that the film was going to be viewed as a typical and ludicrous Hollywood version of Irish history and, as such, was churned up by the critics. With Lennard he was in good hands and was only back in London for a short time when another part was offered in a film entitled *The Wreck of the Mary Deare*, starring Gary Cooper and Charlton Heston – and to be shot in Hollywood.

It transpired to be a sobering experience for him and Elizabeth. In acting terms he was a nobody, and Hollywood does not recognise nobodies. The couple felt like outsiders, he just a cog in the celluloid wheel of a very bad movie, though that may not have been too obvious at the time. Based on a Hammond Innes book, it was about the discovery of an insurance fraud that comes to light when a salvage boat is rescued from the high seas. It was originally intended as a vehicle for Hitchcock, and if he had not opted out the film would have had an entirely different outcome. As it was, the best that could be said of it was that it was a curious, star-studded amalgam of seafaring action and courtroom melodrama.

After Harris's first bittersweet taste of the so-called Mecca of movie making, he would learn that in that rarefied atmosphere things are often not what they seem – and neither are the people. An actor one might have admired on screen is a totally different person in reality, and the foundation of all is built on money and the power of the studio moguls. For the moment, his participation was peripheral and some of the realities of Hollywood might have escaped him. But he would not have long to wait.

One way or another, his career was moving along nicely and, whether he realised it or not, he occupied a pretty safe haven for the moment. He had a new son, a beautiful young wife and the boredom of his last few years in Limerick were behind him. He should have been a happy man. Or at least contented. Yet it transpired that a balanced sense of domesticity was something that did not interest him in the least. His pub life went on, the difference being that he brought a lot of his mates back to the house – a less than ideal situation for mother and baby. He was, as Elizabeth put it later, determined not to be trapped by his marital status and determined that it should not change his life or ambitions as an actor in any way.

There was another film part to follow, filmed on another set in Ireland. *A Terrible Beauty* had a somewhat nonsensical premise – set in a Northern Ireland village, the IRA revive activity on the outbreak of the Second World War. The script suffered from the usual problem of a foreign conception of an Irish problem. The cast was headed by Robert Mitchum and Dan O'Herlihy, with Harris playing a fanatical IRA man. He was reunited with Cyril Cusack for the film, and got on very well with Mitchum, an elder Hollywood statesman by comparison, teak tough in physique and a hard drinker. However, with a weak and melodramatic script the film made no impact and the critics were underwhelmed.

His next project would be in the theatre. *The Ginger Man* was adapted from the best-selling book of the same name by J.P. Donleavy. The producers' first choice for the lead role was Jason Robards but, in what would prove to be a typical act of hustling – a trademark of Harris's future career – Harris called his agent and told him that he was the right actor for the part: 'It's me. It's my life.'

Not quite, in fact, but it is easy to see why Harris would have been attracted to the part. The American author had attended Trinity College, Dublin with a number of his countrymen, supported by the post-war GI Bill, and got the idea for the book when they were all about to leave in 1949.

Following the universal rejection of the book on the grounds of its offensive material, mainly sexual, Donleavy, having tried to sell it in the US, returned to Dublin and showed the manuscript to Brendan Behan who recommended Olympia Press in Paris. Olympia's publisher, Maurice Girodais, agreed to buy the rights and published it in a Traveller's Companion series along with such titles as *Whip Angels*, *The Loins of Amon* and *School of Sin*, which might appropriately have been shelved under the pornographic section in the bookshelves. Its reputation preceded it, without acknowledging undoubted literary qualities, which would thankfully be later recognised.

Set in Dublin in the 1950s, the main character, Sebastian Dangerfield (based on Gainor Crist, a real undergraduate friend of the author), has squandered his GI Bill money and is married to Marion, a well-to-do English girl whose family are unhappy with the marriage and have alienated her. The couple have a young child, Felicity, and he finds distraction from the family through drinking and general debauchery. He displays no care for his wife's feelings and subjects her to a degree of cruelty. He also conducts sexual relations with two women: Miss Lily Frost, a prim and proper woman who works as a botanist for a seed company, and Mary, a young woman who he has seduced and then tries to discard. Dangerfield is a monstrous protagonist whose treatment of women is outrageous. He is terrified of responsibility and fatherhood and is dedicated to drink and debauchery. Finding himself stuck in poverty and squalor, he escapes to London.

It can scarcely be imagined what an impact such a book would have on the arch-conservative Irish society still dominated by the even more conservative Catholic Church, which viewed sex as an evil only to be tolerated within the confines of marriage – and then for the sole purpose of procreation. The book was predictably banned under the appalling terms of the Censorship Act, thus Donleavy was to follow in the footsteps of Joyce and *Ulysses* – a compliment by any manner, which would only affect his pocket for a short while.

Harris landed the part, and rehearsals for the theatre production were postponed until he had finished filming. It was a totally different experience from the rather mechanical and soulless process of film-making, with its starting and stopping all the time for different angles, more takes and technical adjustments. And it was a lead part, portraying a notorious character with whom Harris would have no problem identifying, and included some unfortunate reflections and others quite outside the remit of his wild nature.

For him the process of rehearsal and bringing the character to life was all-consuming; nothing else mattered. This would have been fine if he had left the character in the rehearsal room at the end of the day, but he took it to the bar afterwards and later home with him. The performance would cause endless difficulties for his wife.

She summed it up and the rather unbearable effect for her:

> Had Richard left his performance on stage after the final curtain, all would have been well. Unfortunately, somewhat obsessed by Stanislavsky and all the talk of the Actor's Studio in New York at that time, he continued to live the grotesque Dangerfield off stage. With the characters he liked playing, he assimilated them into his own life for the duration of the play or film.

The play opened to a standing ovation in the Fortune Theatre in London in September 1959, and generally enthusiastic reviews, with top-rated critic Bernard Levin writing: 'Richard Harris as the Ginger Man, Ronald Fraser as his American fellow-candidate for damnation, Miss Wendy Craig as his wife and Miss Isabel Dean as the lodger – each wears his part as if it were his skin.' He made a favourable comparison with John Osborne's *Look Back in Anger* and his lead character Jimmy Porter: 'Like Jimmy, Dangerfield is eternally seeking and knows he will never find. Drowned in debt and dirt and drink, he can yet pop his head out and jeer at fate and spit in salvation's eye.'

While the analogy of that line does not literally apply, the spirit of it did to Harris, who after each performance would retire to the pubs in a perpetual act of celebration instead of having a few to bring himself down from the performance high and then going home. That home was relatively new, and his wife never knew who he would bring home. One night it was the author, Donleavy, to whom Elizabeth took an instant dislike.

The *Daily Express* concurred with Levin's assessment and the favourable comparison with *Look Back in Anger*, with two misogynistic anti-heroes at the centre of the action of tough, uncompromising and realistic plays, both light years away from Noël Coward and Terence Rattigan. In a critical sense it was a personal triumph for Harris and all the signs were that the cast and play would be in for a long run. Godfrey Quigley, a Dublin-based actor and company manager, went to London to see the production and was bowled over, most particularly by the text and the performance by Harris. He wanted to bring the production, with some cast changes, to Dublin when the London run ended, which as it transpired would be sooner rather than later, as the audiences began to drop off after about five weeks. Harris agreed enthusiastically as he saw it as the opportunity for a triumphal homecoming. While London theatre had become dangerous and cosmopolitan, the same could not be said of Dublin, where the staple diet of theatre was still dominated by the Gate, which produced European classics, while the Abbey concentrated on the Irish tradition, which the old-fashioned management thought appropriate for a national institution.

The long and powerful shadow of the Irish Catholic Church stretched over the land and its political and cultural institutions. The arch-conservative Archbishop of Dublin, John Charles McQuaid, ruled the morals of his flock with an iron rod and the politicians genuflected before him. Godfrey Quigley must have had a rush of blood to his head if he imagined that the presentation of the world of the bawdy, drunken, sex-driven and amoral Sebastian Dangerfield in a public venue would encounter no opposition from the guardians of Irish faith and morality.

Just two years before, there had been a controversy surrounding a production of Tennesse Williams's *The Rose Tattoo* when the suggestion of a condom on the stage caused the play to be shut down and was followed by a court case. Any manifestation of sex in a public arena could not but draw the attention of the Catholic Church, whose disapproval was to be avoided at all costs. Yet Quigley's judgement in the matter was left behind by his enthusiasm for the project.

On his return to Dublin he approached Louis Elliman, the well-known impresario and owner of the Gaiety Theatre, to help him as a producing partner. He agreed, and arranged for the show to be produced by Spur Productions in association with Globe at the same venue for a three-week run. There would be some recasting, with Quigley playing Dangerfield's sidekick, O'Keefe, Genevieve Lyons as Marion, with Rosalie Westwater playing Miss Frost. There was not a lot of money in the coffers of the Globe company, but Quigley felt assured that it was a risk worth taking.

He could not have been but affected by the enthusiasm of the leading man. Just about five years after leaving Limerick, Richard Harris had top billing in the most successful commercial theatre in Ireland. It would never have happened had he tried his luck on the Dublin theatre scene. It was vindication of the decision to take the emigrant boat to London. On the evening of 26 October 1959, he took his first steps on the Dublin stage to what the cast members and playwright Donleavy felt was a successful opening show, well received by the first-night audience.

There was, however, one interruption at the start of the second act, when someone shouted from the parterre: 'This has gone far enough.' The players ignored it and at the final curtain their efforts were rewarded by sustained applause. But someone had been spotted taking notes during the performance and was assumed to be a policeman in plain clothes. Also, Elliman, the co-producer and theatre owner, while expressing satisfaction at the performance, suggested to Godfrey Quigley some cuts in the text. One was a reference to a church on the quays mentioned by Dangerfield after Miss Frost says his seduction of her was a mortal sin and she would have to confess to a priest. The director was called and refused point blank to make any cuts, then Elliman made a threat to pull the show. It was a bit late in the day for such antics on the part of the co-producer and created a nervousness among the cast, which the following morning was somewhat added to by the contrasting reviews.

The *Irish Press* review was predictably negative, as the newspaper was owned and run by the De Valera family who had a devoutly Catholic ethos. The second-act seduction scene that bothered Elliman, the critic found: 'the most offensive ever performed on a Dublin stage'. The only others considered so offensive were the condom in the *Rose Tattoo* debacle and the anti-Catholicism allegedly contained in O'Casey's play *The Drums of Father Ned*, a Dublin Theatre Festival production.

The *Evening Herald* panned it, as did the *Evening Mail*, whose critic called it 'tasteless, trivial and empty'. There was no review in the *Irish Independent*, most unusual in a newspaper culture in which theatre reviews were treated as a news item to be always published the morning after.

Despite a fair review in the *Irish Times*, in which Harris was marked out for special praise, the cast and the leading actor had no doubt that the production was now skating on thin ice. As they digested the critical reaction and the threat of cuts, Harris, clearly hurt but totally committed, said: 'Well, what's going to happen? Are we going on or aren't we? Whatever you do I'll play it. I'll go on a soapbox in O'Connell Street if necessary. Just let me know when there is a decision.'

It emerged that Elliman had been put under pressure by a priest, Fr McMahon, the secretary of the Archbishop of Dublin, who was in the audience and had afterwards visited the producer's office. This was a far more dangerous development than mixed or bad reviews, which could be offset by word of mouth. Also the major newspapers, with the exception of the *Irish Times* (with a Protestant ethos), were just as craw thumping and genuflecting to the Catholic Church as the politicians.

This was all a source of great disappointment to Harris, who showed his mettle when insisting that there was no justification for cuts and the show must go on. He also rang the Archbishop's secretary and asked him about the specific nature of his objections, but was brushed off and told to seek counsel with his spiritual advisor – in other words, to examine his conscience.

The play went on stage on Tuesday evening but the following morning a damning review appeared in the *Irish Independent*, which rang the death knell of the production. It could have been written by an emissary from the Archbishop's office:

The current production in the Gaiety of *The Ginger Man* is one of the most nauseating plays ever to appear on a Dublin stage and it is a matter of some concern that its presentation should ever have been considered. It is an insult to religion and an outrage to normal feelings of decency ...

The next show would prove to be the last in a shoddy and shameful episode in Irish theatrical history, after which the management closed down the production. It is a moot point to speculate whether the show would have continued to the end of the three-week run if the requested cuts had been made; the resulting compromise of integrity would have reflected badly on all concerned in the creative process. The Catholic Church had decided that Dublin was not ready for *The Ginger Man*. Harris's homecoming had been transformed into a disappointment of gigantic proportion.

Just three years later, after one more theatre show in London's West End in the interim period, *Diary of a Madman*, which was generally well received, Harris moved into the mainstream of Hollywood.

9

MUTINY ON THE BOUNTY (1962)

'You know *Mutiny on the Bounty* almost made me a drunk and a tramp. It was disgusting. But I survived. I survived and made myself a promise that however poor I got I would never again do anything I didn't really believe in.'

As subsequent events would prove, Harris did not live up to his declaration. But at that early stage in his career such a statement – matched by many other assessments of his time on the *Bounty* – required some courage. Hollywood was still all-powerful in the world of celluloid and the brief intervention of the independent film on centre stage was still some years away.

Later, looking back with the benefit of hindsight, he said:

I caused problems on only one movie in my life. During *Mutiny on the Bounty* I stood up to Marlon Brando at a time when the industry cowed and crumbled before him. I called him a gross misconceived bloody animal. That was a legendary row and it has lived with me ever since.

At the time it was an extraordinary thing to do on a production, in which Brando, the actor, was dictating the course of events, and directors and producers were indeed either unwilling or unable to take on the box office star. That a little-known supporting actor from Limerick would barrel in where the big shots feared to tread said something about either the toughness of Harris's character or his arrogance. Either way, one of the so-called Hollywood screen greats held no fear for him.

His stance earned the admiration of the veteran Irish actor Noel Purcell, who was witness to the unfolding internal drama on the set of the movie in Tahiti. When he finished shooting his role and returned to Dublin, he told reporters that Harris and Trevor Howard were angered by the prima donna behaviour of the star, but added that he was sure in the end a very good film would emerge. He added: 'Take it from me folks, Dickie Harris is going to be a star after this.'

But even John Huston, when asked what it was like working with Harris, said: 'The next time I read he has caused problems on a film, I'll be forced to believe it's because the director or producer hasn't done his homework.'

The film has become legendary for Brando's behaviour during filming, which led to director Carol Reed's departure and then caused confrontations with his successor Lewis Milestone. Richard Harris was the third lead after Brando and Trevor Howard and, in common with other cast members, was outraged by Brando's inability or refusal to remember lines and his constant meddling with the script, which created further insecurity.

Harris said later: 'The picture and Brando were a large dreadful nightmare for me and I would prefer to forget both as soon as my nerves recover.'

Brando, preparing for the scene of Fletcher Christian's death, lay on blocks of ice for intervals of several minutes in order to simulate the burns of the victim. Harris refused to act opposite Brando and he performed to a log. When Brando wanted to film his own close-ups, Harris threw the log down and said: 'Let him talk to this.'

Harris's initial instinct had been to turn down the part when it was first offered to his agent. He felt the part of mutineer John Mills was too small, but a later draft of the script had given the character a higher profile and more screen time. He still was not sure, even after he was offered a bigger financial incentive.

He must have been playing a game when he requested equal billing with the star Brando or alternatively with Trevor Howard. It was pure brinkmanship for the sake of it. If equal billing was appearing third on the poster and credits in same-size type then he did get his way, an achievement in itself. Producer Aaron Rosenberg replied that Trevor Howard was better known; Harris's riposte was that he was better known than Howard was at the same age of 30.

The producer was no pushover. A former All American football player who after college worked for fifteen years as an assistant director at Twentieth Century Fox studios, he had graduated to producer in the early 1950s. He had produced box office hits *The Glenn Miller Story* (1953) and *The Benny Goodman Story* (1955) and had a reputation as a straight talker and for bringing in films on time and on budget.

Rosenberg then sat on his hands and employed silence, his lack of response bringing out sweat on Harris's forehead. It was beginning to appear that he might have gone a bridge too far and for no good tactical advantage or financial reason, as he wasn't driven by the money but by the opportunity to work with Brando, his acting hero. As the weeks crept towards the production date start, 15 October, Harris was convinced that it was all over. The producer waited until the last minute and agreed to the terms. Within a day Harris was on his way to Tahiti.

MGM had hired Carol Reed, the accomplished director of *The Third Man*, to do a remake of the 1935 version with a $5 million budget and twelve-week location shoot in Tahiti, with the rest of the scenes completed at the studios of the production company.

Shooting was scheduled to begin in October 1961, but right from the off things started to go wrong. When the cast arrived at the location – for Harris it involved a trip of over 9,000 miles – the technical end of the production was way behind. The vessel representing the ship HMS *Bounty*, which had been brought from Canada, was not ready. There were 7,000 native extras to be trained for participation and, when filming on location, there is always the problem of the weather affecting continuity: the Pacific was no exception. In the classic tradition of Hollywood, the script was being rewritten on a daily basis, further complicated by the fact that the lead had been given script approval in his contract.

Harris, who had travelled alone to Tahiti, was accommodated in a basic hut. In the evenings Harris, Howard and members of the crew drank in local taverns, and for those thus inclined there was a surfeit of beautiful young girls only too happy to get involved with members of the production, who under normal schedules would not have had the time or energy to be so distracted.

It would be fair to say that whatever money Carol Reed was on, it would not compensate for the myriad and rapidly oncoming problems that were to stalk the production. The weather became unpredictable; rain and tempests appeared from nowhere. Many scenes had to be reshot and many were delayed while waiting for good and consistent light. There were problems with the ship, which had been built for authenticity but creaked and groaned under the weight of technical equipment and personnel, making its sailing pattern and balance difficult to stabilise.

The director was becoming increasingly frustrated by the antics of the leading actor. Right from the beginning, Brando had resisted the director's intention to rehash the 1935 version. He managed to persuade Reed to have the script rewritten. Eric Ambler was brought on board to do the job but Brando was not immediately impressed, hence the constant redrafting. Soon Ambler was doing the fourteenth draft, a nice job as he was on a retainer of $3,000 a week. Not only was Brando foostering around with the script but he was also displaying a curious inability to either learn or remember his lines. That also got to Harris, who remarked: 'He doesn't play a scene with you. Everything is a secret. He doesn't pour on the coal in the first take but lets it go on to the eleventh and suddenly it clicks for him and he walks off. Meanwhile your best take may have been there. It is a self-centred sort of art.'

Brando, who was once a hero and motivating force for the Irish actor, particularly in relation to method acting, now became a source of irritation and annoyance because Harris rightly was coming to the conclusion that Brando's method was entirely self-serving and in no circumstance could he be considered a team player. He was more concerned about playing a political game against the studio bosses who, the way the production was going, would be looking for someone to blame and Harris would be a prime target.

For Harris, it was a disillusioning experience. One of the main reasons he had taken the part was the chance to act with Brando: 'I was being invited to star with

Marlon fucking Brando. All his pictures – right back to the stuff like *The Men* and *On The Waterfront* – were the reasons why I wanted to act and survive as an actor.' What Harris had accepted as the example of the great American art of acting now looked distinctly more like artifice.

He was being exposed early on in his career to the worst aspects of the Hollywood studio system. For Harris, it was an experience that would not easily be forgotten and would induce in him a well-justified cynical attitude. If you wanted the money, just take it and run; if you cared, well that would just invite trouble.

However, the Limerick-born actor was not then, or at any time, fazed about 'trouble'. His instinct was to stand up against and talk about anything that was thrown in his path. It was a characteristic that would mark him out as a man who would take on any challenge put in his way, without fear and seeking no favour.

Richard Harris would prove, as he did on the field for Crescent College or Garryowen, that he would go for the line, come what may. The celluloid arena would be no different in that regard, whether it be in the top echelons of Hollywood or the mean field of small independent production. It was not just a matter of arrogance, of which he was not devoid, but also intellect. Despite the paucity of his conventional education he was hugely well-read and acquainted with the proper provenance of his profession. His understanding of what he was doing was well founded, deeply thought out and underscored by basic instinct. His fondness for life's pleasures and attraction for the camaraderie of drinking would not and could not diminish his formidable intelligence.

Of course, like any man who might have experienced in his youth the height of the success of his father and the relative ignominy of the failure of the family business, he could have something to prove in the realm of generational retrieval of success. But such naked ambition could be too easily ascribed to such simplistic origin. There was a lot more to Richard Harris than that. More a person determined to be his own man and, temporarily at least, to rid himself of the shackles of the past. There is no son born who would not aspire to such status.

But during the shoot there was an ominous reminder of his past:

When I was doing *Mutiny on the Bounty* my father called and asked me when I was coming back to see him. 'Come on now, the next one might take me,' he said. I asked my brother: 'What does that mean?' And he told me: 'He has had a couple of heart attacks since you left.' So I planned with Elizabeth to go back and then I got the call that he had died.

The production, meanwhile, moved from one stuttering crisis to another and the constant problems and delays began to eat through the budget at an alarming rate. Back in Culver City, California, at the headquarters of MGM, Aaron Rosenberg must have longed for the days of his earlier successes as the biggest film of his producing career transformed into an unrelenting nightmare. He had hardly had a wink of sleep for months as he tried to put out one technical or creative fire after another.

Carol Reed, weary of the constant battles off the set, wanted to leave but instead Rosenberg fired him. It was a strange move, because if the British director had left of his own accord or desire he would not have been entitled to any further payment, which could have saved the studio some of the money that the production was haemorrhaging daily. By firing Reed, MGM had to honour his contract, which cost them $200,000 – and then hire a new director and pay him.

Ironically, Brando, Harris, Howard and many others were sorry to see Reed go, as he was generally considered a decent man who had entered a creative lion's den with no conception of the awful difficulties that would arise. He was replaced by Lewis Milestone, who some years before had directed the war classic *All Quiet on the Western Front*.

Brando, meanwhile, had become romantically involved with a native beauty, Tarita, who had been cast as his girlfriend in the film.

It was not long before the new director began to be affected by the general malaise on the film, a lot of it generated by the star. Milestone said later:

> I knew that we were going to have a stormy passage right away. I like to get on with things, but Brando likes to discuss every scene, every line for hours. I felt enough time had been wasted, but time did not seem to mean anything to Brando. He argued about every scene. When eventually the arguments were over, I'd be told that he was ready for the cameras. It was a terrible way to make a picture.

There is a story about an episode between Brando and Harris that may sound like a midshipman's myth but is more than plausible. The script called for Brando to hit Harris and knock him into a camp fire. After delivering his lines he tapped Harris lightly on his cheek but Harris refused to fall down. He told the director that he would fall when Brando hit him hard enough to make it look real. Brando again took the light touch, so Harris went over to him, kissed him on the cheek and asked him if he wanted to dance. Apparently Brando was enraged and both refused to be on set together, the star shooting his scenes opposite a stand-in while Harris performed to a box. Milestone sensibly kept his distance. On the last day of the studio shoot Brando asked for Harris and requested he give his lines one last time but Harris refused and offered him the box he played to, adding insult to injury by commenting that Brando would get as much out of the box as Harris himself had got out of Brando.

The scene had to be abandoned. Later, over a drink, Harris told Howard that he should not be walked on by Brando. The patience and tolerance shown by the British actor subscribed to the Robert Mitchum school of acting rather than the famous and at times infamous Method academy. It was confirmed in a scene between Bligh and Christian in which Bligh did most of the talking. It should have been over in a few takes, as Howard, although a great drinker in his off time, was a thorough professional when it came to being on set. But Brando continually fluffed his few lines, forcing the director to do eight takes until Brando decided to play ball. But Howard kept his cool for the good reason that he knew well what the outcome would be if he lost it – twenty takes. He had been warned before taking the part that Brando would attempt to run the picture and it did not take long for confirmation.

Yet it wasn't all bad for Harris. Elizabeth had arrived with their son Damian and the news that she was pregnant, and they made the best of the rudimentary accommodation and entertained people they befriended on set. He also had an offer for a part in a small budget film to be helmed by first-time director Lindsay Anderson, based on a book by author David Storey entitled *This Sporting Life*.

He loved the book but was not happy with the script, which had been adapted by Storey. Nevertheless, whatever its shortcomings it provided welcome relief from the troubles on the *Bounty*. As he put it: 'I was in a state of absolute desperation at the time, what with Brando's behaviour and the film dragging on interminably. I didn't know where to turn, Suddenly I got this novel and I was a new man. I had a tremendous affinity with it but the first script was terrible.'

Harris made copious notes on the story and persuaded Anderson to fly out to Tahiti and work on the script. After a number of weeks they had, according to Harris, pulled it into shape. Anderson was deeply impressed with the actor's intellect and his instinct about creative matters. For Harris it was a godsend, enabling him to block out the terrible realties of *Bounty* and see light at the end of the tunnel. Already the film had run £10 million over budget and was six months over schedule.

Relief came in January 1961 when the production moved back to Los Angeles to complete the indoor scenes. The Harris family were accommodated in an air-conditioned hotel, which was sheer luxury compared to the previous months. The claustrophobic atmosphere and heat of Tahiti was gone and for the most part the lid had been lifted from the steaming cauldron. The ill-fated film ploughed on.

Milestone threw in the towel and was replaced by a studio director of no flair, named George Seaton. At this stage, the number of writers engaged on the project had exceeded nine or ten. Reshoots in Tahiti resumed and went on from March until the middle of the summer. Elizabeth and Damian went back to London.

In October 1962, a year on from the beginning of the saga, Harris was at last finished with the picture. Brando defended himself against media reports that cast him as the main destructive influence on the mishaps that had beset the film's production. He claimed that there had been no script and the reason for big failures such as this all came from the same origin. He then became a target, in his view, of studio executives trying to cover up their own mistakes.

There may have been some truth in the assertion that the studio was leaking negative stories about Brando towards the end, anticipating the disaster that all expected *Mutiny on the Bounty* to be – and the executives were getting in first on who was to blame. Clearly all the blame could not be apportioned to the notoriously difficult actor, but he shouldered a lot. The idea that there was no script was ludicrous, there had to be a script, but it was not one that Brando approved of, and it did not have an angle and storyline that the leading actor and Carol Reed agreed upon.

MGM was at the time and had been for generations the very essence of the Hollywood film factory, churning out entertainment for the masses at an alarming rate. The cast, of course, was important but actors were just one element of the production line, highly prized for a time and highly dispensable in another. The ghosts of the founding studio father, Louis B. Mayer, and the famous producer Irving Thalberg still walked the studio headquarters at Culver City and their legacy was still predominant in the ethos of MGM.

Thalberg died tragically young after a great blossoming of his career had produced the 1935 version of the film that starred Charles Laughton as Bligh and Clark Gable as Fletcher Christian. In choosing Carol Reed as director, the studio was signalling that it wanted a straight remake, but by bowing to market imperative by going for the most bankable actor with Brando it ensured, unknowingly perhaps, that this was not going to happen.

Worse still, from the studio perspective Brando had an abiding hatred of the system and culture of film-making established by the likes of Mayer. It insulted every fibre of his creative being. Reed, however, was from the old school and would not have empathised. Richard Harris was representative of a new and emerging breed of actor about to replace the English ancient regime of Olivier and Gielgud – and neither could he empathise.

The fact was that, whatever the shortcomings of the producers or scriptwriters, Brando made a strong contribution to the nightmarish experience of the production, which of course had other aspects to contend with, such as the weather which was out of human control. Brando's assertion that they should have known about the weather was laughable.

There are some creative projects that are cursed and it appeared that *Mutiny on the Bounty*, like *Apocalypse Now* years later, was one of them. The expectations for the film were nil, but despite some indifferent reviews it would miraculously prove a commercial success and garner Academy Award nominations. Within weeks of release the film had grossed over $30 million, occupying sixth position in the best earners of the year. All the pain suddenly seemed to have been worth it.

In spite of all Harris's misgivings, he received good notices and the film would have no negative impact on his career. In fact, the opposite. He was up on the posters with Brando and Trevor Howard and his name associated with a successful Hollywood movie. The worst aspects of the film's making ensured him a place in celluloid folklore, with the Irish actor admired for his guts in standing up to Tinselstown's biggest and most awkward name.

Elizabeth had given birth to a second son, Jared, on 24 August 1961 and Harris was embarking on a project that he felt passionate about and in which he would take centre stage. Domestically all was in order, and Harris was driven and full of new ideas and new projects beyond *This Sporting Life*, which would be his film as much as *Bounty* had been Brando's, with the difference that the script would be set, polished and signed off before the camera rolled.

After returning to London he went on to Dublin first and then Limerick. There he would witness the final disintegration of the family business. It was a sad conclusion for his father, who did not live to see his son personally retrieve the success that had once been the mark of the Harris milling operation.

10

RAGING RUGBY BULL

David Storey, the son of a Welsh miner, was a squad member of Leeds Rugby League Club for five years in the mid-1950s, the earnings from which he put towards his further education at Slade College of Fine Art. He was the side's regular half-back and it could be said that no rugby league player combined such aesthetic interest with the rough-and-tumble of sporting activity. He also put his experience on the field to good use, writing a novel entitled *This Sporting Life*, which was published in 1960.

The book is set in a nameless town in the north of England and the central character, Arthur Machin, is a young working-class man employed in a factory as a lathe worker, who sees playing rugby league for his local professional team as a means to escape his boring, poorly paid job and as a path to a more affluent lifestyle. The narrative traces his journey from his first outing on trial until his body begins to fail him in a match ten years later.

Following the success of adapted films from similar working-class arenas such as *Room at the Top* and *Saturday Night and Sunday Morning* it was inevitable that *This Sporting Life* would reach the screen. After its publication it attracted the attention of Lindsay Anderson, an Oscar award-winning documentary film-maker and leader of the radical Free Cinema movement. He took it to Woodfall, a production company run by film director Tony Richardson and playwright John Osborne. They turned it down with the idea that they might make it themselves, but were outbid for the rights by the Rank organisation. Rank offered it to Karol Reisz, who had had a big success with *Saturday Night and Sunday Morning*. Reisz was not interested but saw it as an opportunity to introduce his friend Anderson into feature film, and Reisz would act in the production as a mentor. After visiting the shooting location of *The Guns of Navarone* he became convinced that Richard Harris, even though he had only a small part in that film, would be ideal to play the lead in *This Sporting Life*.

It was the first feature film to be directed by Anderson. The screenplay, adapted by Storey, sets the location as Wakefield, a mining town in Yorkshire, and follows the story of Frank Machin (changed from Arthur), a bitter young coal miner who impresses the captain of a local rugby league team during a nightclub altercation. During a trial for a place on the team, his aggressive playing style convinces the owner Gerald Weaver, played by Alan Badel, and he signs him as a loose forward wearing the number 13 shirt.

The cast of characters in this journey include: the other working-class players; the rich businessmen who own the club, Weaver and Slomer; a probably homosexual loner Johnston, who gets Machin his initial break; and the player's landlady Mrs Hammond (Rachel Roberts), whose husband has died in Weaver's factory, apparently by suicide. Machin has a sexual relationship with her in an effort to break away from his image of himself as a masculine beast on the rugby pitch. But the relationship is fraught by his inability to articulate his desire and her resistance to the worst aspects of his character, which become a mirror of his brutality on the pitch. Set against a landscape of factories, mines and wretched houses occupied by desperate workers, the story makes for an intense and depressing scenario, brilliantly expressed.

At the time that Harris was offered the leading role in *This Sporting Life*, the family business was on its last legs. It is said that Harris's father was blissfully unaware of the situation, but this is unlikely, rather – like many others in his position – there would be a mixture of denial and hope that something might turn up to transform the firm's financial circumstances. At this stage, Rank had taken over the Harris Mills production and distribution. All that was left of the once thriving family enterprise was the mill building. And it was the errant son Richard who, despite his difficult relationship with his father, saved the day by providing the cash to enable his father to hold on to the mill building, thus leaving him some small vestige of self-respect. He told local journalist Gerry Hannan: 'When I bought the building, I swore I would keep it, come hell or high water, until time wore away the Harris name over the door. It was a monument to my father and brothers and my forebears and the work they did. And by God, I did keep it.' He was true to his word and did not sell it for another two decades.

Lindsay Anderson and Harris were a perfect match – both rebellious, anti-establishment and cynical about the film business in general and Hollywood in particular. They got on very well in the many debates that naturally accompany the development of the script, which goes through many drafts as a result of the collaborative effort, including contributions from the director and the leading actor.

Harris originally pointed out that the script had abandoned the flashback structure of the novel and this was taken on board; the main character's first name was also changed from Arthur to Frank.

All were hugely serious about the work in hand and sometimes the intensity led to the odd clash between Harris and Anderson who, the actor claimed, wanted him to invest an enormous emotional aspect to the performance, which Harris felt was a bit too much. He avoided meeting David Storey until late on in the process, but they also hit it off. In the preparation for the film, all the major creative figures were singing from the same hymn sheet, and so, when it came to shooting, the script was in perfect shape.

Rachel Roberts was given the leading female role of the widow Mrs Hammond. She was a highly accomplished performer, a prize-winner at RADA with a solid background in theatre. The British Film Academy had named her Best Actress for her part in *Saturday Night and Sunday Morning*. Her path to the film had been somewhat complicated by her affair with Rex Harrison, who was very much against her being involved in what seemed to him to be a rather grim and grotty project. Harrison had told Anderson that if he was the last film director in the world, he wouldn't work with him. The sentiment was entirely mutual.

Roberts was not only talented but forthright and would stop in mid-flight if she felt something wasn't quite right. There was a certain sadness in her face and demeanour, which fitted the part like a glove. Harris took to her immediately and would amazingly defer to her authority in rehearsal and shooting. There was an instant and powerful rapport between them, obvious to all. Anderson was also in awe of her and felt that his choice of leading actors was probably the most inspired casting he ever did.

Harris was also intent on getting himself into the physical shape necessary to convince the audience that Machin could hack it in the professional rugby league ranks. He trained with a team in Richmond, ran in the mornings and bulked himself up with weight training. He was helped by screenwriter David Storey, who had played rugby league with Leeds for four seasons. This was invaluable, as the game was as much a mystery then as it is now for anyone like Harris steeped in the tradition of rugby union. As well as physique there was a whole ethos to be absorbed by the actor, and Storey provided that. All who were involved in the production recognised a powerful chemistry at play, which was the responsibility of the director to control.

In an article by Robert Sellers, author of *Hellraisers*, in the *Guardian* in 2009, Storey told of the decision to cast Harris in the lead role and its aftermath:

We chose Richard because of his emotional volatility. His enthusiasm was total, he was completely committed, verging on the edge of insanity in some respects and that became infused in the film itself. On the first day of filming in Wakefield, the local rugby league team congregated on the pitch while Harris prepared in his caravan. He was spending ages on his make-up. Then when he came out and saw all the rugby players standing on the other end of the pitch saying, 'Oh look at this flower coming out,' he just took one look at them and ran down the whole pitch towards them.

As he ran he got faster and faster until they suddenly realised with horror he was going to run right into them, which he eventually did. It was that initial gesture of total physical commitment, almost indifference and carelessness that caught the players' imagination and they really took to him in a major way.

Despite the actor's grasp of the physical demands of the role, the character was more complicated, not just by the dint of circumstance but also psychologically. Machin's public persona and masculinity is contrasted with a private striving for a sensitivity that he tries to find in the relationship with Mrs Hammond. It makes nonsense of his materialistic-based philosophy: 'You see something and you get it. It's as simple as that.'

The bleak, northern landscape of the film, the depressing human atmosphere, not alleviated but added to by the sporting element, as polluted and corrupt as the men who effectively ran the town and the crushing sado-masochistic relationship between Machin and Mrs Hammond, provided a powerful celluloid cocktail, but not for the faint-hearted or an audience seeking an escape from grim reality in a weekend trip to the cinema. Nonetheless, the expectation was that it would match, if not exceed, the success of *Saturday Night and Sunday Morning*, the first of the new-wave hits and directed by Karl Reisz, who though he had turned down the same job on this film provided huge support to first-time feature-film director Anderson.

During the pre-production Harris was offered a big part in the upcoming Hollywood production of *The Fall of the Roman Empire*, produced by Samuel Bronston with Anthony Mann on board as director, and Sophia Loren, Stephen Boyd and Alec Guinness already attached. The Irish actor was assigned the part of Commodus, the deranged son of Emperor Marcus Aurelius. He accepted and asked his agent to work out the financial deal.

The fee negotiated was $200,000, a massive amount of money compared to the £25,000 he had got for *This Sporting Life*. After some of his best scenes had hit the cutting-room floor of *Mutiny on the Bounty*, Harris and his agent insisted that there be no dissolution of the character part he was taking on by script changes. This was a bit of a gamble in a business in which the script, not to mention the finished film, is subjected to continual alteration. The bigger the budget, the more changes that would be insisted on by producers nervous about the prospect of not recouping the huge financial outlay at the box office. The fact that many of the changes could be counterproductive to the ambition was beside the point. That was how things were done in Hollywood, and for the creative people it was a matter of swallowing pride if they were going to take the money.

Harris, despite his previous experience, was not totally *au fait* with the rules and, besides, valued integrity, which is not a currency readily recognised by Tinseltown. He and his agent received a redrafted script from the studio, which sent the actor into a rage: 'Suddenly the character Commodus which I wanted was this revamped celluloid lightweight. I said No, no, no.'

His agent gave the producer an ultimatum – the first script or his actor would withdraw. Bronston was not going to be held to ransom by a relatively unknown

Irish actor so he gave the part to a lesser-known Canadian actor, Christopher Plummer. This episode can be viewed from two perspectives. One, Harris and his agent displayed profound naivety and should have taken the money and run. Even if the producer agreed in relation to the script, there could be no guarantee that the part would remain intact after the editing process. Not even a director as established as Anthony Mann would have control over the final cut. Two, it could be said that it was a statement of intent on the actor's behalf that he valued the integrity of his work more than obedience to the Hollywood mogul – he was not interested in playing the game. His judgement may well have been weakened by the intensity of his commitment to the film in hand, which had no outside interfering agent and a modest budget. But the certainty was, given Harris's physique, looks and talent, that he would not be a permanent fixture on the small film scene. He would be going to Hollywood, and there he would be required to play by the rules of its iniquitous game, however much he might protest. In that light, and with the benefit of hindsight, losing the part in *The Fall of the Roman Empire* was a highly expensive mistake, one that upset his bank manager who telephoned to remind the actor of his burgeoning overdraft. Harris said he didn't tell him how to run his bank so 'don't tell me how to run my life'.

This Sporting Life is a remarkable study of working-class angst with a cutting style like no other British feature before it. Despite being lauded on its opening run, it was a commercial flop, prompting the chairman of producing company Rank to declare that he was pulling out of the British new wave of films, kitchen-sink drama, and would never make such a 'squalid' film again.

Despite this rather ignorant assessment the film was well received by US critics, including the influential film magazine *Variety*:

> Among the varied sequences which impress are a horrifying quarrel between Harris and Rachel Roberts; a hospital death scene; a poignant interlude at a wedding when Harris approaches the moment of truth; a rowdy Christmas party and a countryside excursion when Harris plays with the widow's two youngsters.
>
> Harris gives a dominating intelligent performance as the arrogant, blustering, fundamentally simple and insecure footballer.

Critical acclaim was followed by more recognition for Harris in particular, with Oscar and Bafta nominations and the award for Best Actor at the Cannes Festival where, having a few drinks inside him when the victory was announced, he bounded on to the stage. He was handed his award in a plain box by French legend Jeanne Moreau, to which he responded: 'What's this?' 'Cufflinks' was the reply. The unsteady victor instead grabbed a nearby bigger trophy and escaped into the night. He returned the prize for Best Animation later, while the cufflinks were sent to him through the post by the committee.

The director Lindsay Anderson, who developed unrequited feelings for unobtainable heterosexual men, wrote in his diary of 22 April 1962 in the first month or so of production: 'The most striking feature of it all has been the splendour and misery of my work and relationship with Richard.' He felt that Harris was acting better than ever before in his career but feared that his feelings for the actor, whose combination of physicality, affection and cruelty fascinated him, meant that he lacked detachment as a director.

'I ought to be calm and detached with him. Instead I am impulsive, affectionate, infinitely susceptible ... Harris was so attractive that I found I responded to him with a whole-heartedness that made me tremble.'

Malcolm McDowell was quoted in 2006:

I know he [Anderson] was in love with Richard Harris, the star of Anderson's first feature *This Sporting Life*. I am sure it was the same with me, Albert Finney and all the rest. It wasn't a physical thing. But I suppose he fell in love with his leading men. He would always pick someone who was unobtainable because he was heterosexual.

Gavin Lambert's memoir, in which he claimed that the director repressed his homosexuality, was seen as a betrayal by other friends.

Storey told author Robert Sellers of the complex interaction between the lead actor and director:

It was a combination of Richard's Celtic bravado and wildness and Lindsay's homosexuality, that he never really came to terms with and struggles with throughout his life and in *Sporting Life* it came to a climax. In the sense that Richard became the epitome of everything that Lindsay desired sexually. It was a masochistic relationship that went over the edge several times.

It was a great credit to Lindsay's inner sturdiness and intellectual sobriety that he managed to hold on to what he thought it might achieve for the film, but it nearly broke him. We were offered several films afterwards but I felt that the producer in each case wasn't powerful enough to control the ferocity of the relationship between Richard and Lindsay. It had become quite obsessional really on both their parts – particularly on Lindsay's.

Whatever it was that Harris was aware of about Anderson's sexuality, the creative relationship was hugely productive.

In the acting profession there is a right time and a right part – and this was the case for Harris in *This Sporting Life*. He had immersed himself in the process of preparing for the role in a manner akin to that promoted by the method school without any of the pretentious nonsense adopted by some of its practitioners.

His efforts and Anderson's would stand the test of time with reassessments many years later judging *This Sporting Life* as one of if not the best British film of the 1960s. When a reissue of the film occurred in 2009 the highly respected *Guardian* critic Peter Bradshaw, giving a five-star rating, said that it was Lindsay Anderson's best film and certainly Richard Harris's. He adjudged Harris's performance equal to Marlon Brando's in *A Streetcar Named Desire*:

> The thirty-three years old Harris is given a light pancake make-up for his interior scenes, presumably to make him look younger and more boyish, but it actually gives his performance a weird expressionistic intensity. The movie takes a muddy boot to class, celebrity, the North, the South and humbug sham-amateurism of English sport ('I only enjoy it if I get paid a lot for it'). *This Sporting Life* splendidly anticipates modern Britain; a dour yet thrilling and extraordinary film.

In the same year, also with a five-star rating, Sukhdev Sandhu wrote in the *Daily Telegraph*:

> Watching it today, I'm tempted to see it as one of the strongest films of the period; every frame of which pulsates with drama, class confusion and erotic force. Harris is magnificent in the lead role; a drink toting alpha male who dominated the rugby field but who, with his monkish hair and feminine eyelashes, seems less assured in other settings.

Another late assessment reads: 'One of the finest British films ever made with an astonishing, raging performance by a young Richard Harris, an equally blistering performance by fellow Oscar nominee Rachel Roberts.'

Almost a quarter of a century later, Harris gave his own self-effacing assessment in the *Hot Press* interview with Joe Jackson:

> The central character in *This Sporting Life* whom everyone thought they could relate to because he was an 'ordinary guy' – the common man – was not that at all. He was extraordinary. He was the embodiment of many heroic qualities that had always been present in literature. The same applies to *Room at the Top* and *Saturday Night and Sunday Morning*. It was all a con, a beautiful con.
>
> There was a tremendous revolution in Britain then. The old establishment, the upper middle class, was being kicked aside by people like Finney, O'Toole and myself. John Gielgud said it was frightening. But the great deception was that we ruffians were all classically trained actors . There was nothing rebellious about our approach.
>
> The same applies to Clift, Brando and Dean. They were not a new breed of naturalistic actors – they gave highly stylised performances. They painted on their

parts with a coat of theatricality that was so special it grabbed us because we don't want to see the ordinary guy on the screen. There was a glamour to everything Dean and Clift did.

Most of that is true in the sense that the actors mentioned, including Harris, were very well aware of the method they had adopted and the impact of the performance. Nonetheless, they would require some indulgence on the part of their directors to achieve that aim of going from the ordinary to the extraordinary. What Harris fails to mention, and quite understandably, is that they were all in their cinematic prime extraordinary, not just in acting ability but also in looks.

Montgomery Clift with little doubt would come top in that regard and also take the top spot in the area of personal dysfunction. Brando second, Dean third perhaps, though his premature death means he will forever be young and beautiful. Harris possibly fourth, because O'Toole and Finney figured but briefly in that ether and still survive. But Harris underestimates, as would be his wont, the amazing impact and depth of his performance in *This Sporting Life*.

He not only matched Brando in *Streetcar* but made Dean look wimpy in *Rebel Without a Cause*, and comes out on fairly equal terms with *East of Eden*. One could look at those four films and not have too much doubt about who comes out on top.

Half a century on, this is tremendous vindication for the difficult but extraordinary collaboration between a great and driven actor and a director who, despite his ambivalence in that creative relationship, managed to produce a film of worth, intensity and lasting quality.

11

MAJOR DUNDEE (1965)

In a remarkably short period of time Harris had been introduced to a number of Hollywood heavyweights and in his next film, *Major Dundee*, a western directed by Sam Peckinpah, he was cast as second lead behind Charlton Heston. The screenplay by Harry Julian Fink, Oscar Saul and Peckinpah was loosely based on historical incidents but not on a true story.

Heston had expressed a strong interest in working with the director after a screening of MGM's 1962 *Ride the High Country* directed by Peckinpah, which starred the ageing actors Joel McCrea and Randolph Scott playing two retired lawmen transporting gold from a mining camp to the bank, and which had been generally well received. Previously, Peckinpah had directed and written a successful TV series called *The Westerners*.

The director could not have been better qualified to handle the western genre as both sides of his family had migrated to the American West by covered wagon in the mid-nineteenth century. He was an interesting man but with a volatile and combative personality, and he was a hard drinker. It is easy to see why Harris was attracted to working with him. He had not been the first choice for the part: others, including Steve McQueen, had been courted but turned it down.

But that position was ideal for Harris and his agent, and a lot of haggling over the fee went on with producer Jerry Bressler before the handsome sum of $300,000 was secured.

The American story *Major Dundee* centred on a cavalry officer, Dundee (Charlton Heston), who leads a disparate troop of army regulars, Confederate prisoners and scouts on an expedition into Mexico to destroy a band of Apaches who have been raiding US posts in Texas. Harris played the part of Captain Tyreen, who holds a grudge against Dundee and casts the deciding vote in Tyreen's court martial from the army for participating in a duel. Their relationship was superbly written in the script, with a subtlety that let the viewer infer the past without slowing down the film.

When the diverse factions of the expeditionary force are not fighting among themselves they engage the Apaches in a number of bloody battles. Love interests also drive a wedge between Dundee and Tyreen. When the Apaches are finally trapped and the chief Charibba killed, the duo prepare to resume their private battle, but another attack occurs by a French force in which Tyreen is killed.

It was a complex and highly interesting concept with echoes of John Ford's *The Searchers*, Howard Hawk's *Red River* and of all things *Moby Dick*, with Dundee an Ahab of the Wild West.

The Irish actor, who had experienced some of the vagaries of Hollywood film-making and a controlling destructive star in *Mutiny on the Bounty*, was to find another of a different hue in the western. In this instance the controlling destructive influence was the brilliant, tough and abusive director Peckinpah, whose hard drinking might have endeared him to the Irishman in less difficult circumstances.

Harris had just finished filming *The Red Desert*, a frustrating experience that had added to his tiredness. On that film Harris had worked with the enigmatic but disorganised art-house director Michelangelo Antonioni in Italy, opposite Monica Vitti. It was a punishing experience for Harris, not knowing what was going on in the director's head, a problem that was exacerbated by the fact that Antonioni had no command of the English language. European art house had its own problems, as Harris would discover, but Hollywood also had plenty.

Antonioni had held on to Harris after the final shoots until he was late into the pre-production phase of the film, which was already beset by what might later be considered more minor problems, like an unfinished script. As Heston put it: 'If we can't get it right after five and a half months in the typewriter, then we have to get it right in front of the cameras.'

The Italian director's schedule was all over the place and Harris was already due to begin work on *Dundee*. He worked day and night during December and January to finish *The Red Desert* and eventually walked off and booked his flight to Los Angeles. He missed the flight, however, and had to take a long, circuitous route through London, where he drank for six hours. Seventeen hours later he reached his destination in a semi-comatose state from the effects of exhaustion, amplified by the dehydration produced by alcohol consumption and the various flights.

Inevitably it all caught up with him and while on the sound stage at Columbia Studios he collapsed. He recalled it later in a piece he wrote for a magazine:

The rise and fall of the siren wail; tires squealing in a greasy road, rubber-soled shoes squeaking on vinyl floors. A monk in a dark habit is painted on a white wall. No he's not. He's moving. Speaking. Latin. Schooldays. Veni, vidi vici. Amo, amas, amat. But he's not talking schoolboy Latin of the Catholic Church. He's giving somebody the last rites before dying. I open my eyes. That someone is me ...

It was a frightening experience and one of a long line of wake-up calls that the actor would get over the years. Why he chose to ignore them for so long was because the medical tests that Columbia was obliged to carry out both as concern for the actor's health and insurance purposes showed nothing. It had not been a heart attack; physically there was nothing wrong with him. Also, typically, when he was half better he threw himself into the part of Tyreen with total commitment, engaging in long discussions with Heston and Peckinpah.

It was during the shooting of this film that Richard developed the idea that his brother Dermot would take over a managerial role in his career, move to London and form a company, which emerged as Limbridge.

Harris had a strange, ambivalent relationship with both Heston and Peckinpah. Heston was straight-laced, a family man and utterly disciplined about the business of filming, always on time, first on the set and drove Harris (who was late a couple of times) mad by recording his arrival on a stopwatch. He responded by getting a load of alarm clocks and setting them exactly for call time. When they went off, Heston didn't know what was happening and the Irish actor said that it was just him 'clocking in'. They were like chalk and cheese.

On the other hand, although Harris had a lot more in common with the director in the drinking stakes, he was unhappy with Peckinpah because the director did not prepare enough, particularly with the interpretation of character. Harris wanted to know who Ben Tyreen was, where he came from, who his antecedents were, etc. Yet Peckinpah was not too interested in Harris's opinion: he had enough on his plate and was much more concerned with the composition of shots and, of course, the panorama of the Wild West setting. The director veered from being of soft and creative disposition to bouts of rage and verbal rants. He was obsessed with firearms (possibly from his time as a serving Marine, though not on a battlefront) and violence, most particularly the explicit expression of it on screen. None of this bothered Harris, who had struck up a close rapport with James Coburn. Both actors had been recommended for the parts by Heston who effectively, with producer Jerry Bresler, was in charge of the production. Harris would have more in common and empathy with the director's human failings, while he developed a loathing of Heston, who he felt was a tyrant and from a Hollywood mould that he already disliked.

Coburn and Harris concocted practical jokes to annoy Heston, which worked sufficiently well for the pair to be called to the director's caravan. Peckinpah later recalled the incident:

> I was never much good at discipline and the thought of giving these guys, especially two men as tall and fit as Dickie and Jim, a dressing down filled me with dread. I started telling them how important Charlton Heston was to the picture and how they owed him some respect. Suddenly Jim flashed his famous grin at me and I knew I was in trouble. When Dickie started giggling it was all over.

By the time he said 'thank you, gentlemen', concluding that he would see them on the set, 'they had collapsed on the floor, gasping for breath with tears streaming down their faces'.

The schoolboy pranks were in the minor league compared to the director's behaviour. After a month, the production moved from Durango to Mexico City and then to farther flung locations. Even though it was springtime, the sun was hot and the general pressure-pot of filming caused tempers to flare. After the final battle scene with the French, Heston accused Harris of using the wrong rifles in two shots, which had to be filmed again. Heston later acknowledged that he had been unfair to the actor and blamed the heat and the awful location.

Peckinpah was often drunk on set, verbally abusive to both cast and crew, and fired no less than fifteen members of the latter during the shoot. On one occasion he stormed off, declaring he would prefer the company of rattlesnakes to that of actors. During another confrontation Heston threatened him with a cavalry sabre in an effort to stop his abuse. The director's choice of remote location and his behaviour quickly sent the production over budget and the studio, Columbia, began to worry that the film would not be finished.

When the studio contemplated firing Peckinpah, Heston saved him by putting his entire fee into the production. He said it would have been a very bad idea at this stage of proceedings to get rid of Peckinpah: 'Aside from Sam's talent, you don't change horses, if you can help it, in mid-stream. I am positive that the picture's only chance lies in Sam finishing it. I told Jerry Bressler as much.'

The leading actor's faith was sorely tried when the director, drunk as a skunk, disappeared off the set to his trailer to drink more, leaving Heston to finish the scenes in the director's chair. With the schedule spiralling out of control, the studio – with the comfort of knowing how much was in the can – cut the schedule by two weeks and then stopped the production. That was in May 1964. By that stage, the production had overrun by $1.5 million. The first cut was over four hours long, at which point the studio took over control and reduced it to 136 minutes.

It was a commercial flop and castigated by the critics, but with supreme irony many years later the release of a DVD brought it to re-evaluation, with one critic assessing its value as one of the grittiest and most realistic westerns ever made, with terrific supporting performances all round.

Nor, as expected, did it end Peckinpah's career: he went on to have commercial successes with The Wild Bunch (1969) and The Getaway (1972), the latter starring Steve McQueen and Ali McGraw. Peckinpah also had a number of failures still to come. But sharing some of the same self-destructive traits as Harris he would not learn the lessons and eventually succumbed to the effects of alcohol and drugs, dying of heart failure in 1984, aged 59.

Another sense of irony was that much of Major Dundee takes place in the dark, causing an uneasy feeling, and would presage one of Harris's much later triumphs in a western employing the same visual technique, gritty exposition and extreme violence that was not as acceptable at the time that Peckinpah used that cinematic approach. He was known as 'Bloody Sam', and the characters of his films – often lovers and losers forced to compromise to survive in a world of nihilism and brutality – would eventually be accepted as a plausible norm. History would prove that the errant but highly talented director was a man ahead of his time, who would gain much more appreciation and respect after his death.

Harris was different in this respect. He wanted the recognition while he was alive, despite his lifestyle efforts that might prove the contrary. He may have shared the director's obsession about the progress of friendship encapsulated in the film from respect to animosity, loyalty to despair and fear, but redemptive death he could and would leave aside. Survival was always the parachute that the Irish actor employed.

12

CAMELOT (1967)

Three strong roles in Hollywood-backed films were to occupy him for the next twelve months. *The Heroes of Telemark*, set in German-occupied Norway, told of the efforts by the Norwegian Resistance to sabotage the German development of the atomic bomb. Harris as a Resistance leader played second billing to Kirk Douglas as a physicist who reluctantly gets drawn into their plan to blow up a hard water plant. Harris and Douglas clashed off-screen as well as on-screen, and it marked the third time that Harris and Michael Redgrave shared screen billing. Directed by Anthony Mann, historical accuracy about the Telemark raid faded well into the background in favour of strong drama and heroics. The original title, *The Unknown Battle*, was wisely changed to the more stirring *The Heroes of Telemark* shortly before the film's release.

John Huston's *La Bibbia* saw Harris play Cain to Franco Nero's Abel, in a cast that featured fellow Irishmen Peter O'Toole (as three angel messengers) and Stephen Boyd as Nimrod, with George C. Scott as Abraham and Ava Gardner as Sarah. Harris brought a tremendous physicality to the role of Cain, and looked powerfully rugged in a loincloth. He and Huston bonded together while they shot scenes at the foot of Mount Vesuvius in Italy, and they hoped to find another project soon on which they could collaborate.

Then came *Hawaii*, George Roy Hill's adaptation of part of James Michener's epic novel, in which Harris's roving sailor ignites the passions of Julie Andrews, married to a rigid and humourless New England missionary, wonderfully played by Max Von Sydow. Hill and Harris had something in common: Hill, on a GI Bill scholarship, had studied in Trinity College, Dublin, with his army pal Gainor Crist, the inspiration for *The Ginger Man*. Some years later, when Hill's career soared with *Butch Cassidy and the Sundance Kid* and *The Sting*, Hill tried to set up a film of *The Ginger Man*, but abandoned it when Robert Redford declined the role.

After these three films, a major turning point arrived in the career of Richard Harris. In 1959 Alan Jay Lerner and Moss Hart decided to adapt the third and fourth sections of T.H. White's fantasy novel on the Arthurian legend, *The Once and Future*

King, published the previous year as a stage musical. White's book in turn had been based on Sir Thomas Mallory's fifteenth-century book *Le Morte d'Arthur*, written by an extraordinary man under even more extraordinary circumstances, prompting White and the adaptors to introduce him as a character.

Mallory, knighted in 1442, came from a rich, landed background in Warwickshire. He was a Member of Parliament but as a result of the complex politics of the time and opposition to the Duke of Buckingham had been charged with extortion, robbery, rape and spent a lot of time in and out of various prisons in the provinces and London. Whether he was guilty or not of the many charges set against him, he clearly had a wild marauding side to his character, but accompanied by deep sensitivity and ultimately a proven creative side.

It was that last quality that would come to the fore in the later part of his life, perhaps to seek some sort of redemption. The choice of his subject of Arthurian legend would provide evidence of that aspiration. In June 1468 he was imprisoned in the Tower of London, in relative comfort and with access to one of the best libraries in the country. It was during his time in prison that he wrote *Le Morte d'Arthur*, which he completed in March 1470.

He was freed in October of that year by the returning Lancastrians and six months later died in London. He was buried under a marble tombstone in St Francis's Chapel, one of the most fashionable churches in the city. His epitaph called him valiant knight of the parish of Monks Kirby. His reputation had been restored in dramatic fashion in death and even more so by the legacy of his work.

In relation to his character, P.J.C. Field put it thus in his very insightful entry in the *Oxford Dictionary of National Biography*: 'If an author's life and writings must echo one another, the criminal charges must be false, or perceived idealism exaggerated, or the author's personality must have changed in the course of eighteen years, mostly spent in fifteenth-century prisons. It seems likely that all three notions contain an element of truth.'

It would be replicated over half a millennium later by an actor who would take on the mantle of the crown of Mallory's King Arthur and who would, in some small measure, share some of the originator's character.

Mallory made his story the rise and fall of a great king and his kingdom in Camelot. Symbolic power was provided by this, the innumerable quests and adventures in the book and by the half-strange world of chivalric romance, re-enforced by a transparent colloquial style that made events free of any controlling author, which quickly made it a popular and definitive telling of the Arthurian story.

Nineteenth-century interest in medieval life raised the status of Mallory's book to unimagined heights. Dante Gabriel Rossetti put the book second only to the Bible. The question would now arise as to whether or not this would be the case in 1960. The genesis of the new version of *Camelot* would prove almost as complicated as its medieval origin.

Frederick Loewe, who had no interest in the project, agreed to write the music on the understanding that if things went wrong, it would be his last score. Following the collaboration between Lerner and Loewe on the hugely successful *My Fair Lady*, expectations were high for the new stage musical. But right from the beginning the production was beset with complications. Firstly, Lerner suffered health problems during the writing process, resulting in him seeking medical attention which delayed the production.

A strong cast had been put together with Richard Burton as King Arthur and Julie Andrews as Lady Guinevere, and included Roddy McDowell. The first out-of-town try-out was in Toronto at the O'Keefe Centre in 1960. The show was far too long and the curtain fell forty minutes after midnight. The reviews were positive but agreed the show needed a lot more work to make it a success. However, Lerner was rushed to hospital with a bleeding ulcer and was off the scene for a while. When he recovered, producer-director Moss Hart suffered a heart attack and Lerner, at the urging of his wife, stepped into the breach. This caused problems between Lerner and Lowe, the latter reluctant to make changes without the guidance of Hart. It seemed to everyone involved that the production was cursed.

The star Richard Burton provided a stabilising influence, accepting cuts and changes and calming the cast, unnerved by the constant shifts in the treatment of the story. Guinevere's song 'Before I Gaze at You Again' was handed to Andrews at the last minute before the first New York preview, prompting her classic response: 'Of course darling, but do try to get it to me the night before.'

After the show opened on Broadway, Hart was released from hospital and with Lerner began to introduce more cuts. The reviews were mixed and it seemed that the show would not have a long run. But fate intervened when Ed Sullivan approached Lerner and Loewe to create a segment on his show to celebrate the fifth anniversary of *My Fair Lady*. They decided to include little from that musical and four highlights from *Camelot*. That moment, though Harris had no idea at the time, would have a huge impact on his future fortune in two distinctive ways.

The impact of the segment on the hugely popular and influential television show took *Camelot* from the brink of extinction to instant success. The ticket sales of the production went through the roof, achieving unprecedented advance sales of $3.5 million. The show, which opened at the Majestic Theatre on Broadway on 3 December 1960, ran until 5 January 1963, with a total of 873 performances.

There followed an Australian production that ran for two years and a London production that opened in August 1964 at the Theatre Royal in Drury Lane, starring Laurence Harvey as King Arthur, which ran for 518 performances. Nowhere, in all that successful equation, despite its difficult gestation, did the name of Richard Harris figure. But that was about to change.

The huge success of the stage version made it as inevitable that, as day follows night, it would make its way to the silver screen. Whether it would retain the magic of the live experience in a theatre was quite another matter. The rights had been bought by Warner Brothers and Jack Warner was prepared to invest a lot of money in the production. It was equally obvious that the mogul would look for the stars Richard Burton and Julie Andrews. The Welshman was at the height of his fame and hugely bankable by Hollywood standards.

Julie Andrews was not a great actress but was a terrific singer with a powerful stage presence. It would have been natural for her to revive the stage role on film. But she had been rejected in favour of Audrey Hepburn for *My Fair Lady*, so she would probably refuse any offer from the producers of *Camelot*, or at least play hard to get. But director Joshua Logan was not too worried. While he searched for his perfect Guinevere, he also tried to cast King Arthur. Along with the help of Lerner, Warner pursued Burton and in classic Hollywood fashion a game of cat and mouse ensued. Burton was on board and then not. It was ultimately clear he did not want to be involved and his demand for double the fee finally convinced the studio to look elsewhere.

Harris watched the game with great interest and, when it was up for Burton, declared his interest by pursuing Lerner, Warner and director Joshua Logan. When the director flew to London to begin casting, he was immediately contacted by Harris's agent. Logan told him that he hadn't seen anything in the actor's previous work that might prompt him to consider casting him in the lead. The following day a telegram delivered to Logan's suite in Claridge's read: Only Harris For Arthur.

Harris then literally stalked Logan, a tactic that contained the risk of annoying the director to such an extent that Harris would blow any chance of getting the part. It was a risk the actor was prepared to take. He was driven to the point of obsession to get the role, and the attention of his overbearing tactic was an old-style figure of the musical theatre and film tradition, who on paper should have no truck with such an intrusive campaign.

Then again Logan, who was over twenty years older than Harris, was a tough man who had served as a PR man and intelligence officer in the Second World War. An emotional character, he had abandoned his diploma course in Princeton to study with Stanislavsky in Moscow on a scholarship. His first marriage had been short-lived and in 1945 he had married Wedda Harrigan.

Logan had been hugely successful on Broadway, directing *Annie Get Your Gun*, *South Pacific* and *Fanny*. But he had suffered the vicissitudes of the business when he was at first ignored for recognition of the Pulitzer Prize in 1950, which was awarded to Rodgers and Hammerstein for *South Pacific* despite the fact that Logan had been a co-writer. That was amended later and he got his credit.

He had hit films in Hollywood with *Picnic* (1955), *Bus Stop* (1956), *Sayonara* (1957) and *South Pacific* (1958). Nonetheless, he was known for emotional outbursts and huge mood swings, which some years later would be diagnosed as bipolar disorder. But when he was dealing with Harris, this diagnosis was eight years down the line. They might not have known it, but the two men were close in temperament, both driven and with big egos.

Harris confronted Logan at a party in Palm Springs and passed him a handwritten note announcing himself as King Richard Harris. The problem was that however he might fit the heroic role of King Arthur, he had no track record as a singer and no background in musicals. However vigorous his campaign to convince Logan, Warner did not want him. But Logan's problem was finding an alternative. Whoever was chosen for the king had to be able to act and the singing would follow – it would not work the other way round.

Harris eventually landed the part. His campaign, however outrageously conceived, had worked. But his demons had also begun to work overtime.

During the *Camelot* merry-go-round Harris landed a part opposite Doris Day in a comedy thriller directed by Frank Tashlin, *Caprice*, a movie that he might have been better advised to avoid. He was drinking heavily and his marriage was falling apart, with rows in the expensive rented villa in Bel Air attracting the notice of the well-heeled neighbours. Twice during the shooting of the movie he collapsed on the sound stage of the Fox studio. He told the writer Henry Gris that he had been drinking with Jason Robards, a first-division boozer by any standards.

He ended up in hospital where he was dried out, thus stalling the production. He was ordered off the drink and told to get plenty of rest. But it had all been too much for Elizabeth, who flew back to London and filed for divorce. In July 1966 she applied for a court order to prevent him molesting her and restrict his access to the children. Her affidavit stated that she was afraid of him and sought the court's protection in that regard. She was given that protection until October, when he could make an application to have the injunction discharged.

The press, of course, had a field day and Harris felt humiliated and hurt, but with the benefit of hindsight would accept the blame. There could be little argument about the fact that he had behaved like a maniac, indulging himself in a welter of booze and womanising. He was now on the cusp of taking on a far more heroic role, that of King Arthur in a production with a huge budget for the time – £13 million. He could ill afford to dance with his demons.

He got a flight to London in an effort to effect some sort of reasonable conciliation with Elizabeth but was met by a herd of reporters at Heathrow. He gave an interview in which he feebly tried to make an excuse for the inexcusable:

> I am absolutely shattered by this divorce action. I have always tried to treat my wife like a delicate flower. I flew here intending to give her a pleasant surprise. She did not know I was coming. She did the exact same thing two weeks ago. It is just one of our little games.

There had been far too many unpleasant surprises and Elizabeth had had enough. He flew back to Los Angeles and tried to settle into the most high-profile role of his career to date. It had finally dawned on him that his wife was serious and this time there would be no way back. He must have realised that his errant ways, which might add to the allure of his status an actor in the cauldron of Hollywood, had an entirely different effect on his domestic life. Financial provision was one thing that he had never or would never shirk from; true commitment was another matter. He could not have been in a worse position to take on a role that would transpire to be one with which he would be identified for the rest of his career.

There was not only a lot at stake on a professional level, but a lot to prove for Harris in particular, who was diving into the untried waters of a big screen musical. But, as always, it was his wont to relish a challenge, and the focus of his mental and creative energy on the role of King Arthur also helped him to forget for a while the slings and arrows of his personal life. Nevertheless, the prospect was frightening and he was afraid of letting people down. Singing in front of a huge orchestra was a daunting task. He had a stuttering start in the first few recordings but then settled in.

The film version differed from the stage rendering in that the main plot was presented as a long flashback. In the opening scene King Arthur is preparing for a great battle against Lancelot, one he does not want to fight but into which he has been forced. The king reflects on the sad circumstances that have led him to this situation and asks his childhood mentor, Merlin, for advice. Merlin appears to him and tells him to think back – and this is where the main plot kicks in.

After two weeks of filming, he returned to London for the court hearing. The divorce petition had been lodged the morning of the hearing and mentioned drinking bouts and violence and the adverse influence of this behaviour on his children, including the use of foul language. Harris returned to the Burbank Studios to continue filming.

He would be helped by his deep immersion and love for the part, which in its essence, a royal triumph over human frailty and embracing of goodness and compassion, provided an example of how the actor could find a path out of the forest of his own troubles. The press attention on him was also relieved by the concentration on the big love affair between his co-stars Vanessa Redgrave and Franco Nero.

Everyone on the set was impressed with the Irish actor's professionalism, most importantly the director, Logan, who had in the heel of the hunt taken a huge jump by casting Harris and Redgrave. He was delighted with both, describing Harris as 'methodical and involved'. This was in spite of the fact that Harris still continued to involve himself in the continuous party circuit and yet arrived bright-eyed and bushy-tailed on set each morning.

Paradoxically, his discipline was noted and the technicians at Warners were unstinting in their praise for Harris as a highly focused craftsman. His huge enthusiasm, energy and commitment allowed him to persuade Jack Warner to let him sing his songs live on set as opposed to pre-recorded and mime. But when

Harris tried to persuade the mogul to back a rewrite of the seduction scene between Lancelot and Guinevere, on the basis that it somehow reduced the king's dignity, Warner took him for a walk to the studio gates.

He pointed at the sign and asked the actor what it said, and he replied 'Warner Brothers'. When it read Harris Brothers, said Jack Warner, he would be entitled to rewrite *Camelot* any way he wanted – but not until then.

It was a good time for Harris, although he was close to exhaustion from the nearly nine months of filming he felt creatively fulfilled: 'I attribute it to my work on *Camelot*. I think I have done some terrific stuff in the film. It is some of my greatest and yet I am fed up and tired of it all.' But it did not stop after the film was wrapped up: during the dubbing process he maintained his professional search for perfection, for example by spending an hour on one word – Camelot – repeating it seventy times.

The bubble of the involvement in the extended production protected him from his family troubles; the high associated with the rarefied atmosphere, like the end of a theatre run, was inevitably replaced by anti-climactic feeling. Harris, by his own assessment, was a man who hated doing nothing.

Despite putting on an act for the press, he began to feel miserable and started looking out for something else to sink his teeth into.

13

'MACARTHUR PARK' (1968)

With his rich, deep, gravelly voice, Richard Harris took the poetic words of songwriter Jimmy Webb and turned 'Macarthur Park' into an unlikely worldwide hit.

Jimmy Webb was born in 1946 in Elk City, Oklahoma, the son of a Baptist minister. He learned to play the piano and organ at a very young age and played in the choir of his father's churches, accompanied by his father on guitar and his mother on accordion. His home life was conservative and religious, and radio play was restricted to country and gospel music. During the 1960s he started writing songs that were influenced by church music on the one hand and Elvis Presley on the other.

In 1964, the family moved to Southern California where he attended San Bernadino Valley College. He studied music after which he decided to pursue a career as a songwriter. His father warned him that 'this songwriting thing is going to break your heart', but gave him $40 and told him that it was all he had. Little did his father realise it would be the best investment he would ever make.

In 1966 Jimmy met singer and producer Johnny Rivers, who signed him to a publishing deal and recorded Webb's song 'By the Time I Get to Phoenix' on his album *Changes*. The following year, Rivers asked the young writer for songs for a new group, The 5th Dimension, and he came up with five songs for the album entitled *Up, Up and Away*.

The title song was released as a single in May 1967 and reached the top ten, and the group's follow-up album the same year contained eleven of Webb's songs. In November, Glen Campbell released his version of 'By the Time I Get to Phoenix', which reached number twenty-six in the Billboard Chart and became a pop standard. Webb's songs landed eight Grammies at the awards ceremony that year.

The following year, *Time* magazine recognised the songwriter's range and proficiency and 'a gift for varied rhythms, inventive structures and rich, sometimes surprising harmonies'. That year there was further success with 5th Dimension, and Glen Campbell's single written by Webb, 'Wichita Linesman', sold over a million copies. That $40 had gone a long way and Webb decided to form his own production and publishing company.

His first project would come in the shape of the most unlikely musical source, an actor from Limerick by the name of Richard Harris. Webb had written a song called 'MacArthur Park', inspired by his break-up with his girlfriend Susan Ronstadt, a cousin of the singer Linda Ronstadt. In the first flush of love they used to meet in the park in the Westlake district of Los Angeles, named after the famous American general Douglas MacArthur. At the time, Ronstadt worked for an insurance company, the offices of which were located in a street just opposite the park.

In the summer of 1967 Webb had written a twenty-two-minute cantata that ended with a seven-minute coda called MacArthur Park. It was a song redolent of the good memories of a love affair in the abiding image of the place of meetings and the bittersweet aftermath of the loss. Nothing new, perhaps, in the arena of love songs, but Webb departed from the normal structure and convention of the three-minute, radio-friendly pop song. The song began as a poem about love and then progressed into a lover's lament. The lyrics were pitched to be symbolic. His musical influence, quite apart from the emotion involved, or maybe because of it, was cantata – a vocal composition with instrumental composition, typically in several movements, often involving a choir. Radically different was the length – over seven minutes: radio-play friendly it was not.

There was also the matter of the lyrics, which could have been seen as somewhat cheesy and sentimental – leaving the cake out in the rain and it took so long to bake it, a case in point. Webb would say later: 'The lyrics were very real to me, there was nothing psychedelic to me. The cake was an available object. I saw it at the park on birthday parties. But people have strong reactions to the song. There has been a lot of intellectual venom.'

At the time, Webb probably did not have a chance of getting any singer to record it, but sometimes an artist has to follow his instinct and forget the challenges to his expression, and this is the path Webb followed. He offered it to Bones Howe, the producer of a band called The Association, for possible inclusion in their fourth album. He loved it but the band rejected it on account of its length. It appeared that the song would not get an airing.

Richard Harris met Webb at a fundraiser in East Lost Angeles in late 1967. The songwriter had been invited to provide a musical backdrop on the piano. He explained the genesis of the collaboration:

I met Richard on the stage of the Coronet Theatre in Los Angeles where we were doing an anti-war pageant involving Walter Pidgeon, Edward G. Robinson, Mia Farrow and some other people, and I was doing the music. In our off-time, we used to play the piano backstage, sing and have a few beers.

Richard and I got to be really good friends and we were tossing the idea about that wow one of these days we ought to make a record. I used to say that to everybody. One day I got a telegram over at my house on Camino Palermo. 'Dear Jimmy Webb, come to London, make a record, Love, Richard.' It was the first time I was ever out of the country. I got on a 707 and flew to London and started to do this record with Richard. MacArthur Park was in the pile but we had a lot of songs we were interested in doing.

The album was *A Tramp Shining* and some people wondered why would you get an actor who was a singer. He was a singer. He had just done a very successful top grossing movie, a musical version of Camelot. He had sung all the Lerner and Loewe stuff. He wasn't perfect but he had sung it. He had gotten through the score and it was considered successful. I thought I could make a record with him.

He knew every Irish song that I had ever heard, he could and did sing all of them. His favourite drink was Black Velvet, champagne and Guinness, and after a couple of them he would start singing Irish songs. I still know a lot of them he taught me. We ended up making a very successful album, it would be hard to find a more successful album. He brought a great sense of theatrical dignity to 'MacArthur Park'. If he missed a note or he didn't carry it off particularly well as a singer, he had the actor's ability to step his way through the lyric, speak some of the lines and carry it off.

He did carry it off and met his match in terms of not giving a damn about convention. Webb found Harris a very positive energetic presence, driven to do everything in the present as if there was some imaginary sword of Damocles hanging over him. And that he needed the involvement and focus of work to avoid getting into trouble, as Harris put it to a *Daily Mail* reporter: 'It's boredom, frustration, not drink that makes me aggressive ... I felt so ashamed after the last fight, I swore it would be the last time. The worst thing I do in life was nothing. There must always be a new challenge.'

After listening to all Webb's compositions Harris selected 'MacArthur Park' as his pop-music debut, as part of an album of all Webb songs entitled *A Tramp Shining*. 'MacArthur Park' would prove the most challenging.

Webb, possibly influenced by 'Sgt Pepper's Lonely Hearts Club Band' by The Beatles, envisaged big sweeping arrangements, combining a full thirty-five-member orchestra as well as a range of top session musicians. The cost for a debut album by an unrecognised singer was prohibitive for a record company and Columbia passed. Webb's ABC Dunhill came in with a funding deal and the songwriter returned to Los Angeles to start the project at Sound Recorders. The Harris recording of the song was planned and executed in four sections or movements: a mid-tempo arrangement, called 'In the Park', in original session notes built around piano and harpsichord and with horns and orchestra coming in; at about two and a half minutes into the song, it shifts to a slow tempo and quiet arrangement, parted with an alternative lyric 'After the loves of my life'; at about five minutes in there is a sudden switch

1. Looking every inch the rugby star in *This Sporting Life*. (Courtesy of The Rank Organisation)

2. With Rachael Roberts in *This Sporting Life*. (Courtesy of The Rank Organisation)

3. Harris in *Major Dundee*. (Courtesy of Columbia Pictures)

4. With Vanessa Redgrave in *Camelot*. (Courtesy of Warner Bros/Seven Arts)

5. *A Tramp Shining* established Harris as a major recording artist. (Courtesy of Dunhill Records)

6. In his beloved Kilkee, Richard Harris is remembered as a racquet ball champion. (Courtesy of Tim Mason)

7. Richard Harris speaking out in support of a new university for Limerick in 1968. (Courtesy of *Limerick Leader*)

8. Harris liked to support his native Limerick, putting his weight behind the campaign for a new university. (Courtesy of *Limerick Leader*)

9. Playing the English aristocrat John Morgan in *A Man Called Horse*. (Courtesy of Cinema Center Films/CBS)

10. As the bomb-disposal expert in *Juggernaut*. (Courtesy of United Artists)

11. Harris as The Bull McCabe in *The Field*, for which he received an Oscar nomination. (Courtesy of Granada Films/ Noel Pearson)

12. Limerick icons – Harris with socialist firebrand and mayor, Jim Kemmy. (Courtesy of *Limerick Leader*)

13. Harris was a familiar figure to Limerick rugby fans; he is seen here making his way in to watch his beloved Munster. (Courtesy of *Limerick Leader*)

14. Harris with pal Russell Crowe on *Gladiator*. (Courtesy of DreamWorks/ MCA Universal Pictures)

15. Harris brought gravitas to the role of the emperor in *Gladiator*. (Courtesy of DreamWorks/ MCA Universal Pictures)

16. As Albus Dumbledore in *Harry Potter and the Philosopher's Stone*, his final great role. (Courtesy of Warner Bros Pictures)

17. Richard Harris, ageing disgracefully, in Limerick near the end of his life. (Courtesy of *Limerick Leader*)

to an up-tempo instrumental section, allegro, led by drums and percussion and punctuated by horn riffs, building up to an orchestral climax; at about six and a half minutes, a reprise of the first section's arrangement accompanying final choruses and another climax.

The recording was made on 21 December 1967 at Armin Steiner Recorders in Hollywood, with more work done on 29 and 30 December. Musicians in the original studio recording included members of the famous Wrecking Crew of LA-based musicians who played on many hits of the 1960s and 1970s including Hal Blaine on drums, Larry Knechtel on keyboards, Joe Osborne on bass guitar and Mike Deasey on guitar, with Webb on harpsichord.

If ever a song could have been written by or for Harris, this was it. It summed up a lot of the sentiments of his romantic life, by coincidence perhaps as opposed to design. He sang it with the required passion but also the distance that underlines its emotion and thus its effect. Little wonder it was a big hit.

As the songwriter observed, the song had been long in his own experience when Harris got to it, but Harris put so much into it that he made it seem like his own. Webb saw that this suited the project and the synchronicity was to both their advantage. He watched his own songs delivered with, as he put it, 'incredible vocal sensitivity'.

Webb had put down the backing tracks in a studio in Los Angeles and immediately afterwards came to Ireland with them to record the vocals. First he was brought to Limerick and Kilkee and then back to stay with Harris in a rented house in Dublin. The songs for the album *A Tramp Shining* were recorded in Lansdowne Studios.

Webb found it a very pleasant task working with the actor. Though Harris brought a bottle of Pimm's to the studio every day, it was only to wet his whistle and he was totally focused on delivering a top-class performance, which he did. 'MacArthur Park' stood out amongst the tracks, with its sweeping and dramatic orchestral arrangements, but it was very long. This made the record label nervous that it would not get airplay. Efforts were made to reduce the time but Harris and Webb stood their ground and won the battle.

It is quite possible that the song might never have been recorded if not for the actor's passion and commitment. That is not to suggest any weakness on Webb's part, but he was sixteen years younger than Harris and was taking the first step with his own production and publishing company in an industry notorious for exploitation and control. Harris's uncompromising nature in an equally exploitative industry provided great comfort to the young songwriter in what was, and would prove to be, a very fruitful creative relationship. Both were highly accomplished in their respective professions, but it could have been viewed that Harris was not a recognised singer – as other interpreters of Webb's songs had been. Both would confound any critical doubts with their passion, which can upset the predictions of the most hardened doubters. Webb and Harris were not lacking in that department. Though coming from entirely different directions and disciplines, in their collaboration they were personal and musical soul brothers and uncompromising in their vision.

Whatever doubts that might arise about the album would rest with the single release of 'MacArthur Park'. Webb recalls:

> I was fortunate. If it wasn't for FM 'underground' radio 'MacArthur Park' would never have been broken as a single because the Top 40 was not going to play it. It was seven minutes twenty seconds long. I remember Ron Jacobs calling me from KHJ in Los Angeles and saying they would go with 'MacArthur Park' but you have to edit it for us and I said that I'm not going to do that. He told me that you realise what you are doing – you are throwing away a hit record. I replied that I was not going to do it because that was what the song was.
>
> A week later they were on it. As soon as a station like KHJ started playing 'MacArthur Park' in its entirety, forget it – it rolled across the country – it was inescapable.

'MacArthur Park' as a single proved to be a massive success, topping the charts in Europe and Australia and reaching number two in the US Billboard Chart, while *A Tramp Shining* would remain in the same chart for a year. Another collaboration followed with the album *The Yard Went On Forever*, which peaked at number twenty-seven in the Billboard Chart but was considered by many critics to be superior to *A Tramp Shining*.

The obvious question is if either album was of its period or somehow stands the test of time. Thirty-five years on, Bruce Eder of AllMusic gave his considered opinion as an entirely credible critic with no axe to grind and entirely objectively. Giving *A Tramp Shining* four out of five stars, this was his assessment: 'A great record, even 35 years later, encompassing pop, rock, elements of classical music and even pop-soul in a body of bitter-sweet romantic songs by Webb, all preserved in a consistently affecting and powerful vocal performance by Harris marked by its sheer bravado.' Assessing the singer's rendition of 'Didn't We':

> Harris treaded into Frank Sinatra territory here and he did it with a voice not remotely as good or well-trained as his, yet he pulled it off by sheer bravado and his ability as an actor, coupled with his vocal talents – his performance was manly and vulnerable enough to make women swoon but powerful and manly enough to allow their husbands and boyfriends to feel okay listening to a man's man like Harris singing on such matters.

Eder also was impressed by Webb's arrangements: 'some of the lushest ever heard on a pop album of the period.' He concluded: 'Strangely enough, MacArthur Park – the massive hit of the album – is not that representative of the rest of the record, which relies more on strings than base or drums than brass or horns and has a somewhat lower-key feel but also a great deal more subtlety.'

Eder was even more effusive about *The Yard Went On Forever*, assessing it as other critics did as a stronger album:

Recorded a year after the hit record, it was conceived by Webb as a Harris project from the beginning, so the register is right and his singing voice slips perfectly into each song – the lyrics are dazzling in their cascading imagery and the music is richer and more vividly conceived and recorded, and the entire album works magnificently, juxtaposing grandeur of expression and intimacy of feeling at different moments, all most effectively.

The Billboard review of the time confirmed this assessment: 'Webb's material is treated with class and finesse by Harris. The track Lucky Me was "a shimmering gem".'

There was a symbiotic relationship between singer and songwriter that would not become parallel into their respective experience until the next decade after their brilliant success. Webb puts it this way: 'In the '70s I lost it pretty badly, but unlike some others, I never wanted to die – not really.' He said that he had never performed on stage even 'remotely sober'.

Webb and Harris had met at a time when neither of their personal demons were in the ascendancy, but both had similar inclinations in that regard. Webb recalls his own: 'When you are in your early twenties, nobody can tell you anything, you're burning through this money and you think you are going to always be able to write hit songs and the world is always going to be the way you want it to be.'

He went to say he hadn't a smidgeon of co-operation in him and he made life difficult for everybody. As it transpired that was not the case with Richard Harris; their collaboration was fruitful in every sense, and that probably had to do with the fact that they were two free spirits working in tandem with similar personality traits – 'us' against the world. In addition, there was the circumstance that Harris was hugely successful in his own right at the time, but not at all proprietorial towards his young and successful collaborator. Both were cognisant and admiring of each other's individual talents. A perfect match, as it transpired, brought about by the instinct of the actor to think about and grasp the moment.

The unfortunate thing in relation to Harris was that the media, particularly the print hounds, were not interested in anything about him but his private life or his partying image. As he put it to writer Robert Ottaway in an interview for the *TV Times*: 'Acting is not enough. Singing, especially if you have written the songs yourself, is a great form of expression.' But he complained that only his acting or brawling made the headlines: 'I was in New York recently to read some of my poems to the city's Poetry Society. It gave me the greatest creative satisfaction I've ever had.

A few days later I went on a pub crawl, and that's what the papers covered. Not a mention of my poetry reading.'

The endurance of 'MacArthur Park' in spite of critical attention on the lyrics was more than proved by the fact that it was covered more than fifty times by high-profile artists (among others) such as Frank Sinatra, Diana Ross, Aretha Franklin, Liza Minnelli, Andy Willliams, Sammy Davis Jnr, Justin Hayward, Waylon Jennings and Donna Summer, whose version hit number one in the Billboard Chart.

14

BURNING UP THE SCREEN

There was an interesting backdrop to *Cromwell*. The producer Irving Allen had won an Academy Award in 1948 for his short film *Climbing the Matterhorn*. In the early 1950s he formed an independent production company, Warrick Films, with Albert 'Cubby' Broccoli and they relocated to England to avail themselves of the government subsidy incentive for the indigenous film industry. Also, American films were forbidden under the Marshall Plan to take profits in the form of foreign exchange; Americans working outside the country for over 510 days in an eighteen-month period would not be taxed by the IRS.

Working on the notion that they would have more control of the films they produced outside Hollywood, they struck a deal with Columbia and the studio agreed to match the funds they raised dollar for pound. Broccoli, a former agent, contacted Alan Ladd after Ladd had left Paramount over a money dispute, and the actor agreed to a three-picture deal with Warwick.

The Red Beret (1953) was the first production starring Ladd, which cost £700,000 and took $8 million at the box office. More successes followed until the relationship with Columbia ended in 1957. Allen was a producer driven by the financial as opposed to artistic imperative, with an arrogant assessment of his nose for vehicles that would make a profit. Time would quickly prove that he, no more than the best moguls that Hollywood could produce, was capable of making stupid and costly decisions.

At the height of his power in 1959 he outlined his philistine philosophy in an interview:

If somebody sends me a literate script do you know what I do with it? I throw it in the waste paper basket, that's what I do with it. I make films to appeal to the lowest common denominator. That's why I am still in the business while the other arty-farty boys are not.

I just want to make films to make money. The art of surviving in this business is to never let on whether you've got fifty million bucks or fifty cents. I couldn't see my own films. I've got more taste than that.

Towards the end of that year Warwick announced that it would be producing only one film a year as costs had doubled and earnings halved – and when those two graphs meet you are out of business. Despite Allen's commercial inclinations, he and Broccoli produced the critically acclaimed *The Trials of Oscar Wilde* in 1960, which proved to be a box-office disaster.

Worse still, while Broccoli was dealing with his wife's terminal illness, Allen met Ian Fleming's representatives to discuss the matter of turning his books into film, and insulted them by saying the books were not even worthy of television production. Broccoli was furious: he saw the potential of the Bond franchise and resented having to leave his sick wife to rectify the deal. This led to a parting of ways between Allen and Broccoli, and Broccoli teamed up with veteran producer Harry Saltzman, who had been at the helm of so-called arty-farty films such as *Look Back in Anger* (1958); *Saturday Night and Sunday Morning* (1960); and the brilliant *The Entertainer* (1960), starring Laurence Olivier. They formed Eon Productions, which went on to acquire and produce the hugely profitable Bond films. Allen's arrogance had stripped him of a fortune, but he was one of those beings who just got on with producing. Broccoli and Saltzman would go on to make huge amounts of money from the Bond movies, which starred Sean Connery, among others.

Meanwhile, much later, Allen teamed up with writer-director Ken Hughes who, despite directing the Wilde failure, had gone on to much better things with *Casino Royale* (1967) and most notably the children's classic *Chitty Chitty Bang Bang*, produced by Broccoli in 1968.

It was not, however, a combination of producer and director who might tackle such a hugely interesting subject as Cromwell in a manner to find satisfaction with critics, never mind audiences, however divergent their expectations and experience might be. The bar had been set just a couple of years previously in English costume drama by *A Man For All Seasons* (1966), adapted from the play by Robert Bolt, directed by Fred Zinnemann and starring Paul Scofield as Sir Thomas More, who had taken on Henry VIII as Cromwell had Charles I. There was also a stellar cast including Susannah York, Nigel Davenport, Robert Shaw, Orson Welles, Leo McKern, John Hurt and Corin Redgrave and the film won five Oscars and the same number of BAFTAS. To say it would be a hard act to follow would be an understatement. But that never stopped genre-hunting or imitating producers or directors from going down the same road, even if comparison might be on the agenda.

One way or another, the subject of Cromwell was one worthy of bringing to the screen depending on how the subject was treated, for unlike Sir Thomas More, where integrity and sacrifice in the face of royal brutality could engage empathy with the audience, Oliver Cromwell was more noted in history for brutality and blood lust, justified by some missionary zeal to replace the corruption of the royalty with a 'democratic' alternative.

Cromwell is one of the most controversial figures in British history, considered by some historians as a regicidal dictator and by others as a hero of liberty. He was born in 1599 in Huntingdon to Robert Cromwell and Elizabeth Steward. He was descended from Katherine Cromwell, the elder sister of Thomas Cromwell (1485–1540) who had been a minister of Henry VIII.

In the film, there would be the inevitable horsing around with historical accuracy. As the prince of film critics, the late Roger Ebert, put it: 'I have argued as a principle that it does not matter if a movie is faithful to a book; what matters is whether the movie is any good in its own right. If the movie works, I am not concerned with its accuracy.'

The publicists boasted that the movie had been made 'after ten years' research', which is hardly likely given the career track of Hughes, except on a part-time basis. He would take the usual liberties with the script, which in the process of dramatic reconstruction was not unusual. As Friedrich Nietzsche observed: 'Historians begin by looking backward and often end by thinking backward.' Film-makers are capable of doing the same and much more with events that should never get in the way of narrative prejudice or facts that may spoil a good story. But at the end of the day, dramatic licence is allowed even in the face of such blatant twisting of fact as in a scene where Henry Ireton appears with a delegation of MPs to offer Cromwell the throne. In reality, by the time Cromwell was offered the Crown towards the end of his life in 1657, Ireton, his son-in-law, had been dead for nearly six years.

The screenplay (in traditional fashion for the film industry) had been around for a few years in what is known in the business as 'development hell' when the green light is at the end of the tunnel of expectations. During the process, the director usually attempts to attach a star name to the project to give it more credibility with the prospective financiers. Richard Harris might have seemed the most unlikely candidate for the main part, given Cromwell's campaign of slaughter in Ireland. But the script did not deal with that awful episode; it was a mighty and interesting role covering the story of the English Civil War, the execution of Charles I and the dramatic political events that followed – and it was very attractive to Harris. In a telegram to Hughes, he said: 'I want to play the part of Cromwell. I want to do this film.'

What had attracted him to the project was the script's exploration of the central character's concern for the common man and opposition to the corrupt practices of the monarchy and hypocritical religious practice. Charles I regards himself as a devout Anglican but allows his French queen to practise Roman Catholicism in private, as long as she does not bring up the young Prince of Wales in that faith. Cromwell plans to take his family to the New World but is convinced by friends to stay and play a role in the increasing dangerous politics of the time.

Charles summons Parliament for the first time in eleven years as he needs money to fight wars against the Scottish and the Irish. Parliament will not grant him the money unless he agrees to reforms that will lead to a constitutional monarchy. Believing in the divine right of kings, and under pressure from the queen, he refuses. When he attempts to arrest five members of Parliament, war breaks out in England.

The Parliamentary forces in which Cromwell is a cavalry officer get nowhere and so he sets up the New Model Army, which takes on the Royalist forces to great effect and is ultimately responsible for the defeat of Charles. Charles stubbornly refuses to give in to the demands of Cromwell for a system of government that will allow Parliament as much say in the control of the country as the monarchy.

The story moves on, awash with battles and political intrigue, betrayal and the news that Charles has secretly been raising a Catholic army after his initial defeat in order to resume war. This leads to the king being put to trial for treason. Found guilty he faces his fate with great bravery, moving even his most ardent enemies by his dignity. His execution provides little celebration.

Cromwell then ironically assumes the role of the dead king, dissolving Parliament and assuming the role of dictator. The film ends with a voice-over stating that Cromwell spent a successful five years as Lord Protector before Charles I's son, Charles II, brought back the rule of monarchy in an England 'never to be the same again'.

Like all directors of the time, Hughes was wary of Harris's off-screen reputation, but once they met he was convinced that Harris was right for the part – though they both agreed that no self-respecting Irishman should play the part of Oliver Cromwell. More importantly, both were agreed on the angle of the script and the interpretation of the central character. The writer-director had lived a long time with his project and was sure of his vision, and Harris respected that commitment as much as he had with Lindsay Anderson in the genesis of *This Sporting Life*.

However, that was not enough to draw the finance. The studios felt that the days of costume epics were gone and could not justify the investment of the roughly $7–8 million needed to mount the production. Eventually, Hughes persuaded Irving Allen to come on board as producer and he went to his old ally Columbia for the finance. Allen proved a very effective advocate and managed to convince the doubting executives to stump up the budget. It was a considerable achievement in the face of the conventional wisdom that the time was up for such projects.

The question could have been easily put as to what possible connection could be made by an American audience with a historical figure completely unknown to them, against an even more obscure background of historical events of seventeenth-century England – and with an Irishman in the lead and an all-English cast. Not a very attractive proposition and so it is little wonder that the script had been around for so long.

Even taking into account that Hollywood studios were as capable of backing turkeys as producing blockbusters – and given Allen's track record as a producer who, as a rule, sought profit before artistic worth – there was no doubt some financial incentive in backing the movie. Genre movies shot away from Hollywood could still be successful and profitable. For example, the spaghetti westerns of Sergio Leone were shot in Spain and were huge hits.

Harris was announced in the lead role, with Alec Guinness cast as King Charles I. The Limerick actor was getting a whopping $500,000 as a fee. The location work was to be shot in Spain, England and Ireland, and interiors at Shepperton Studios, just outside London. It was a massive logistical operation involving a huge outdoor set and thousands of period costumes and props.

Before and after starting work on the film, the leading actor ended up in court twice, with both hearings extensively covered in the tabloids. The first incident occurred during a *Talk of the Town* show featuring Sammy Davis Jnr, when Harris punched a heckler. Subsequently he was involved in an altercation with a policeman who had been called after the incident in an effort to restrain and detain the actor. Harris told the hearing in Bow Street Magistrates' Court that he found the remarks of the heckler offensive and distasteful, so he hit him. He got off lightly, considering the altercation with the police who were only doing their job, and was given a £12 fine with the same sum towards costs.

Harris's next appearance in court was of an entirely farcical nature. As reported in the *Irish Times* on Wednesday 8 October 1969:

Harris (38) of Tower House, Kensington was given a six-month conditional discharge at Bow Street Magistrates Court after being booked by a meter maid, despite not having a car. But he stopped her putting a ticket on a friend's car, 'when he danced an Irish jig with her.' She said that he put his arms around her and she was squashed and it hurt.

The magistrate Mr Kenneth Barraclough told him: 'I think it was misplaced friendliness. You must not think that everyone enjoys being hugged and jigged around by a film star.'

As well as Harris and Guinness, the top-class cast assembled by Hughes included Robert Morley, Dorothy Tutin, Frank Finlay, Patrick Wymark, Timothy Dalton, Patrick Magee and Nigel Stock, among others. The shooting schedule for *Cromwell*, which began in Spring 1969 in Spain, proved to be a marathon and far more physically demanding for the lead actor than *Camelot*, with take after take of exhausting battle scenes in stifling conditions added to by the wearing of costume armour. As if this was not enough energy to be expending, more was often sacrificed to drink. Under the pressure of the combination of work, sleep deprivation and drink, Harris began to get wound up and started hallucinating:

I woke up one morning, it was during the time that the scene of the execution was coming up and I thought we were about to cut off Charles I's head in real time. I grabbed the telephone and roared that we must give him a second chance, we must think twice about this. It was a terrifying experience.

The production nurse and a doctor were summoned and Harris was given a strong tranquilliser by injection. He had driven himself over the edge: 'I had finally crossed the line from sanity to madness.'

After a day's rest Harris was back in the saddle as Cromwell, but he had received a severe fright and knew that he had to do something about his drinking. He knew that he had reached a crossroad. The very memory of this experience would draw a shiver from him many years afterwards. He considered the possibility of psychotherapy but then rejected it. He intended to continue the treadmill of film-making but would try it without the crutch of alcohol.

There was an element of loneliness that he had to contend with; he would deal with the 'comedown' from the daily performance of Cromwell by staying late in nightclubs and restaurants. But he was also as manically driven when it came to acting and literally inhabited the part, which gave him pause many years later when he contemplated the film-acting cliché that 'less is more'. But he accepted that this could never be his technique. He had a tendency to give too much but that was an ingrained part of his personality, which in creative terms would never change.

The trick might have been not to allow that inclination to spill into life after the day on the set, but it would take some time for that to sink in. Burn the candle at both ends and the flame will begin to flicker. He obviously realised this but, as was his wont, he would go to the edge of the abyss before pulling back. That abyss, in fact, would wait for him for another decade – and even then he would face it on his own terms.

Even the worst of scary situations can fade with the passage of time, as any climber of mountains would know. One slide to the edge was not sufficient for Richard Harris to pull back instantly. It was a lesson, but there would need to be more. He was a man convinced of his indestructability, even with the chimes of middle age ringing in his ears. Pushing himself to extremes was part of his psyche and there could be all sorts of psychological explanations offered for that fact. He was what he was and self-destruction would ultimately be balanced by an acute instinct for survival.

The director of *Cromwell*, however, had no time to worry about the off-the-set life of his lead, only in so far as it might impact on his shooting schedule. His lead was, after all, approaching 40 and should have been able to look after himself. Hughes was very happy with the performance of his leading man and also Alec Guinness, who in personality and acting technique could not have been more different to the Irishman.

Hughes had been very well aware of the so-called hellraising exploits when he had offered the part to Harris, but he had experienced far more discommoding relationships with his leads, most notably Kim Novak in *Of Human Bondage* (1964), of whom he said that his instant love transformed into instant hate. By contrast, he found Harris to be utterly professional on the set. With one exception, Harris's night-time activities never interfered with his punishing schedule.

The problems would begin for the director in the post-production period, when the studio became concerned about the length of the film and started insisting on cuts, including all the battles scenes in Ireland. The first cut was 180 minutes long and trimmed back to 139 for release, losing performances from a number of prominent English actors, and poignantly Felix Alymer as an archbishop in what would prove to be his final film.

Hughes fought as hard as he could, but Columbia insisted on the cuts in order to make it accessible to audiences and maximise the commercial potential. There were mixed but generally favourable reviews, and the majority gave high praise. As one put it: 'Whether wielding his sword in battle or dominating politicians by the strength of his personality and the courage of his convictions, Harris gives a magnificent, commanding performance.'

The movie was a commercial flop in the US but did very well in Britain, Europe and Australia. It ran for three months at the Odeon in Leicester Square and topped the box-office charts in other countries. King Arthur had big appeal for American audiences but Oliver Cromwell obviously did not. It was nominated for two Oscars in 1971 and won one for Best Costume Design by Vittorio Nino Novarese. There were also BAFTA and Golden Globe nominations. At the seventh Moscow International Film Festival, Harris won the award for Best Actor and the film was nominated for Best Picture.

15

A MAN CALLED HORSE (1970)

It might have occurred to Harris to take a break after the rigours of playing such a demanding role as Cromwell and the hair-raising experience that he would always recall when talking about it, but he went straight on to another film with a most unusual story and a part that was challenging, not least in a physical sense. In December 1969 he flew to Mexico and the location for *A Man Called Horse*.

It was the third story adapted for the screen from the writings of Dorothy M. Johnson. She was born in 1905 in McGregor, Clinton County, Iowa, and in high school worked as a stringer for a newspaper in Montana. In the 1930s she sold a magazine article to the *Saturday Evening Post* for what was a princely sum at the time – $400 – which was some indication of her talent. After the Second World War, which interrupted her writing career, she produced some of the best western stories of the time.

Between 1956 and 1960 she taught creative writing at the University of Montana, from which she also graduated, and wrote numerous articles and fictional stories for a variety of magazines. During the same period she had posts as secretary and researcher for the Montana Historical Society and secretary-manager of the Montana Press Association.

In 1957 she was awarded the prestigious Spur Award from Western Writers of America for a short story 'Lost Sister' from her collection titled *The Hanging Tree*. The story deals with the reintegration into white settler society of Cynthia Ann Power, who was kidnapped as a child by a Comanche Indian tribe. Two years later she was made an honorary member of the Blackfoot tribe.

The first of Johnson's stories adapted for screen was *The Hanging Tree*, released in 1959, directed by Delmer Davies and starring Gary Cooper, George C. Scott (in his first film) and Karl Malden, set in the gold fields of Montana during the gold rush of the 1860s and 1870s.

The second was *The Man Who Shot Liberty Valance*, released four years later, directed by John Ford and starring John Wayne and James Stewart. The film is remembered (among other things) for the famous line: 'When the truth becomes a legend, print the legend.'

But the premise for the next film was, as the saying goes, a horse of a different colour. It was from a collection of short stories published in 1968 and was only five pages long. But such was the skill of the author that her plain but dense prose gave a reading experience more akin to a novel. Entitled *A Man Called Horse* it had an existential quality, quite apart from an intriguing storyline that was redolent of those great masters of the art Albert Camus and Jean-Paul Sartre, albeit in a Wild West setting. It was not surprising that Richard Harris became interested and committed to the expression of the subject matter.

The opening paragraphs of the story would have been sufficient to hook him:

He was a young man of a good family, as the phrase went in the New England of a hundred odd years ago, and the reasons for his bitter discontent were unclear, even to himself. He grew up in the gracious old Boston home under his grandmother's care, for his mother had died in giving him birth; and all his life he had known every comfort and privilege his father's wealth could provide.

But still there was the discontent, which puzzled him, because he could not even define it. He wanted to live among his equals – people whom were no better than he and no worse either. That was as close as he could come to describing the source of his unhappiness in Boston and his restless desire to go somewhere else.

The latter paragraph could be describing Harris to a T. Although this story was set in another country and another time, still its dramatic ebbs would, by dint of circumstance, pull him into the flow. It may have been 'no country for old men' in W.B. Yeats's phrase, but it would prove perfect for the Irish actor.

In Johnson's story the man from Boston with no name left home in 1845 and went to seek his identity and equality in Indian country, where danger would sharpen and perhaps prove the efficacy of his instinct. He hired companions but they were killed and he ended up a captive of the Crow tribe of Indians. It is there that the real tale and examination of his pursuit begins, and when he acquires the name, self-given and accepted by the tribe, of Horse.

He begins the period of captivity, practically naked, lapping rainwater from the ground. Thrown a chunk of meat by an old woman, he has to fight the dogs for his share of it. He realises that he has to bury his pride and restrain his emotion if he is to survive. The captive becomes a horse, 'a docile bearer of burdens, careful and patient'. The old woman, Greasy Hand, lives in a tepee with her warrior son Yellow Robe and his wife, and his little sister Pretty Calf, with whom the man/horse's fate becomes inextricably linked.

There follows a hideous chronicle of the privileged man's submission to and acceptance by the Indian tribe, during which he has to murder members of another tribe in order to acquire status. He captures his victim's horses and this dowry allows him to marry Pretty Calf whom he loves, and she him. She educates him in tribal customs. He prospers with the acquisition of more horses and achieves equality with his Indian peers.

It is a brilliant exposition of the merging of one culture with another and the subsuming of the educated white man into the primitive mores of a tribal community. By a quirk of good fortune, it becomes a rite of passage to share and attain the respect and status that had been given rather than earned in his previous life.

But tragedy, in the shape of the deaths of Yellow Robe and Pretty Calf in battle, reduces him to the depths that marked the beginning of his captivity. By recognising Greasy Hand after her entreaty as mother he must, according to custom, protect her until she dies. He does, and finally, three years later, returns to Boston. The last line of the story sums up the result of his extraordinary journey: 'He did not find it necessary to either apologise or boast, because he was the equal of any man on earth.'

Producer Sandford Howard had read the story in an anthology of western stories and instantly recognised the potential for a movie. He bought the rights for a song and began to develop it. He hired veteran Jack De Witt to write the script, for which Johnson would get an agreed credit, and when it was completed went looking for a bankable actor to play the central role of the young English aristocrat John Morgan. He also got on board Elliot Silverstein, who had directed the 1965 production of *Cat Ballou*, which got four nominations and an Academy Award for Lee Marvin in the leading role.

But the choice of Silverstein was strange as he had an unremarkable career and *Cat Ballou* was a spoof on the western genre, a clever but light film. *A Man Called Horse* was a serious piece, unrelentingly brutal and potentially of controversial subject matter. Howard had put the wrong man in charge and this may have had some influence on the fact that a number of actors, including Robert Redford, passed on the project. Harris, however, never one to avoid a challenge, accepted the role.

Silverstein proved to be a disaster and fought with his leading man, who as usual was putting all his energy and talent into a part and a picture he believed in, and could see that the director just did not get the concept or the potential of the story. The director's final cut outraged Harris, who was proved right in his attitude when a test screening produced a hugely negative reaction from the audience. With the help of a colleague at the production company, Howard re-edited the film until a version was produced that all were happy to release and which conformed to the original vision and spirit of Dorothy Johnson's story.

This of course both added to the delay of the release and considerably increased the cost of the production, which the producer claimed was over $1 million. There might have been some exaggeration in this respect, but in the long term the effort would prove worthwhile as it would transpire that there would be two sequels (at admittedly long intervals) to the original production, not a bad result considering the difficulties involved.

The impact of the film when released in 1970 was immediate, with excellent reviews. An element of controversy surrounded the graphic initiation rite of Morgan being raised by hooks to his pectoral, and audiences were fascinated by the newness and authenticity of the depiction of a white man adapting to the ancient rituals of an Indian tribe. As Harris put it in an interview: 'The public has never seen the American Indian as he was before the white man. In this movie, we see the truth.'

The sequels that would appear in 1976 and 1982 were much less engaging, had no surprise and could never match the impact of *A Man Called Horse*, a movie that would for many years to come be largely associated with Harris's central and powerful part in it. The experience had also cemented a fruitful working relationship between Harris and the film's producer.

Of course, without Johnson's incredibly brief but mightily effective short story, there would have been no films. Even if no one could connect her name to either *The Hanging Tree* or *The Man Who Shot Liberty Valance*, the Montana-based writer could have derived at least some financial satisfaction from her association with Hollywood.

While a relatively young woman Johnson had experienced a failed marriage and ever afterwards was proud of her own self-sufficiency, which would have been helped in later life by the translation of her stories to the silver screen. She died in 1984, two years after the last of the movies, *The Triumphs of a Man Called Horse*, was released. She wanted her epitaph to read 'Paid in Full'. The headstone on her grave in a Montana cemetery simply reads 'Paid'.

16

THE MOLLY MAGUIRES (1970)

*T*he *Molly Maguires* had been Harris's next after *Camelot*, but it did not reach the screen until long after it had been completed. The director, Martin Ritt, had been blacklisted during the infamous McCarthy era and the political foundation of the story and the theme of injustice captured in the script of his long-time friend Walter Bernstein appealed to Harris, as well as the fact that his co-star was to be Sean Connery, who was anxious to throw off the yoke of the Bond series and was still the industry's most bankable actor.

Nevertheless, the Scot had been cast in the second lead after Harris, a credit that should have been unthinkable at the time. Yet with a wry smile Connery, in reply to a journalist's question on the matter, said: 'They are paying me a million dollars for this picture. For that money they can put a mule ahead of me.'

Samantha Eggar had been cast in the female lead role. While she had been pushed into the spotlight by her excellent performance in *The Collector*, five years previously, nothing much had happened for her in the interim.

Set in the latter half of the nineteenth century in the coalfields of Pennsylvania and West Virginia, the story follows the true life exploits of a secret organisation of immigrant coal workers, the Molly Maguires, who were dynamiting the trainloads of coal coming out of the mines as a protest against the appalling working conditions and poor pay. Irish-American miners were at the forefront of the terrorist campaign, and the group was named after an Irish widow who had led a band of land agitators in the 1840s.

The pit owners contacted the famous (or even infamous) Pinkerton Detective Agency who, as well as the usual private-eye activities, had developed an expertise as strike breakers and had been engaged by big business all over the country when there were labour disputes. The agents specialised in undercover work and acting as agents provocateurs.

Harris was cast as Jack McParlan, based on a real-life detective, whose job is to infiltrate the group. His job is made harder by the fact that he comes to admire the miners' leader Jack Kehoe, the role played by Connery. Both characters are Irish immigrants who share the same aspiration of advancement in a new society but come at it from different routes. A natural alliance between them is made impossible by the divergence of their respective interests. The detective's testimony leads, however, to the conviction and execution of ten members of the secret organisation.

Ritt was looking for an authentic backdrop to the story, so the location of the action was where much of the true events had taken place. This was Eckley, Pennsylvania, a town so unchanged from its appearance in the 1870s that little dressing had to be done. It had been condemned and was due for demolition but the movie saved it and it was transformed into a museum of a mining town of the time.

In production through spring 1968 the location was hot, uncomfortable and dusty and Connery was treated for dehydration at one stage. He and Harris got on very well. The Irish actor was revelling in the role and was at the height of his physical and creative power. Eggar, somewhat left out from this male bonding, at first seemed fragile and aloof, but as she watched them help each other out and share mutual advice she relaxed. As Harris recalled later in an interview: 'I think Sam was amazed to see two actors of our calibre helping each other, not trying to upstage each other. Once we got to know her, she was the darling of the crew. They adored her.'

Despite poor conditions, it was a happy shoot and Harris and Connery insisted on doing their own physical work without the intervention of stuntmen. One scene was a football match that was a mixture of soccer and rugby. Harris had brought along his New York boozing buddy Malachy McCourt to play a small part and he was appointed referee. Harris clearly thought it was a replay of *This Sporting Life*, while Connery felt that he still possessed the physical attributes of his Bond days. But this was not the case. Harris sustained a black eye, battered nose and sore ribs while Connery twisted his knee and bruised his shoulder.

Eggar was beguiled by the Irish actor's crazy energy and enthusiasm: 'Mad as Richard was, he poured out so much energy that you simply had to try to match up to him.'

After the film wrapped and the post-production process was complete, Paramount was uncertain about the film's content and marketability and the $11 million investment. It was not released for over a year and then for one reason and another it flopped. The critical responses were mixed, yet by all accounts the film should have succeeded, given the mix and the standard of talent involved in its making.

The highly regarded critic Pauline Kael, writing in the *New Yorker*, came closest to identifying the problem:

> *The Molly Maguires* is a failure, nailed on its own aspirations to the tragic and the epic, yet it's an impressive failure ... in the end it is too sombre and portentous for the rather dubious story it carries, but it feels like a reminder of a bitter, tragic past and when you come away you know you have seen something.

Harris got more than faint praise from Kael:

> Richard Harris whose devious, hangdog expression makes him a natural for the role, is wily and complex as a smart but weak man. He has a volatile edginess that draws us into the spy's divided spirit and contributes most of the suspense in the film.

While he was making the film Harris felt it was one of the best he had made and observers on the set felt the same. But what happens in the making, and what survives the cutting-room floor in the film business, particularly with a nervous studio, can be entirely different. Harris would reflect on the experience – not the making of the film but watching the final product – as heartbreaking.

He recalled that the director, Ritt, took the story and related it to those people who had betrayed their own kind during the witch-hunt of the McCarthy era. Ritt was also attempting something more subtle: exposing the treachery on which America exists and the men who climb any kind of ladder to reach the top. Harris comments: 'When I saw Ritt's first version of the movie, it was shattering and brutal, but because of whatever pressures one must assume were placed on Ritt during the editing, the film was watered down. The film became a great compromise on the screen.'

It was an aspect of large-budget Hollywood film-making that Harris would remain highly critical of, prompting him some years later to return to the sort of small-budget independent films that launched his career: 'In big-budget pictures that cost $15 million everybody tells everyone what to do because it costs so much, and it makes me want to get involved in films like *This Sporting Life*, small, intimate and with substance.'

This he would do, while equally conscious that a jobbing actor would never really be able to afford to turn down the sort of income that only Hollywood can afford. It would be a pattern that he would maintain without completely abandoning his integrity. But he would prove capable of turning down the main chance when he became passionately involved in a vehicle that he believed in.

One thing that characterised Richard Harris was his commitment – whether big or small picture, he gave it his all, even in a celluloid vehicle that, given the many vagaries of the business, had no chance of success. One of these was his only directorial credit – *Bloomfield*.

17

BLOOMFIELD AND BEYOND (1970)

Harris had an adversarial relationship with Limerick, rather like two boxers who have slugged it out in the ring. There is a grudging respect, an outward bonhomie, but behind the joviality there is the knowledge that they have knocked sparks out of each other, and could again.

Harris also had a very tetchy relationship with its local newspaper, the *Limerick Leader*. In the early days of his career, it was a love-in. When he spotted actress Rita Gam out shopping in Limerick in the mid-1950s, before he had made the break for London, he posed with her for a photograph – then went to the *Leader* with the picture, which they were happy to publish. They continued to celebrate his success. This is from 1960:

> Limerick-born stage and screen actor Richard (Dickie) Harris is at the Grand Central all this week, in *Alive and Kicking*. Next week he co-stars with Robert Mitchum in *A Terrible Beauty*, and with Charlton Heston and Gary Cooper in *The Wreck of the Mary Deare*.
>
> Mr Harris has also scored big successes on television and has been hailed as one of the most promising young actors of this decade.

Three years later Earl Connolly wrote:

> The highlight of my recent visit to London was seeing for myself the brilliant performance of Richard Harris in the *Diary of a Madman*, at the Royal Court Theatre.
>
> The sight of Richard Harris was exciting enough, but on entering the theatre I found to my surprise that I was expected, and that two guest seats had been left for me at the office by the ever thoughtful Dickie Harris.
>
> Harris proved he is now an actor of stature and ability, with a voice which rings loud and clear, rising and falling as the occasion demanded. It was a tour de force

in every sense of the word, and the best tributes were paid to him at the end, when he took no less than eight curtain calls.

I hurried backstage after the performance to find several Limerick people in the number one dressing room, including Dick Naughton of the Customs and Excise, and Mr Kennedy of Thomondgate. Richard was very pleased to find that we liked the show, which had run the gauntlet of the critics.

I learned that New York, Paris, Munich, Dublin and other world capitals are waiting eagerly to see his marathon one-man performance. I asked Dickie would it be possible for him to include Limerick. He felt elated at the idea of playing in his native city.

For the next decade Harris did his best to help Limerick. When a campaign was launched for a university for the city he threw himself into it, flying in to attend and address public meetings. The campaign was successful. The National Institute for Higher Education was established in 1972, becoming the University of Limerick in 1989.

But the actor's relationship with Limerick, and the *Limerick Leader*, soured considerably in 1970.

'He wasn't a nice man to meet,' said Eugene Phelan, the newspaper's deputy editor, who had joined the paper a decade or more after those golden days. 'You couldn't just walk up to him and say: How's it going, Richard? He'd tell you where to go. Sometimes you'd catch him in the right mood, and he could be fun. But if he wasn't on form, then it was best to stay out of his way.'

What caused the change was the reaction to Harris's directorial debut in 1969/70. At the height of his fame, when he could do no wrong, he decided to broaden his horizons, by directing. Directors often get a bigger slice of the financial pie and make a bigger creative impact on the business than actors, so the move was a shrewd one. Significantly, few of his hellraising colleagues had the courage or ability to make the switch. However, Harris's foray into directing happened largely by accident.

Harris's production company, Limbridge, was financing a British/Israeli production called *Bloomfield*. The actor believed in the project, and poured £300,000 of his own money into it. The story had a sporting theme. Harris's big breakthrough had come as a rugby player in *This Sporting Life*, but rugby – despite its popularity in Britain – is a minority sport worldwide. In *Bloomfield* Harris would play an ageing soccer star, with a script by the highly regarded Wolf Mankowitz and produced by his good friend John Heyman.

Harris played Eitan, a former star of an Israeli soccer team who is facing the end of his career. He still believes that he is essential for the team, but is beginning to face up to the fact that his day is over. He desperately needs a new direction in life, but his girlfriend, played by Romy Schneider, does not understand what he is going through. Then salvation arrives in the form of a runaway boy. Eitan goes on a road trip with the boy.

While Harris dived into the project with characteristic enthusiasm, he was somewhat blind to or unprepared for the implication of his role in the project. Having committed his fee, he was effectively an investor/producer. Thus he had crossed a line and would naturally feel entitled as somewhat of a proprietor to more control of both the storyline and production schedule. By doing this he would be putting the independence and integrity of the director under threat. If this relationship was not defined in advance of production and agreed, there was every likelihood of trouble coming down the track.

Before filming started, along with producer Heyman, he scouted for locations in Israel and went into a programme of physical training for the part, as he had first done in *This Sporting Life*, although this time around he had a personal trainer and jogging routine. The actor was putting everything into preparation and his commitment was unquestionable. It was also obvious to all involved that he was running the show and on a path to conflict with the director.

Work began well, under experienced Israeli director Uri Zohar. But then Harris arrived in Tel Aviv. He started altering the script and making suggestions on set. Within ten days Zohar walked off. Undaunted, Harris decided he had the experience to take over direction, on the basis that he already had fifteen years' experience in the business at the highest level. He had done it successfully on stage.

But this was more complicated. Harris admitted that he was learning as he went along – a risky thing in a movie on such a tight budget. And to compound matters, the dialogue was in both English and Hebrew. Harris was fast approaching 40 and was not the physical machine he had been a decade earlier, but playing a washed-up sports star was well within his physical capabilities; a year later he was still fit enough to make the semi-finals of the annual racquets tournament on the beach of his beloved Kilkee, so the years of hard living were not leaving their mark too badly.

In early February 1970, the filming was complete and Harris flew back with Heyman to London to begin the post-production process. There he learned from his brother-in-law Jack Donnelly that his beloved sister Harmay was seriously ill and he immediately moved on to Dublin. Harmay underwent surgery but due to post-operative complications she died. He and his family were devastated. The extent of the actor's grief would be more adequately expressed in the poems he wrote in her memory, which would be published three years later.

His marriage had ended a short time before and now his sister had passed away. It was not that he was not affected by both events, but as was his wont he got on with life. Regarding his former marriage he would not discuss anything about Elizabeth or her relationship with Rex Harrison – the only clue was in a newspaper interview in which he said that he was all for making love, as in satisfying bodily appetite, but was all against falling in love as it was far too time-consuming.

There was perhaps a trace of misogyny running through his attitude to women, claiming that they played games while making love and their trouble was that they needed men to an emotional degree that men could not provide. There was more than a smidgeon of post-marital bitterness here. For the moment, however, *Bloomfield* and the gruelling editing process, normally the territory of the director, occupied his main attention. He sought the advice of his old friend Lindsay Anderson for the post-production process, which in a film is dominated by the editing of both visual and sound, the laying of the music and the dubbing of dialogue.

There was a lot of pressure on Harris as a small budget means less time and he must have been keenly aware of the attention that his directorial debut would draw. He had put his money where his mouth was, but would this vocal and opinionated man have any talent when it came to producing a work of art or worth, as opposed to being merely a participant? He was particularly exposed as he had not been the director from the start of the project and the departure of Zohar could be interpreted as the worst aspect of a vanity project.

All this was underlined by the gigantic waves of publicity that had accompanied the recent releases of *Cromwell* and *A Man Called Horse*. Harris finally finished his labours in the tunnel of the editing room, while all over London his image was carried on cinema posters. His original ambition when moving to London had been to train as a director, so many must have asked the question, was that ambition justified and had Harris added another string to his massive bow of talent?

The film, released in 1970, moved with funereal slowness, and lacked the emotional punch that such sentimental tales need in order to be a hit. It was a commercial failure when it opened in the UK and Ireland, and was renamed *The Hero* for its US release in 1971. The rename, and a re-edit, was not enough to make it successful, and it sank into obscurity.

A review in *Time Out* magazine gives an idea of how it was received:

Harris, directing himself (an embarrassing debut in that department) as an ageing Israeli soccer star, has a row with his plump sculptress girlfriend (Schneider). 'Give eet up!' she begs. 'You don't understand. They need me' he says, miming exasperation. There's even a clock ticking in the background. All this plus potted music and long shots of architecture and desertscapes.

Bloomfield never approaches even the energy level of those hilariously dated commercials which send you scurrying to the ice-cream girl as a hero-worshipping kid hovers and Harris is offered a car to throw the game. Hanging up by your nipples may be masochism, but this is suicide.

Harsh words. It is against this backdrop that Harris fell out with the *Limerick Leader* – and with much of Limerick society – for a while.

He had decided to stage the world premiere of *Bloomfield* in the Savoy in Limerick, as a fundraiser for charity. It would be a black-tie event, and a significant milestone for the city. Hollywood was coming to Ireland.

The event, on 6 November 1970, was hosted by the Limerick Lions Club, in association with Limbridge Productions. The funds raised would go to the Limerick Handicapped Children Fund, and the Christian Leadership Movement. The event was sponsored by Halpin's Tea, who had a number of free tickets to distribute.

Harris must have known that his enterprise was doubtful at best; it was a sentimental story, filmed in two languages. But he had faith in the forbearance of his audience, and believed they would give him the rousing reception he yearned for. And he had an ace up his sleeve; the musical score was composed by two Limerick men, Bill Whelan (who went on to compose the music for *Riverdance*) and Niall Connery.

The build-up was intense. There were acres of coverage in the local papers, including the *Leader*: 'The world premiere of a feature film in Limerick is a history making event, but the fringe attractions planned for *Bloomfield* on 6 November promise to rival in brilliance the film itself.'

The paper went on: 'Richard Harris, with characteristic showmanship, has gathered quite a galaxy of stars for Bloomfield's premiere in the Savoy; a specially chartered plane will fly in some sixty top names in the entertainment business, and they should make Limerick a centre of world attention on premiere night.'

The celebs included Dusty Springfield, Lulu and the Bee Gees. Honor Blackman was there with her husband Maurice Kaufmann, and rising talent Leonard Whiting, who starred in Franco Zeffirelli's *Romeo and Juliet*, also flew in. They all toured the west of Ireland with Harris, hanging out at Dromoland Castle and visiting Kilkee. Harris also had a special guest – bubbly blonde Linda Hayden. Then just 17, she was beginning to make a name for herself in the risqué sex comedies that the British film industry churned out in the 1970s. She had three films under her belt, and had bared all for her art at the tender age of 15. Linda Hayden was Harris's mistress, but it was a brief affair.

As the premiere approached, the army decided that the Band of the Southern Command was going to play the patrons into the cinema. It was a grand affair. Pharmacist Dermot Foley, the chairman of the Lions Club, was one of the key figures instrumental in planning the event. He was the same man who had photographed Harris with actress Rita Gam on O'Connell Street fifteen years previously.

Harris arrived a week before the premiere, and enjoyed all the hospitality that Limerick had to offer. He took over Dromoland Castle, one of the finest luxury hotels in the country, set in extensive grounds about 10 miles north of Limerick, where he often stayed when he returned home. During the build-up to the big night he took some of his showbiz buddies to Bunratty Castle. The Norman castle is Ireland's top tourist attraction, with nightly medieval banquets. Harris stood grinning as Maurice Gibb of the Bee Gees was crowned King of the Castle, and Lulu, his wife, Queen, in a mock ceremony at the banquet.

Manuel Di Lucia recalls the events of the day: 'My wife and I were invited. We were invited up to Dromoland, and booked in with all these stars. We went into the Savoy by coach, tuxedos on the lot of us, big fashion gowns on the women.'

Huge crowds gathered outside to cheer on those lucky enough to have got their hands on a treasured ticket. One person who had tried to get a ticket was Helen Buckley, proprietor of the *Limerick Leader*. Ms Buckley was a socialite who edited the fashion and social pages of the newspaper, and was a bit of a party animal. She was the sort of woman who should have appealed to Dickie; like Ava Gardener, one of his flames, Helen Buckley could drink him and smoke him under the table. But the two did not hit it off. Harris was incensed that someone could ask for free tickets for a charity event and he refused to give Ms Buckley the tickets.

The spat, minor though it was, preyed on his mind. He was worried about how the film would be received. Things began to go wrong before the film was even loaded. Television personality Bunny Carr was master of ceremonies, and the event overran badly. There were 1,500 people in attendance, including the mayor, two government ministers and the cream of the showbiz world. As they were preparing to begin the screening it was already an hour late. Then Detective J.J. Masterson received a phone call. There was a bomb in the cinema!

The Troubles in Northern Ireland were a few years old by that stage, and bomb scares were becoming a feature of Irish life. Most were hoaxes, but all had to be checked out. Bunny Carr calmly asked people to quit their seats for ten minutes and go to the foyer. He did not mention the word 'bomb', but everyone knew – except the visiting celebrities. A hasty search confirmed that the call had been a hoax, then everyone was allowed back in.

Carr remarked: 'I was told that things would go with a bang in Limerick, but I did not think it would be so close!'

Harris himself commented wryly: 'Two in one week is a bit much, as we had also to get out of our plane in London for an hour while a bomb scare held us up.'

The film was initially well received, but mainly because everyone wanted it to be a great success. Every appearance by Dickie was greeted with wild whoops and cheers. But as the film went on it was noticeable that the cheering grew more muted. The local lad come good was being applauded, not his artistic work. By the end it was obvious that the crowd were not enthused. But it didn't stop them celebrating. The event raised £3,500 for the charities, a large sum for those days. And the Irish love a party.

After the screening the festivities raged on until well into the early hours, with a lavish reception, followed by dancing to the sounds of a big band. Then the principals went back to Dromoland Castle for the post-mortem.

Di Lucia recalls:

The film was a dodo. It dive-bombed. Harris even admitted it himself. He was asking us afterwards in the bar in Dromoland what we thought of the film. 'It was shite, wasn't it?' he said. I said: 'If you say it Richard, it was. You'll have to rejig it.'

Harris said he'd go back to the cutting room with it. It never saw the light of day after that.

The film flopped in the UK, then opened in America, and flopped again. The failure threw Harris into a depression. He was used to success, but his first directorial effort had bombed. Forgetting the huge amount of positive publicity and uncritical support he had been given, he blamed the people of Limerick – and their paper – for turning against him, ranting that he would never again appear in Ireland and condemning the 'mind-set of Limerick'.

Harris was being unjust. The *Limerick Leader* recorded: 'Last Friday will long be remembered as a night of triumph for Richard Harris.' But it went on:

> The film itself was generally well received, though many claimed that Harris has often been seen to better effect in such films as *Camelot*, *Cromwell* and *This Sporting Life*.
>
> But it was Richard's big night and the crowd rose to him magnificently. His every move inside the theatre had the crowd cheering, and how he lapped it all up. The native son had come home to be treated like a hero in his home city. Crowds had mobbed him outside the theatre as he tried to enter, and once inside he was given a standing ovation. Again at the end of the film he was greeted with a standing ovation and he gained more applause as he lifted his two boy stars onto his shoulders by way of tribute for their display.

But perception is more important than reality sometimes. Richard Harris felt he had been slighted by his native city. It would be a number of years before the damage was undone.

In a broader sense the artistic failure also hit him because it dashed any aspiration he harboured of climbing on to the creative level of actor-director, which others such as Laurence Olivier had reached. There is no doubt that he had the ability to direct, as he would show to great effect many years later in a stage production of Pirandello's *Henry IV*. But two things defeated him in this instance: the weakness of the material and his headlong rush into everything he took on.

His plan had been to emulate Olivier by directing and starring in a film of *Hamlet*; with himself as the moody Dane, Mia Farrow as his Ophelia, George C. Scott as Claudius, and Peter Ustinov as Polonius. He had scouted location in The Burren in County Clare with his cameraman Geoffrey Unsworth, who had shot *Cromwell* and Olivier's *Othello*, and also had Kubrick's *2001 – A Space Odyssey* on his CV.

But now, Harris withdrew, into himself. He also made a disastrous career move by turning down an offer from the great Alfred Hitchcock to star in *Frenzy*, his penultimate film, to be shot in London. Harris was offered the role of a former RAF officer who is falsely accused of a series of gruesome murders in Covent Garden by 'the Necktie Killer'. He passed, and the little known Jon Finch, who had just completed Polanski's film of *Macbeth*, got the role.

Perhaps the intense disappointment of artistic failure, combined with that of his marriage, was in some way responsible for hurtling him on a journey in the 1970s that was largely, as he said himself, a rush from one crap movie to another. The previous decade had been largely a triumph of artistic accomplishment, which had unfortunately ended with the destruction of his marriage. Now he could and did concentrate on self-destruction, consciously or not, which on an incremental basis included a daily dose of over two bottles of vodka. That was bad enough, but he later experimented with cocaine and this came close to killing him. That was all on top of a work schedule that itself was capable of producing detrimental effects on his health.

As a result of a cocaine overdose, Harris ended up in the A&E department of the Cedars-Sinai Hospital in Los Angeles, where he was put on a life support machine and the doctors were so worried about his condition that his family were told that there was little hope for survival. But the planned obituary notices had to be left aside for another time after Harris made a miraculous recovery.

There was no doubt in anyone's mind that there would be another time like this one, even though the actor was not to indulge in drugs again. Just as with the episode during the filming of *Cromwell*, the actor had not just suffered a fright but was given a strong warning – whatever he might have thought of his physical power, this was another instance to prove that he was not indestructible. Or was it the opposite – 'If I can survive this I can survive anything'? The human mind has an infinite capacity for self-delusion and denial. Richard Harris was a very lucky man but, yet again, it would take him a number of years and more frights to take positive and lasting action.

An innate aspect of the man and the actor was an ability to bounce back from any crisis, both personal and artistic. It was something deeply ingrained in his character. In the moment and in retrospect he viewed failure as part of the human condition, the trick was to face it and move on. 'You are living today and you must be part of that, even if that part includes failure,' he said. He was equally philosophical about whatever the future offered:

> I have to contemplate the day when no one is going to ask me to act in a movie. I might last like Tracy or Cooper. I don't think about tomorrow because I am not interested in ten years' time. If you do you become that age. You can worry yourself into an older frame of mind.

He would, however, never lack ambition or energy in spite of lifestyle interventions. The breadth of his creative aspirations was as wide as ever. He held the opinion, often expressed, that acting was simply not enough.

He persisted with the long-held ambition to do a film version of *Hamlet* and was not going to be dragged down by the obstacles to making it actually happen. The time for projects in the film business, as he well knew, has to be when the circumstances are right; luck – as in the bounce of the ball in sport – always plays its part. In the interim he got on with his role as a jobbing actor, which he did with Sandy Howard and writer Jack De Witt in *Man in the Wilderness*, which was completed in 1971.

It was a reprise of the creative relationship responsible for *A Man Called Horse*, the story set in the Canadian north-west in 1820 in which a trapper, played by Harris, is mauled by a grizzly bear and learns to survive, and sets out for revenge against the assailant.

Meanwhile, in his Tower House abode in Kensington, west London in the autumn of 1971 he was embarking on a return to his singing career, this time with some of his own songs in a musical collaboration with Derryman Phil Coulter, who had garnered international recognition with his song 'Puppet on a String', which was performed by Sandie Shaw and won the Eurovision Song Contest in 1967. He had also come close a year later with 'Congratulations', sung by Cliff Richard.

Coulter was an utter professional but also a sensitive artist whose song 'The Town I Love So Well', first beautifully interpreted by Luke Kelly of The Dubliners, would enter the canon of great Irish traditional music. The popular appeal of his hit songs in the Tin Pan Alley of music belied his real talent; in another realm he was the Irish equivalent of Jimmy Webb, he had the facility with his music and lyrical ability to tear at the heart of the listener.

Coulter was a perfect collaborator with Harris and according to Coulter the two men established an immediate rapport. Harris's material was a personal journey of love lost and the impact of the breakdown of his marriage on his children, most affectingly captured in 'All the Broken Children' and 'My Boy'. The lyrics of the songs, like his poetry, expressed the deeper, emotional and sensitive nature of Harris, quite at odds with his public image and persona of the hard man.

The song, which would be recorded by Elvis Presley, could bring tears to the eye and was a hit when Harris performed it in October that year on *Top of the Pops*. He worked incredibly hard with Coulter on the songs in Tower House in Kensington, all the more so because he had no training in the art of music. He more than made up for this by his intrinsic talent and choice of collaborator. He voiced his feelings in an interview on the subject at the time:

Singing doesn't come second with me after acting. If I wake up in the morning and have a great idea for a film, it takes at least six months to get the thing off the ground. By that time I am likely to get bored. Now if it is an idea for a song I call up a songwriter or a producer, get into the studio and a week later we've got the finished product.

As well as the album, he planned a concert tour with Coulter with a thirty-piece orchestra, incorporating clips from his films and TV recordings. They rehearsed for months but Harris was nervous about the prospect of appearing in such a show in front of a live audience. Straight theatre and film are distinctly different to musical performance. Harris was worried that his talent might not stretch that far.

'I just don't want to sing a few songs and call that an evening's entertainment. I think audiences deserve something a bit different. If they even want me to talk, I'll only be too happy to oblige,' he said. This betrayed a sense that he was not sure exactly what he was undertaking and that he could not be sure of its success. As the start of the concert tour in January 1972 closed in, his doubts increased:

> I'm scared bloody stiff. They'll literally have to push me up the steps to get on. But it is something that I want to do. If you really want to communicate with a live audience you can't do it on Broadway and certainly not on Shaftesbury Avenue. The people with heads, the thinking people have gone from the theatre and they are going to concerts now.

The underlying problem that must have affected him was that he had mastered the art of film acting and that had been proved and recognised, as had his huge success with *A Tramp Shining* and most particularly 'MacArthur Park', but he could not be all artists to all audiences. However all-encompassing his creative urges, he could not possibly match Sinatra or suddenly invent a musical formula that would surpass the traditional and long-established forms. He would be too easily viewed as a dilettante as opposed to a master – and this proved to be the case. Inevitably the tour had a poor response. Not that Harris would have given a damn one way or another, he could well afford the slings of the critics, and financially he was not dependent on its success. The well-appointed music critic Robin Denselow was particularly scathing:

> Is it conceit or sheer self-deception? Why should a first-rate actor parade himself like a shambling tenth-rate Sinatra? True he has handled a musical successfully and gone on to record a series of albums but when it comes to a full solo concert, there is no hiding behind a name or studio techniques. He tried to play it straight and just couldn't do it: the lights dimmed to a flickering clip from *Camelot*, up went the screen to reveal an orchestra, and Harris wandered on, dinner jacketed and hand in pocket and launched straight into a batch of sentimental standards.

The consensus of opinion was that the show would have been better placed in a cabaret setting – and that was possibly true. He tried it out in New Orleans, where he achieved some success and had a great time in the Maison Bourbon, where he stayed up until the early hours of the morning listening to jazz. He gave a number of interviews at the venue to journalists and displayed no disappointment on the result of his latest

musical venture. He presented himself as a nomadic and nocturnal animal, 42 years
of age, full of energy and aspirations and intending to continue living his life in the
way he had until that moment.

He moved on to New York, where he made a concert debut at the Philharmonic Hall
in the Lincoln Centre, where he was much appreciated by the audience. There was
nothing stopping Harris on his journey and he seemed immune to both any perceived
achievement or the lack of it attributed to his professional pursuits:

> I've done so many things in my life and accumulated so many experiences that
> it won't make any difference to me. I'll go on as long as I am capable of going on.
> Although I'm 42 I feel marvellous, full of vigour. I plan to continue my life as it is,
> regardless of criticism and regardless of accolades.

The rest of the decade would confirm his strange and peripatetic existence, including
many films of not much value, a book of poetry of the opposite, many interviews in
which he would lead the journalists a merry dance and a new marriage. He made
pretty outrageous statements about women, which no doubt were deliberately made
to inspire sensation as opposed to firmly held personal belief:

> Girls just don't get the hang of doing things for pleasure. It is as if they have all been
> brought up in a puritan climate, where everything is necessarily sin, so they have to
> assure themselves that they are wanted for their inner selves. Who wants to eat the
> apple for the core all the time?

Pure bravado from a man with a proven sensitive soul and there is little likelihood
that he believed one word of it; there was no one better to wind up the media interest
in him, which was intense and would increase when he apparently ate his own words.
Not even Richard Harris, with his fabulous energy, creativity and high film profile,
was immune from the passing of the years and the mid-life crisis.

His crisis might well have been said to have happened some years earlier, but he
must have longed for some anchor in the midst of the turbulent seas of his career, with
its upswings followed by downswings. There is an inevitable sense of loneliness for the
troubadour moving from film to film, town to town, bar to bar.

He had long pursued the idea of a film of *Hamlet* and must have understood the
role of the Player King, which he could easily identify with. In the 1948 film, the
central role of Hamlet had been played by Laurence Olivier, aged 41, far too old for
the young man that Shakespeare portrayed. Harris was also subject to the obvious
temptation of the leading man falling for the leading lady, more so as a result of the
encroaching years.

That is exactly what happened. Back in Hollywood he was starring in the absurdly
titled *99 and 44/100% Dead*, a so-called spoof of 1940s gangster movies. The director,

John Frankenheimer, would later call it the worst movie he ever made. A beautiful young actress, Ann Turkel, almost twenty years Harris's junior, was playing the female lead after Jacqueline Bisset had turned it down. At the time she was engaged to David Niven Jnr, but soon came under the spell of the famous Harris charisma.

It should not be easily forgotten that the Irish actor, quite apart from his wit, humour and knowledge of all things artistic, was an incredibly handsome man. The extremities of his hectic, creative undertakings and dissipated life had made no impact on his physique or looks. There are some men who are just built like that, either from genetic favour or luck. He was one of them.

Turkel was smitten by him and he by her. For entirely different reasons, as it would later emerge. However, unless he found some new formula for personal stability and professional wandering it would be hard to see how a permanent relationship would work. There would have to be a number of compromises introduced by Harris (which is unlikely by leopards and humans of a certain age). His new amour summed it up in part:

> This was my total opposite – a guy from Ireland, a hellraiser and a brawler. He was also much older than me. We fell in love before we had ever gone to bed together. If I believed all the wild stories about him I wouldn't be going out with Richard. There is no need to tame him; he is more a lamb than a lion.

There was a certain truth in the young actress's assessment. Harris was acutely aware when he entered the relationship of the appalling behaviour that had led to the breakdown of his marriage. He was up front to Ann about his close connection to Elizabeth and his abiding love for his children, which she accepted as an honourable act that carried no threat to her.

She was also transparent to the public about his previous relationships, which she said meant something to her: 'I hear all about those women who are supposed to have passed through his life. They were one-night affairs which had no meaning.' It was clear to friends of the actor that Ann Turkel was no pushover. She appeared to be confident and determined. For Harris, he made the mistake in their relationship, as he would later admit, of over-compensating for his previous failure.

At the beginning there was no hint of marriage, but that was the route the couple took and in early 1974 the engagement was announced, the date being fixed for April. He brought her to London and to Ireland to introduce her to his friends. He also decided to sell Tower House in Kensington, a transaction that brought a handsome profit of £200,000 and, on the advice of Kevin McClory, allied with some tax advantage, he purchased a large house on Paradise Island in the Bahamas with no fewer than ten bedrooms.

It had been the abode of American millionaire Huntington Hartford, who also owned the entire island. It was to be the idyllic home for the engaged couple. Harris was now living the dream existence so beloved of the high-end magazine world, a far cry from his roots in Limerick and somewhat alien to his brash and down-to-earth personality. It remained to be seen whether this would suit his apparent desire to settle down.

After some unexplained delay and rumours of arguments, the couple were married in Beverly Hills in June and departed to the Bahamas for the honeymoon. It might have been more appropriate at this juncture of seeming happiness to keep his personal life a private matter, but Harris had no problem, as ever, in talking about it to the media. The obvious danger did not seem to impact on him. Public pronouncement on the private life of high-profile people when things are going well has the inevitable consequence of unwarranted attention when things go wrong.

When invited to comment on the reason for marriage he said: 'Ann is a well-brought-up girl, whatever that means. She is also very nice and talented. I've made no bones that I'm bad news for any girl.' He went on to say that he had told her father as much and he had just laughed. At the same time, his ex-wife was experiencing difficulties with her marriage to Rex Harrison.

Even though the films Harris made in the 1970s were viewed as a low point in his career, as always he got on with the job. It was never the responsibility of the actor to judge how a film might turn out in the end. There were too many variables at play between the concept of the script and the journey to the screen. In a notoriously uncertain industry like the film industry, if the actor is on a high and in demand then the chances have to be embraced. The greatest actors in the business have made bad choices, terrible movies and commercial failures – as have directors.

Longevity was an unusual thing in film, as it was in sport. The 1970s was the decade of disaster movies and a rather good British attempt at matching the Americans in the genre was *Juggernaut*. In the pre-production phase, two directors, Bryan Forbes and Don Taylor, had been shown the door and the baton was handed to the England-based American Richard Lester, who had come to prominence with two films starring The Beatles, *Help* (1965) and *A Hard Day's Night* (1964), and the successful *The Three Musketeers: The Queen's Diamonds* (1973).

Lester started by rewriting the entire script for *Juggernaut*, with writer Alan Plater. He also added to the existing top line-up of cast: Harris, Omar Sharif and David Hemmings, with a very strong ensemble including Ian Holm, Shirley Knight, Roy Kinnear, Freddie Jones and Irish actor Cyril Cusack, who had first acted with Harris in *Shake Hands with the Devil*, fifteen years previously.

Harris was playing the lead, Lieutenant Commander Anthony Fallon, a bomb-disposal expert who with his team is parachuted on to the cruise liner *Brittanic* in the middle of the Atlantic in rough weather and heavy seas. A number of explosive-packed barrels have been placed on the ship by a shadowy figure who goes by the name of Juggernaut and who threatens to allow the barrels to explode and sink the ship if he is not given $1 million ransom. Back in England, a police team headed by Supt. John McLeod (Anthony Hopkins) is given the task of tracking down Juggernaut. His job is given increased tension by the fact that his wife and children are on the ship. A real cruise ship was hired for the sea shoot, the SS *Hamburg*, which had recently been sold by German owners to a Russian company and renamed the SS *Maxim Gorky*.

Lester was not only a good director but highly efficient and fast, a method that suited the cast, crew and over 200 extras assembled on the ship. When the sea scenes were complete, the production team moved to Twickenham Studios to shoot the interior scenes there and in other locations in England. The result was a gritty, realistic suspense thriller with stand-out scenes such as the parachute landing on the ship and one where Fallon is being directed by the villain (now captured on land) as to which wire to cut to defuse a barrel bomb.

He tells Fallon to cut the blue wire but the expert, in the midst of sweat-inducing tension, suspects he is being led into a trap, which will spell death for all. He chooses the red wire. Then, following his example, his team defuse the other bombs. Harris was in top form in the part and received excellent reviews. Though he would not rate his performance in his own top ten, it confirmed the breadth of his acting range and how he effortlessly crossed from one film genre to another.

Lester said that he enjoyed working with him and shared his opinion of the boredom of location work. Harris got on with the job, which suited the director. It was not in Lester's opinion the best part Harris played: 'I don't think you can say that. Richard did, after all, play some other splendid roles, so one cannot be categorical. I enjoyed working with him. He caused me no worry at all.' There would be more splendid roles to come for Harris, but not in that decade. Richard Lester would go on to greater things in the movie business, most notably the *Superman* series in the 1980s.

Harris made pronouncements around the time to try in some way to diminish the effects of ghastly films he had chosen to act in such as *Gulliver's Travels* (1977) and *Robin and Marian* (1976). One such pronouncement was: 'I can tell you what the next Steve McQueen movie will be and exactly how he's going to play it – the same way he's been playing it for fifteen years. In the motion picture business you cannot have tremendous artistic ambition. And that's why I couldn't care less anymore.'

There was another reason. His brother Dermot had been the long-time manager of their production company, Limbridge, and despite Harris's big success in acting, singing and poetry writing, the financial health of the company was poor and there was need for both the sale of assets and more careful investment. This resulted in the sale of the London home and the tax-efficient move to the Bahamas. Most of the time during this period he was working for the cheques, which were the major influence on his acceptance of the roles.

He also signed a production deal with producer Sandy Howard, which had an attractive profit-sharing clause and among the planned movies was a sequel to *A Man Called Horse*. Shot in 1976, again in Mexico, like most sequels it failed to impress but did manage to make a profit in the US. There were good reviews but the consensus of opinion was that the violence was off-putting for the Middle American audience.

Also in 1976, Harris missed an opportunity that would have been a milestone in his acting career. The great Swedish director Ingmar Bergman, marooned in Germany after fleeing the Swedish authorities for alleged tax evasion, was about to film *The Serpent's Egg* for producer Dino de Laurentiis; the story of an unemployed circus acrobat trying to survive in Berlin during the turbulent days of 1923 as the early signs of Nazism ferment. The broody Bergman, who liked to probe the human psyche with a scalpel, wanted Harris to star opposite his muse Liv Ullmann and *Goldfinger* villain Gert Froebe. But Harris was laid low by a debilitating illness that sapped his energy for months, and was obliged to pass. The role went to David Carradine.

Over the following eighteen months, Harris starred in no less than three turkeys: *Golden Rendezvous* (1977), *Orca, The Killer Whale* (1977) and *The Cassandra Crossing* (1976), in which his wife had a part. He always knew instinctively whether the film would work during the production period and he would do his best to avoid watching the finished product. He never saw *The Cassandra Crossing*: an added reason to avoid it was that during the shoot his wife, who was pregnant, began to suffer dreadful pain. He insisted on putting her on a plane from Rome to New York but she miscarried during the flight. The couple were devastated. Harris dreamed of having a daughter and it made him bitter and angry.

At the same time, Harris's drinking habits, at 47 years of age, began to affect his body. His condition was not helped by a developing cocaine habit. He collapsed a number of times but seemed to bounce back and the doctors could not find any immediate explanation for the incidents. He then began to go into coma-like states, similar to but not as dramatic as those experienced by diabetics.

The doctors recommended that he stay off alcohol. He did, but still took cocaine and smoked weed. During one coma episode Ann took him to the Cedars-Sinai Hospital in Los Angeles, where he had been taken previously for a drug overdose. His body appeared to be in working order, but the genesis of the problem would have to be solved. He flushed away his drug stash at home. He had been frightened by the last lapse into unconsciousness and was determined to kick his habit.

His brother Dermot was a big drinker and smoker, and his wife, Cassandra, was a casualty of his habit. There was, no doubt, a sibling rivalry in the area of drink but Richard was now worried by the effects of his lifestyle. Blood tests in a New York clinic found that he was suffering from hyperglycaemia. No alcohol and a rigid diet avoiding fats and sugars was recommended. But, of course, there is a psychological barrier to be breached in relation to alcohol, in Richard's case his unshaken belief in his own indestructibility. It would take two more years for Richard Harris to adopt the regimen recommended by the doctors, and that would only come about when he was told that if he did not adhere to it, he would die.

His marriage was also in trouble. Harris would make many excuses for this in later years:

> When you marry a girl so much younger, you lose your identity in trying to be what they want you to be and trying to keep up with them. It is very novel to begin with, but gradually it gets tiring. I soon found out that I was modifying my behaviour, tastes and outlook just for her. I began to neglect a lot of things because of Ann, particularly my career.

He told Joe Jackson:

> Ann Turkel married King Arthur. I discovered a cuttings book she'd had since she was 14. She'd been in love with that celluloid image of me from *Camelot*. She's seen the movie twenty-eight times. So she married Arthur. She then woke up one morning and thought this isn't Arthur at all and punishes you for not living up to her expectations.

Of course, it takes two to tango and this viewpoint is just a little too self-serving. Richard Harris was not a man who would live too easily with compromise and he hated their Beverly Hills life, which he thought utterly false. Although he had houses in several parts of the world, by this point he felt most at home away from the Hollywood set, either on Paradise Island or in Kilkee, Ireland. The cult of youth in Beverly Hills would have annoyed him, a thing that Ann might justifiably not have been bothered by, being young herself. One way or another, blame in the break-up of a relationship is a waste of time. He moved out of the Beverly Hills home into a hotel.

It was disastrous for him because, whatever his faults, he would suffer emotionally from another failure of marriage – and this would not help his health problem. Predictably he turned to the bottle and, worse still, the bad trajectory of his film career continued its downward spiral; the quality of scripts he was being offered also went downhill. Even the titles of the movies he was in at the time told the story: *The Ravagers, High Point, Game for Vultures, The Last Word.*

For these and many reasons, as 1980 approached Richard Harris would have some sense of relief from the passing of the 1970s – what could be described as his Lost Decade in artistic, personal and health terms. The notable exception was his book of poetry, *I, In the Membership of My Days*, published in 1973, which sold very respectably but more importantly provided a lasting testament to his creative power and the breadth and depth of the sensitive side of his nature

Published by Michael Joseph in 1973, the collection provided a surprise for people who thought they knew Richard Harris by his much chronicled public persona. The collection had the following dedication:

It was dedicated to:

Harriet-Mary who is still in my heart and Flanny who is still in my head.
Requiem Aeternum dona eis, Domine,
Et Lux perpetua Luceat eis.

Harris says of the collection:

> I am known as someone who drinks too much, womanises too much, raises too much hell. But this book shows how I have fooled them. I have always played a double game, one in public and the other in private. This is the private me, the real Richard Harris.

This volume of poetry represented the continuous work from his childhood in Ireland to the year of its publication. The poems describe a young boy growing into manhood, racked by the sadness of death, touched by the wonder of love, strongly aware of the sorrow and joy in the world around him. They reflect the lyricism and richness of the author's native Ireland; they are angry, loving, lusty and joyous.

The poems by and large are beautifully pitched sentiments of times past, they aimed to capture the sense of the child in the simple appreciation of the family environment marked by elation and a certain sadness. There are two poems in which the parents are seen on the telephone which are gut-wrenching in the expression of the child not being able to help the mother and father in the midst of their grief.

The poems certainly display, as the actor himself rightly points out, his other side, the artistic sensitive nature that his public persona was able to hide or deliberately concealed. Here is contained ample evidence of the two sides of the man and the artist, the divided self that is contained in all humans, whether admitted or not. Humans are not of one dimension, whether this is expressed or not. This is particularly true, perhaps, for those who espouse artistry or creativity as their occupation.

No more than the mask is the exclusive possession of the actor, the mask can provide a very convenient and comforting cloak to ward off the sting of reality. Richard Harris would have to face the length and depth of his escapism and escapades over the decade during which, professionally and personally, he was facing a form of oblivion not allowed by his lifestyle preferences. By dint of pure luck he had managed to avoid the clutches of the Grim Reaper, but not by so far that the trumpet of change was not ringing in his ears and in his heart.

The tide of fortune would change in his favour but as much by his own efforts as any favour bestowed by the perfidious veiled lady of chance. The first and most significant step was his decision in 1981 – when confronted by the reality of his mortality – to give up drink. He remembered the time and the place: 11 August 1981 at 11.20 p.m. in the Jockey Club in Washington:

I had the discipline to stop. Just like that. I had been collapsing in the street and on the stage. I passed out at dinner one night and a doctor friend warned me that it wasn't the booze. I had been in a coma: the alcohol was shooting up too much insulin in the system.

So I sat in the Jockey Club with a friend and said, 'This is my last drink.' I took the wine list and there were two bottles of Chateau Margaux at $325 a bottle. I drank them both and that was that.

The second step was to virtually abandon the world of film to return to the stage in the shape of King Arthur in *Camelot*. But for this stage show, Harris might have disappeared from sight for all time, as it was in the 1980s that he was sinking slowly and painfully into a celluloid marsh. The start was playing Bo Derek's father in *Tarzan the Apeman*, an excruciating experience for the actor and audience alike. He was becoming totally disillusioned by the film business, but if he was playing in 'such crap' – as he described it – he had only himself to blame.

During a movie shoot in Sri Lanka, Harris kept a diary, marking off the days until the completion of the shoot, like a boy watching and willing the school clock to the end of class. He then got a call from Los Angeles when he got back to London, offering him the part of King Arthur in a touring production of *Camelot*. His old friend Burton, who was playing the part, had had enough.

The tour had started in June 1980 and garnered rave notices in New York. It had moved on a criss-cross tour of the country but after a long and exhausting schedule of travel and performance, when the show hit Los Angeles Burton signalled his intention of quitting. Harris accepted the unenviable task of taking Burton's place, but drove a hard bargain, insisting on £25,000 a week and a percentage of the box office takings.

Harris not only stepped into the shoes of one of the great actors, but in his usual fashion he totally immersed himself in the part and grasped the opportunity. The opening night in April 1981 was a sell-out and the reviews hugely rewarded his effort. The critic for the *Los Angeles Herald Examiner* wrote: 'Harris has pulled off an astonishing feat in stepping into Burton's shoes and delivering a performance that looks like it had months of thought and preparation poured into it.' The demand for tickets was huge and in one week the show took in $500,000. Harris's decision to take a cut of the box office takings was looking to be a very lucrative move, and his grasp of and love of the part of the knight king ensured that there would be a long run. He was 51 years of age and the gruelling effects of constant performance would lead to him being physically depleted, and even hospitalised on one occasion with severe chest pain. He admitted to being totally exhausted but kept going.

A frequent visitor to the show was Ann Turkel; the couple had remained friendly after the split. He insisted that both were pursuing their own independence, and a coming divorce would prove it. She said, however, that they still loved each other, which was entirely possible, but the fact was that they could not live together.

She stayed with him at the Savoy Hotel before the London opening. He was in effusive form and giving the media hounds loads of very quotable material. Such as:

> My burning desire is to be a monk ... Women prefer women's company ... I've had enough women in my life to know that lurking under that Helena Rubenstein exterior is a very vicious animal ... absolutely ruthless ... I've tired of being loved by women. It's the most dangerous trap you can get into ... I've humiliated people – lost my temper – I've hurt people – actors, directors, all sorts of people.

Camelot came a cropper in London for it seemed that the English audience did not have the same affection and empathy for the musical that the Americans did. The reviewers only confirmed the general attitude in rather overstated and vicious attacks. Milton Schulman in the *Evening Standard* summed it up: 'Back in 1964 I assessed the musical *Camelot* as wholesome, pretty and empty. Seeing it again at the Apollo Victoria I felt I had been caught in a time warp, It is still wholesome, pretty and empty.' The *Daily Express* critic spent most of the review telling the reader that Harris was too old for the part. It was a gratuitous piece of nonsense, as Schulman's was an effort in smart-alec phraseology.

There was an added suggestion that some statement Harris had made about the IRA had contributed to its demise. For whatever reason, the audience stayed away and after eight weeks the show closed.

Harris, naturally enough, was bitterly disappointed that the great success in America had not been replicated in England, the provenance of the whole legend at the centre of the story of King Arthur. His relationship with *Camelot* was far from over. Back in his bolt-hole on Paradise Island he hatched another plan to bring the musical back to life. And it would make him a fortune. In 1983 he bought the stage rights to the musical and spent the next four years under his own direction touring America incessantly. In that period the show grossed over $92 million.

The actor who in 1955 had left his native Limerick with little prospects was now a multi-millionaire and could have retired, aged 57, and written poetry for the rest of his years. But the great triumph was tinged with tragedy.

His brother Dermot had been his long-time manager in charge of his business affairs and a close friend. In previous years they used to rent a house in Stroud in the Cotswolds and bring both their families there. When Harris bought the rights to *Camelot*, Dermot had been installed as producer. They had a great personal and professional relationship. Dermot was also a hard drinker, but had no inclination to stop as long as it did not interfere with business, which it most assuredly did not. He shared the rogue-like character of his brother as Harris recalled: 'Dermot was such a rogue. You can take me and magnify me ten times, that was my brother.

He'd say to me. "You go and do that picture so I can live in the style to which I've become accustomed."'

The show was playing in Chicago in 1986. Dermot as usual was living the hectic life of the producer and the drinker. One night before the show opened he said to his brother that he was not feeling very well and that he was going to lie down. By the time the curtain came down and Richard Harris had taken his bows, his beloved Dermot was dead. Harris says:

> The great mystery was solved when I saw him on a slab in the hospital, his face purple from a massive heart attack. And that's what it's all about isn't it? Here and gone. Why do we mess it up? We want too much and we're not pleased with what we have.

After the funeral, the *Camelot* juggernaut rolled on, stuffing the cash coffers. But the tour eventually reduced Harris to a gaunt shadow of his former self. He was not feeling well and doctors insisted on rest. In 1987 the curtain finally fell on *Camelot*, the lead actor having physically hit the wall.

In time, he would return to film with new vigour and the same mixture of indifferent choices and brilliant performances – though now with the luxury of financial stability. With the autumn and winter of his life and career approaching, Richard Harris would probably surprise himself and once again confound all the worst expectations of his critics. The 1990s would be both a swansong and a decade of selective triumph for an extraordinary man with a talent to match.

In America, as F. Scott Fitzgerald pointed out, there are no second acts. Harris was the exception that proved the rule: his career was capable of and would play out a third act in the classic theatrical convention. Ironically, before the curtain came, his career was neatly summed up by Ann Turkel, who held her ex-husband in high esteem:

> I can't think of any other actor who has starred in movies, starred on Broadway in musicals, won awards, collected Emmys and gold discs and directed plays and movies. He has had careers in almost every field of activity in the arts – except painting. I remember when we went to Richard Burton's memorial service in Hollywood, people were saying how versatile he had been. But really, nobody has done as much as Richard, and he hasn't been given the credit.

He had got plenty of offers during his sabbatical from the screen but clearly was not in the mood: 'I turned down most of the offers because there are too many artless savages out there who simply want to rent your face and then ruin what you do.' The sentiment is true of the business as the financiers decide the shape of the film even though cinema history is riddled with proof that their interference makes matters worse. But interference or not, the directors and writers are also capable of producing celluloid muck.

Harris also shared some of the blame:

> I went through a time when I didn't care what films I did – I just hired them my body and my voice. Work had taken a secondary place in my life. I picked easy scripts that I could walk through and not have to deliver or really perform. It was easy money.

Harris was adept at giving the quote that suited the time and his mood. This, of course, was true but the record showed that when he believed in a project every molecule in his body was attached to it.

His first venture on the small screen was in a two-hour TV special in which he was cast as the famous French detective Maigret. When the 85-year-old Georges Simenon heard of the casting he remarked: 'I would have never thought of him in a million years. My favourite was Jean Gabin in France who made seven films, but now you say it, I can see him.' The problem would be to erase the memory of the original English Maigret, Rupert Davies, who received universal acclaim in the part.

Filmed on location in Paris, it was not a success when screened: the critics were fairly savage, the audience lacking and indifferent. Plans for a follow-up were shelved.

It was television, toe in the water stuff and no big deal: there comes a time in life when disappointment loses its edge. Nevertheless, Harris was just revving up. There would follow a mix of art-house and blockbuster films, a brief interlude in an at-first troubled production of Pirandello's *Henry IV* in the West End, and some stunning performances matching those of his earlier career. It was the final period of his acting career, if a film could have been entitled *The Indian Summer of Richard Harris.*

THE FIELD (1990)

It had been a decade since Harris had been involved in any film of note. He had been given the script of a film entitled *The Field*, written and to be directed by Jim Sheridan, who was fresh from his double Oscar success with *My Left Foot* (1989). Coming from a theatre background, Sheridan had posted the script to Harris at his Paradise Island home and had offered a small cameo role as the priest.

The script was based on the play of the same title by the hugely popular John B. Keane, whose rural dramas – many set in his native Kerry – were highly in demand, first on the amateur circles and then in the larger professional houses in Dublin. Keane, who ran the family pub in the small town of Listowel, was a writer of great skill yet was modest and down to earth. He was in every sense a rural poet, and the universal themes of his plays were set in a world a million miles away from mainstream Dublin theatre.

Jim Sheridan was from a working-class inner-city area in Dublin and had cut his theatrical teeth in Dramsoc, the university theatre society at University College Dublin. Afterwards he ran the Project Arts Theatre, which under his stewardship caused plenty of controversy and was marked out by consistently mouthwatering productions. One of the great successes was *The Risen People*, a play set in the poverty-stricken tenements of Dublin in 1913 and featuring the great hero of the working classes, the famous trade unionist Jim Larkin.

To say that Sheridan would not easily grasp the essence and spirit of the rural metier of Keane's work was obvious to theatre and film professionals when the planned production was announced. The story concerned the legacy of land hunger and ownership that had bedevilled Irish history through the iniquities of colonial experience under the British and remained in the wake of independence. In rural communities in particular the land was a man's wealth and only means of survival.

The central character had rented his field but worked it as if it was his own. He had spent many years of hard labour cultivating the small plot of land and transforming it from barren rock into a fertile piece of land. He considers the land, rightly or wrongly, his own and dreams of buying it.

The field is then put up for auction and Bull McCabe makes sure, by means of intimidation, that none of the local community will emerge as a purchaser. An emigrant from England appears to buy it with his own plans to develop the land.

The murder of the prospective buyer of the land is the consequence, which is followed by a cover-up by the local community. Handled properly, with the original creative intentions intact, it could have had the universal resonance that Jim Sheridan had achieved so tellingly in *My Left Foot*, and that French director Claude Berri had achieved four years earlier with Marcel Pagnol's novel *Jean de Florette*, with a not dissimilar rural theme and starring Yves Montand and Gérard Depardieu.

While there were the usual film compromises made to the playwright's work such as the portrayal of the victim as an American (Tom Berenger), Harris would have identified with the subject hugely. Not merely from his republican sympathies but also from the memories of the dismantling of his father's business by the British Rank conglomerate. There was more than a subconscious parallel. His father had, as a result, become a renter as opposed to an owner.

Quite apart from Harris's determination to re-establish his film career, he would have had the same passion and identification with the role that he had adopted in *The Ginger Man*, *This Sporting Life* and *Camelot*. That sense of identification and thus passionate commitment had always driven his best performances. The part of Bull McCabe was one that he could literally live, to the exclusion of everything else in his life and abandon any degree of proportion.

Ray McAnally, a fine Irish actor, had been cast in the main part but he died suddenly from a heart attack. As Sheridan put it: 'He created the role in 1965 and he believed in it passionately as a major film. He was in *My Left Foot* but in *The Field* he would be the star.'

Harris knew instinctively from the cameo role he had been originally offered as the priest that he had a great chance of stepping into the shoes of Bull McCabe. Within the bounds of decency he let his feelings be known with a call to the producer Noel Pearson. The producer found out quickly enough that the main financier, Granada Television, did not want Harris as they felt he was old hat. At one stage someone said that Harris had not been heard of for so long that they thought he was dead. The signs were not good. There was talk of Brando or Connery, the sort of absurd notions that film people get in the heat of the moment. But Harris was by far the better candidate and Pearson knew it. After lengthy discussions with Granada they agreed to the recasting with John Hurt and Tom Berenger as the under-leads. Harris was utterly revitalised and set about his usual preparation, reading as much material about the background as he could lay his hands on and taking longs walks to get fit. The shoot was to take place in the beautiful landscape of Connemara as opposed to the setting of the play in Kerry.

The film shoot began in October in the village of Leenane. Harris arrived a few days late, sporting a beard that would have been more appropriate for the part of King Lear than Bull McCabe. The director got a shock but just got on with the job. It was clear in a visual sense that Harris had made up his mind on the approach he was going to take to the role.

It was a classic part but the issue would be how the actor interpreted the role. Bull McCabe got his sobriquet for good reason. The bull in the field is always a dangerous animal. In human form the physicality is not necessarily so obvious.

The sense of danger in the film could be effectively employed with subtlety, but it was not this route that Harris took, it was a far more overwhelming bombastic approach. He annoyed some members of the crew with his forthright views, which they felt were undermining the director, but that was Harris and always had been. For his part he seized the opportunity and poured every last ounce of sweat into the work. He was well aware that if this performance made the impression he hoped for – and anticipated – he would be back on the celluloid trail with a bang.

The fee of £100,000, paltry by his standards, did not matter. He was back and in an Irish film. His appetite for the medium had returned. The production wrapped in December 1989 and he moved on to a return to the London stage in Pirandello's *Henry IV*. In the middle of 1990 there was a call for a small reshoot of the completed film. It was released in the autumn but did not do well at the box office and failed to breach the US market.

But there was talk of awards for Harris's performance and he was delighted, despite the poor showing in cinemas. And so it came to pass, with nominations for Best Actor at the BAFTAs and the Oscars. However, he lost out to Jeremy Irons for *Reversal of Fortune*. Sheridan would go on to get seven Academy Award nominations for the stunning *In the Name of the Father* (1993). Richard Harris was back on the film scene in a big way, and although he was in the autumn of his career, it would just get better and better. And better.

After the critical and commercial success in the West End of *Henry IV* in 1990, the actor felt that not only was he back on the true road of his original ambition, but he was personally and professionally in a good place:

You do a piece of work that you like and think, perhaps arrogantly, that after everything you have been through you can still do your job. You can still deliver the goods and you are actually pretty good at what you do. Now I am deadly serious. I turn down all the crap, whatever money they are throwing around. I am enjoying myself more than I ever did.

19

INDIAN SUMMER

The 1992 western *Unforgiven*, produced and directed by and starring Clint Eastwood, was a film that had an incredibly long gestation. It was written by David Webb Peoples, who had written the Oscar-nominated *The Day After Trinity* (1981) and co-wrote Ridley Scott's *Blade Runner* (1982), and it had been bought by Clintwood's production company, Malpaso. The concept of the film had dated back to 1976 under the titles *The Cut-Whore Killings* and *The William Munny Killings*. It tells the story of William Munny, an ageing outlaw and killer who takes up one more job after years of retirement in which he had turned to a legitimate way of life in subsistence farming. But after his wife dies and he has no way of looking after his children he is forced to return to his old evil ways.

Eastwood delayed the project, partly because he wanted to wait until he was old enough to play the part of Munny and add to his great western roles in the spaghetti westerns of Sergio Leone and later ones such as *High Plains Drifter* (1971) and *Pale Rider* (1985). Eastwood comments on the film:

> I bought it in 1983 and I kind of nurtured it like a little jewel you put on the shelf and polish now and then. I figured I'd age into it a little bit. It's a fictional story about a renegade, very stylised, a little different. What appealed to me was the idea that the good guys weren't all that good and the bad guys weren't all that bad.

Be that as it may, it could also have been influenced by the 1990 success of *Dances With Wolves*, starring Kevin Costner.

It was hardly the right time for westerns, which had been dying a death for many years (with the exceptions noted). Also, the main parts were old men and women, not usually welcome in the traditional ageist arena of Hollywood. *Unforgiven* was a vehicle distinctly for character actors, an advantage in this case as Eastwood cast some bankable talent.

These included Gene Hackman, born the same year as Eastwood in 1930, and Morgan Freeman, born in 1937. Another would be added in an important cameo role, Richard Harris, who was in the over-60s category. In addition, the concept was a dark and intense examination of the worst aspects of violence and the myth of the Old West. There was therefore little to intimate that it would make any impact on the box office.

But Eastwood was no fool, nor was the studio that would back the film, Warners, employing an old adage that if the film was made for $14 million or under then no matter what happens in the box office, there was a very good chance that the film would at the very least break even. It would, however, confound all expectations.

The story was paramount, followed by the film's treatment, the direction and performances. In the first instance, it was a powerful story. A group of prostitutes in Big Whiskey, Wyoming, offer a $1,000 reward to whoever can kill two cowboys who have disfigured one of their own. This upsets the local keeper of law, a corrupt former gunfighter who does not allow guns or criminals in his town.

Meanwhile, a young gun has approached Munny to seek his help in doing the job. Reluctantly, Munny takes the invitation and recruits another old friend. There are other suitors for the job, notably English Bob, a vicious assassin who arrives on the scene with his biographer W.W. Beauchamp, hired to chronicle his dastardly deeds.

English Bob has made his living shooting Chinamen for the railroad company. Beauchamp has written a book about Bob's exploits as a gunfighter entitled *The Duke of Death*. To win a bet, Bob demonstrates his accuracy with the pistol by shooting pheasants from the train on the way to Big Whiskey. When he arrives, the sheriff Little Bill, who knows him and his associates from a previous life, beats English Bob to pulp.

There follows a chronicle of extreme betrayal and violence during which the original perpetrators are dispatched, Munny's friend is brutally killed and he comes back to the town to seek revenge and kills the corrupt sheriff and his hirelings. Munny rides off into the distance, threatening that if his friend is not buried properly, or if the prostitutes are harmed, he will come back. Munny then goes on to a better life in San Francisco, where he prospers.

Much of the cinematography was shot in Alberta in August 1991 by director of photography Jack Green. Principal photography took place over fifty-two days in September and October 1991. Production designer Henry Bumstead, who had worked with the director on *High Plains Drifter*, was hired to create the dark wintry look of the film.

Harris delivered a stunningly good performance as English Bob, the imperialist blow-hard who gives himself civilised airs quite at odds with his profession, and achieves added credibility via the presence of his biographer Beauchamp (Saul Rubinek).

In a nice and less-than-subtle dig at the newspaper writer turned biographer, the story of the gunslinger Bob is now transferred to Little Bill by the yellow-livered Beauchamp, a media rat with the lashless eye always focused on the main chance.

He would be given his comeuppance while watching the latest subject of his literary attention being despatched to eternity by Munny's shot to the head.

Harris not only played the part to a T but also looked great on screen, as fit, slim and powerful as he had been for years and looking about twenty years younger than his long-bearded, grizzled image in *The Field*. Even though he didn't know it at the time, this film would put him on the map in an even more effective fashion than *The Field*.

The reviews were close to ecstatic. 'The movie's grizzled male ensemble, its gradual build and its juxtaposition of brutality and sardonic humour testify to its disdain for box office conventions', wrote Michael Sragow in the *New Yorker*. Iain Johnstone in the *Sunday Times* wrote: 'Eastwood climbs back into the saddle to make a classic western.' *Variety* summed up with: 'A tense, hard edged, superbly dramatic yarn that is also an exceedingly intelligent meditation on the West, its myths and heroes.'

The film was not only greeted with almost universal critical acclaim, it won four Academy Awards: Best Picture, Best Director, Best Actor in a Supporting Role (Hackman) and Best Editing, one of only three westerns to win an Oscar for Best Picture. It was a huge commercial success, clocking up $160 million in worldwide ticket sales, $101 million of which was in the domestic US market.

There had been the usual media gossip anticipating the end of Eastwood's directorial career and concerning Harris's acting future. However, Harris's performance in and association with *Unforgiven* resulted in nothing but positive publicity. It was a very important platform. He had been up there with the contemporary elder heavyweights of Hollywood – Eastwood, Hackman and Freeman – and more than held his own. He was back in the spotlight and some other celluloid heavies would notice.

Harris then moved from the wilds of Calgary to South Africa for his next film, a remake of the 1951 movie *Cry, the Beloved Country*, based on Alan Paton's classic novel about the paths of two men, a black minister and a white landowner, brought together by the tragic fate of their sons in apartheid South Africa. It was a historic production, the first post-apartheid film, and Harris was proud to be involved. 'One has visited and seen the injustice, and coming from a country where this is integral, where we have fought our own wars and now see justice in sight, it's a great privilege to be part of its awakening.'

On set, Harris told a local *Natal* reporter:

It's a wonderful part. In the world of movie-making today, scripts like this do not come along very often. And it's a change for me. I'm always being offered these histrionic parts and then the critics accuse me of over-balancing films. But the great chance with this is that it's the very opposite – Jarvis is this very quiet internal guy.

Produced by American company Miramax, the film premiered at the Ziegfeld Theatre in New York on 23 October 1995. Among the distinguished audience were South African president Nelson Mandela and Hilary Clinton. Mandela had already seen the film and gave a speech before the showing in which he said:

> Today's premiere of *Cry, The Beloved Country* confirms once more our confidence in the future. It is causes such as this which bring to the fore men and women of goodwill and talent – Anant Singh, Darrell Roodt, Visi Kunene, Leleti Khumalo. The talent and creativity that was virtually unrecognised under apartheid is able today to shine, combined with the skill of compassionate friends of Africa, such as James Earl Jones and Richard Harris.

It was a touching and unique moment for Harris to receive acknowledgement from a great South African hero and a world figure. The whole experience was made all the more fruitful when the critics heaped praise on the production and the performances.

20

LIMERICK GIANTS COME TO BLOWS

L imerick produces few giants in any sphere, apart from on the rugby field. But the locals of the Shannonside city have always had a way with words. From the poet of the proletariat, Mike Hogan (the nineteenth-century Bard of Thomond), to the more schooled and sophisticated Kate O'Brien, wordsmiths have always been appreciated.

Richard Harris considered himself a man of letters. He wrote poetry, told long rambling stories in drunken stupors, and involved himself heavily in the fight for a university for his town. But in local literary circles, at least, Harris is best known not for his verse, or his championing of academia, but for a feud with Limerick's most famous man of letters. His public clash with Frank McCourt – which broke out into physical violence between the two middle-aged men – was the stuff of legend and propelled both into the headlines.

And it was all because of his intense love of his native place – and his desire to put in his place any man who dared criticise Limerick.

Frank McCourt was born less than six weeks before Richard Harris in America, but he was raised in Limerick when his family came home after failing to make their fortune. McCourt and Harris grew up side by side without ever meeting. In some ways their stories paralleled each other: both walked the same streets, snuck into the same cinemas, and studied the same curriculum for the same exams in school; both encountered the scourge of TB in their teens (Harris personally, McCourt in the person of his first love); and both left Limerick as young men to earn their fortunes.

But there was one massive difference: McCourt was not born with a silver spoon in his mouth. His father was an unemployed alcoholic, and he grew up in poverty in the lanes around Hartstonge Street, from where Harris's great-grandfather and grandfather had founded their business empire. The lanes were infamous in

Limerick. As the elegant Georgian buildings of Newtown faded into genteel poverty many were converted to tenements. Some families had to share a single room with a second or third family, and several families would frequently share a single outside toilet. Sanitation was poor, and heating was provided by the weight of bodies in a small space. Children would miss school so that they could spend the morning scrabbling on the ground near the docks, picking up lumps of coal that had fallen from the carts of the hauliers.

This was where McCourt grew up. His father drank every penny that came into the house, and his mother struggled to cope with her young children. It was miserable, but it gave McCourt the material for one of the most successful memoirs of the last century, *Angela's Ashes*. The opening lines summed up the story:

> When I look back on my childhood I wonder how I survived at all. It was, of course, a miserable childhood: the happy childhood is hardly worth your while. Worse than the ordinary miserable childhood is the miserable Irish childhood, and worse yet is the miserable Irish Catholic childhood.

The book was published in 1996 and propelled McCourt from another Irish dreamer in the Big Apple to a literary giant. The book was a worldwide bestseller and launched the genre of misery memoirs, which accounted for 9 per cent of the UK book market by 2009. It sold five million copies, was adapted into a film, and made McCourt a rich man in his final years; in 1997 it won him the prestigious Pulitzer Prize. It was also the most controversial book to come out of Limerick.

McCourt's brother Malachy was a larger-than-life figure – a writer, an actor and a politician; he ran unsuccessfully for governor of New York in 2006, representing the Green Party. He had a number of roles in various US soaps, and a number of film credits. One of his most significant movie credits was *The Molly Maguires*, in 1970. Appearing beside him – considerably further up the billing – was, of course, Richard Harris.

During the production Harris and Malachy McCourt became firm friends. They were both raconteurs and drinkers, and shared boozy nights on set. The friendship endured after the shoot ended. Malachy owned a bar on Third Avenue in Manhattan. Called Malachy's, it became a bit of a legend, attracting celebrities who mingled with the regular patrons in an atmosphere of unmatched conviviality. It was as close to the atmosphere of an Irish watering hole as New York could manage, and became a favourite hang-out of Harris's whenever his work took him to America. Harris, ever up for a laugh, even stood behind the bar and pulled pints on occasion.

Through his friendship with Malachy, Harris got to know Frank, the older brother. Frank was a smaller, quieter man, though still fond of a pint and capable of raising hell when the spirit moved him. From the start there was tension between the two. Harris found McCourt to be bitter and angry. He also felt that McCourt did not like him because of his more privileged background. As he told Radio Limerick One, in a lengthy interview:

> I knew Frank in his New York days and I found him to be probably the ugliest and the most bitter human being I have ever met in my entire life. Frank was full of bitterness. I don't think I ever confronted a man that was so angry. Every fibre of his being was in rebellion against something.
>
> I believe he hated me with a passion because according to him I came from an elitist part of Limerick, and because I became so successful. Though he would use my success to promote himself, he very much resented my success.

Their first meeting was not auspicious:

> I first met Frank years ago in his brother's pub in New York, and he was very derogative and derisive in his attitude and remarks about Limerick. I was in discussion about Limerick with Malachy when Frank raised his fist and hit me a terrible belt on the nose. Like a hare running from a hound he raced towards the exit door, and ran out of the pub. I said to Malachy: 'I am afraid your brother is not really a Limerick man.' When Malachy asked why not, I told him that I have never yet been confronted by a Limerick man who ran away from a fight.
>
> We don't do that in Limerick. We stand and fight. To run from a fight is not part of the Limerick character at all.

McCourt's memory of the event is different. He admitted striking Harris, but said: 'He provoked me. But we reconciled a long time ago.' Harris and Malachy did not fall out over Frank's performance that night, though later their friendship did deteriorate.

Frank had ambitions both as a writer and a performer, and with Malachy he put together a two-man show about his early life in Limerick. *A Couple of Blackguards* actually played in Limerick, to reasonable reviews. But even then there were questions about the accuracy of Frank's memories. Their mother described the work as a 'pack of lies'. Harris recalls:

> I knew Angela McCourt quite well. I visited her regularly, and I spent a lot of time with her, and they (Frank and Malachy) treated her really badly. The way they spoke about their mother made me very angry. They had an obvious disdain for her, and I remember on one occasion in the pub where I grabbed Malachy by the neck, and shouted that she is your mother, and you cannot treat her like this.
>
> Malachy's only answer to me was that they were bringing her lots of beer and cigarettes in the hope that she would die, because she was costing them rent money.

After that, the relationship between the brothers and Harris began to go rapidly downhill.

When Angela died in 1981 her sons decided to cremate her and take the ashes back to her native Limerick. She had wanted to be buried in her home town, but the brothers were unwilling to pay the cost of flying the coffin home. Cremation was a compromise – a compromise that Harris felt would have repulsed their mother.

The scattering of the ashes in Limerick is described in the book – but Harris maintained that this was another example of fiction. He said that both brothers went on the piss in New York before their flight. They got on separate flights, and one plane was diverted back to New York. Between all the jigs and reels, Angela's ashes got left behind.

'It is a commonly held opinion among the Irish in New York that Angela's ashes are buried away in some far distant remote lost property corner of Kennedy Airport,' Harris claimed.

In another interview he said:

> You ask McCourt what happened to his mother's ashes. I know he fucking lost them. When his mother died he hadn't a bob to rub together. He wanted to ship her ashes to Limerick to be scattered over the family grave. I was touring in *Camelot* and helped him out with cash to pay for the shipping.

This generosity would have been in keeping with Harris's character, despite his simmering feud with the fellow Limerick man.

'Frank went to a cheap shipper in Queens, and he lost his mother's ashes. He fucking lost them.'

Frank McCourt strongly denied the allegation, saying: 'That is not true. We brought the ashes and spread them in Mungret graveyard.' Yet he did admit to journalist John McEntee some years later that there was some truth in Harris's account: 'Yes, we did lose our mother's ashes. I had too much to drink in a Manhattan bar, and we left them behind. But we did eventually retrieve them.'

The tension between the men simmered beneath the surface for years. Harris was not often enough in New York, and neither man was often enough in Limerick, for the embers to fan into flame. But it exploded when McCourt's memoirs came out.

The book was published in September 1996 and the protesters began to attack it almost immediately, seeing it as an affront on the city. Book signings were disrupted and protesters tore up copies of the book.

Richard Harris was never a man to jump on a bandwagon unless he held the whip in his hand and was driving it. He immediately wrote a letter to the *Irish Times* denouncing this attack on his beloved city. The simmering feud had become public, and escalated sharply when director Alan Parker announced that he was going to make a film of the book and shoot it on location in Limerick.

The resulting production will probably be best remembered as the wettest film since *20,000 Leagues Under the Sea*. Every scene seemed to be flooded with driving rain, and the misery was painted thick. Limerick people had mixed views about the whole thing. While they welcomed the money that the filming brought to the town, no one was looking forward to the final product.

Harris agreed to appear with local shock-jock Gerry Hannon to discuss the film. Hannon had a show on pirate radio station Radio Limerick One, and no holds were barred. He was a vocal critic of McCourt. In a two-hour interview on 20 January 2000, Harris held nothing back:

> If Limerick is, as he claims, a city of begrudgers, why did they give him an honorary doctorate at the University of Limerick? And why did the Mayor propose making him a Freeman of Limerick? Are these the acts of begrudgers? I was offered an honorary doctorate by UL, and though I never say never, I would have to think very seriously about it, because I don't want to link myself to totally mediocre non-entities like McCourt.
>
> There is a friendly tribal rivalry which exists in the rugby world in Limerick, but when an outside team comes in to play we all come together in unison to support our own. It is for that very reason that Limerick is unique. The loyalty is absolutely astonishing and, I believe, that element of Limerick totally by-passed the McCourts. They [Frank and Malachy] are devoid of any sense of loyalty, and are filled with hate for Limerick.
>
> Limerick is a sporting city and when, as a young man, I had TB, legions of my mates from the Young Munster Rugby Club came to see me in my sick bed. These guys were from the same background as the McCourts. They came from the lanes of Limerick, and they had just as tough a time but, in spite of the poverty and hardship, they had an almost indestructible loyalty to Limerick.
>
> You never heard from them one condemnation about Limerick. Not even one utterance of disloyalty, and this was a quality that Frank never inherited. Limerick people have a passion about each other. When I go back to Limerick they will attack me and they will make fun of me, and they will pass jokes about me. But God help if somebody from Dublin or London said anything nasty about a Limerick man. That kind of loyalty is something that McCourt just did not have.

He was equally scathing about Alan Parker, the director of the movie. 'I have made sixty-three movies, and I know how these guys operate,' he said. 'Alan Parker hasn't directed a good movie in years.'

He went on to describe the movie as boring, dull, repetitive and totally unmoving, and said it should be nominated for an Oscar for best rain effects. 'The movie is one long perpetual moan,' he concluded.

Harris was preaching to the converted. Though he might jinx Young Munster when he attended their games, and though he might have been born in a different social class than the common people of Limerick, he was now their champion and they loved him for it.

McCourt responded to the interview, saying that he was annoyed but also puzzled by the outburst of the actor. 'Why is he bringing it all up now?' he asked.

Harris never forgave either of the McCourt brothers, or Alan Parker. When he died in 2002 the dispute was still going strong, though McCourt did reveal that Harris had thought of extending the hand of friendship. In an interview in 2009, McCourt said that on his last visit to London he had stayed at the Savoy Hotel and was put in the Harris suite:

It amused me because he and I had a very turbulent relationship. He was angry with me for what I'd said about Limerick, and wrote to *The Times* denouncing me. But his wife told me that before he died, he said to her: 'Maybe I should call McCourt. Maybe we should have a reconciliation.' He never did, though. She invited me to the memorial service, but I couldn't go.

Considering the character of the big man, and his love of his native town, this death-bed conversion may have been another fabrication on behalf of McCourt.

21

GLADIATOR (2000)

The late 1990s had been a time of ups and downs in Harris's career. In *Trojan Eddie* (1996) he played a fiery godfather to a network of itinerant Irish gypsies and petty thieves, who is cuckolded by his much younger gypsy bride. It is a brave performance, which Harris fearlessly plays with a gaunt ravaged face and snow-white hair. In *Smilla's Sense of Snow* (1997) he and Gabriel Byrne help massacre Peter Hoeg's marvellous book, in a misguided version directed by Bille August. Harris teamed up again with Gabriel Byrne in the ghastly Irish film *This Is The Sea* (1998); and he was bitterly disappointed when director Pat O'Connor, against producer Noel Pearson's wishes, declined to have him as Father Jack opposite Meryl Streep in *Dancing at Lughnasa* (1998), a role then blandly played by Michael Gambon.

In the summer of 1999 Harris was filming Ridley Scott's *Gladiator*, which critic Philip French described as a remake of Anthony Mann's *The Fall of the Roman Empire* (1964), for which Harris had been offered, but turned down, the part of Commodus.

This time around, the Irish actor was playing the part of Emperor Marcus Aurelius, who has been impressed by General Maximus (Russell Crowe) in his defeat of the Germanic tribes in AD 180. Although the dying emperor has a male heir, Commodus (Joaquin Phoenix), he wishes to grant temporary leadership to Maximus, hoping to eventually return power to the Senate. But when Commodus's father tells him of his decision, he murders his father and claims the throne. There the convoluted plot of the story and film begins.

Harris explained his acceptance of the role. Every movie in the past decade had been, in his mind, the last one. He was tiring of film but he could not resist the vast and astonishing scale of the director's vision. It was also a tough shoot for him, eight weeks in length, but he had a sense that he was in something big and he also had the bonus of striking up a symbiotic relationship with the box-office star Russell Crowe, copper-fastened by their shared passion for rugby.

Harris had other attributes in common with Crowe: their shared ability to immerse themselves in a part; a healthy disregard for Hollywood mores; and a readiness to question a director on the shortcomings of a script. Generational differences apart, they were artistic soulmates in a graphic manner expressed in the genesis of *Gladiator*.

It was classic Hollywood stuff in the beginning, somewhat redolent of *Mutiny on the Bounty*. David Franzoni had written the first script, but when director Ridley Scott was brought in he had problems with the dialogue and hired John Logan to do a rewrite. With just two weeks to go before the start of filming, the actors had problems with the script, so a third writer, William Nicholson, was brought on board to develop it further. Franzoni was then brought back to add to the rewrites of his predecessors. The screenplay was then subjected to suggestions by Russell Crowe. This process recalled for Harris the genesis of *This Sporting Life*. Crowe questioned every part of the evolution of the screenplay, to the great annoyance of the studio executives. Nicholson, the final screenwriter, recalls Crowe telling him: 'Your lines are garbage but I'm the greatest actor in the world and I can make garbage sound good.'

It was no wonder, perhaps, that Crowe struck up such a good relationship with Harris. The Irish actor had the same talent to turn turgid dialogue to good account, which can happen only when the part is inhabited in the method the actor had practised for years, that is, when the role captured his imagination. The younger actor followed a similar path, though neither were disciples of the method school, Strasberg style.

It was an epic production in every sense, the film being shot in three main locations between January and May 1999 in England, Morocco and Malta. Harris was fascinated by the scale and loved every minute of his involvement, which he expressed with great enthusiasm to the director.

During the shoot in Malta, Oliver Reed, Harris's old adversary and hellraiser, died suddenly in a bar after quaffing an enormous amount of drink and before all his scenes had been shot. The miracles of modern CGI technology solved the problem in post-production – to great cost but also to great effect.

Despite the enormous difficulties in its gestation and production, *Gladiator* proved to be a huge success, grossing $457 million worldwide and being nominated for multiple awards, which it won, including five Academy Awards, with Best Picture and Best Actor for Crowe. Harris made a big impression with a performance imbued with quiet dignity and whispered wisdom, and in leading actor Russell Crowe he made a great friend for the remainder of his life.

As he said of Crowe: 'Top bloke loves his rugby, doesn't give a stuff, brilliant actor, much loved new friend. He will carry the baton on. He irritates the hell out of the Hollywood bigwigs, but he's much too good for them to ignore.' He could have been talking to the mirror.

The love of rugby that first struck a chord between the actors is worth examining for it was a durable and abiding passion with Harris that transcended and remained constant while other obsessions were subject to the ebb and flow of his interests and moods.

22

THE ONGOING PASSION

Limerick is a tribal city. But the tribal markings are not clan tartans, family names or even places. The tribal markings are rugby colours. Rugby is an English game, born on the playing fields of their great public schools. Its greatest exponents are the southern hemisphere teams – the All Blacks, the Wallabies and the Springboks. But Limerick calls itself the rugby capital of the world, and no one seriously disputes that claim.

The game is like a religion in the city. When the All Ireland League was set up, Limerick teams won for the first several years on the trot. There is an old expression that soccer is a game for toffs, played by ruffians, while rugby is a game for ruffians, played by toffs. In Dublin and Cork that is true. But in Limerick, rugby is played by everyone, and followed by everyone.

The city has a number of thriving clubs – Bohemians, Old Crescent, Garryowen, Shannon, and Young Munster among the better known. Each club has a strong structure, with its own playing ground, club house, even its own traditional pubs. Rivalry between the clubs is intense, but when Limerick men get together, either to play for Munster or Ireland, then the rivalries are put behind them and everyone gets behind the team. In his famous feud with the McCourt brothers, Harris invoked tribal loyalties in order to have a go at them. In a radio interview with Limerick local radio he said:

> When Malachy McCourt played rugby he didn't play with his own people. He didn't play with Young Munster, St Mary's, or Presentation, which were the clubs around his area. Instead he played for Bohemians, and in those days they were the snobs, the most right-wing club in Limerick. Malachy elected not to play with his own class, but to upgrade himself and play for Bohemians.

Dickie conveniently forgot that he also togged out for a number of teams, before turning away from his own to support the amber-and-black army of Young Munster.

Although Harris was a late convert, he became a loyal supporter. He often appeared at matches, especially if he was home visiting. He would visit the club house the day before a game, hanging out and chatting with the other fans. He was down to earth, with time for everyone. The following day, probably either still drunk or hung over from the night before, he would be on the terraces, singing and waving his scarf with the others.

Despite this intense loyalty, he had never played for Young Munster. Although he regained his strength and fitness after the TB, he knew his days as a top-flight player were in the past. Rather than become a weekend warrior, lining out with the seconds – or even the thirds – he switched his passion to acting, but remained a committed fan.

The closest he ever came to playing again was when he starred in *This Sporting Life*, which was shot in 1962. Aged 32, and almost a decade from his sporting glory days, he felt that he needed to match brawn with the extras, hardy footballers drawn from the rugby league clubs of the north of England. They were the type of men he enjoyed back in Limerick, and he desperately wanted their respect. The only way to earn it was to match them on the field. He went into training.

'I take my roles extremely seriously, despite my reputation in the press, which is Rabelaisian. I went up to Leeds and Wakefield, and I studied with the players for three or four weeks. I togged out with the second team, and it was hard,' he told Parkinson. He continues:

These football players from up the north, they always maintain that actors are poofs, with their long hair and their mascara on their eyes. When I went up first there were odd remarks – 'Better watch him, lad. Don't turn your back on him, I tell you lad.' What was I going to do? I had to play football with them.

I went back to London, to Richmond Rugby Club. They had a great goal kicker there. When I was at school I was pretty good at football. And I had a great facility to kick a goal. But years had passed since then. So I went to this goal kicker, and I asked him to teach me to kick a goal, to get the precision of it right. And I went to a gym, worked on the legs, got the precision timing like clockwork. I went every single night for six weeks before the movie, just to kick a goal.

Now came the first day of shooting. I said to them: 'Is that what you have to do to make a living? Chase a ball around a field like that. You're a strange lot. I was watching you last night. All of you getting into the tub together naked. I was watching. Can't fool Harris. I know what's going on. And you have to kick that little ball over the bar?'

'Aye, bloody hell you 'ave to,' they said. 'Simple,' I said. 'Give us a decent kick.'

The players put the marker down about 40 yards out. Harris's outward bluster belying his nervousness, he took the ball and placed it.

Six weeks training. I placed the ball on the ground. I took a step back and they were all waiting. And I closed my eyes and I said a little prayer. I said if there ever was a God in heaven, put wings on that ball and carry it over. And I stood back and I kicked it and it went over. And from that moment on, I was in. I became a chum of them all. Fantastic.

Respect gained, the film became a pleasure to shoot, and was the breakthrough that made him a star.

In his early years he had had to concentrate on building up his acting credentials, and on his young family. But as the wealth increased, his opportunities for travelling home grew. He often took a flight to Dublin for the big games. He told Michael Parkinson during an interview in 1973 about a typical trip home for an international game. Ireland was playing New Zealand on 20 January 1973 in which the southern visitors won an undistinguished game. Harris arrived at the airport in typical dishevelled style. He never wore a shirt, preferring to bulk-buy cheap football shirts. They could take the spills and knocks of his lifestyle:

They are cheaper than wearing suits when you go out for the night, and fall down in the street. I hate to see something out of order, unless I did it myself. So if I see a wet bar, I will wipe it with my sleeve. And that would ruin a jacket. I took to wearing football jerseys, which were cheaper, at thirty bob a time.

I went home to Ireland last week to see Ireland playing New Zealand. I had this bunch of football jerseys – four or five dozen. And I put three or four in the bag because I knew it was going to be one of those weekends. I call Dublin the glue pot – once you get there you cannot get out of it! I prepared myself for a long, long weekend.

But he put no consideration into what jersey to wear:

I put a jersey on, got on the plane. I took my coat off. I was talking to a chap, he said: 'How is it now an actor who is obviously extremely wealthy wears a thirty shilling football jersey?' So I went through the whole thing. 'Oh I see,' he said. 'But don't you think you have picked the wrong colours?'

Harris had put on a red, white and blue jersey – the England colours: 'Could you believe it? I am going back to Dublin for a football match wearing red white and blue. So quickly I jumped up, dashed down to the toilet, stripped it off and put my coat on, and arrived back in Dublin naked. Naked but safe.'

Many of the trips home became extended drinking sessions. On one famous occasion he had left his home in London to get some cigarettes, but instead had a few drinks, then got the notion to fly to Dublin for a game. He arrived home about four days later.

As one of his Limerick drinking buddies recalled:

> He came over, and he went back home about four days later, after being on the piss. Knocked on the door, langers drunk. He saw the shadow coming down – the missus, the first missus (Elizabeth). 'Jesus Christ, what will I fucking say to her, being gone for the last four days. I told her I was only gone for the newspaper.' Then she opened the door.
>
> 'Why didn't you pay the fucking ransom money?' he says. Very quick, very witty man.

Some of the stories are exaggerated in the retelling, but in his drinking days the trips to games were extended drinking sessions. He loved going to Dublin and staying in the Burlington – which was managed by his brother-in-law Jack Donnelly for many years. In Limerick he often stayed in Dromoland Castle, the height of regal luxury.

Confusingly, he decided to call his Bahamas property 'Kilkee'. So when he announced he was going to Kilkee he could be slipping over to Ireland for a few days, perhaps catching a rugby game, or he could be heading to the sun for a month.

As the years progressed, the trips home to Limerick became more frequent.

'It was only later on in life that we saw Harris at matches,' one Young Munster fan revealed. 'We didn't see Harris at Young Munster matches in the 1960s as such. It was only later on when he came to prominence that he was seen to be a Young Munster man.'

But his commitment was total when it came. He even wore the Young Munster tie in the movie *Patriot Games* in 1992. He played an old IRA man opposite Sean Bean and Harrison Ford. Throughout the 1980s and 1990s Harris became a fixture at Irish internationals, and he also followed Munster and Young Munster.

'He might come over for the odd game. If Munster were in a final he might be there. It depended on what was on. But if he was home, he would come out for the game,' said Tommy Monahan, who was president of Young Munster in 1996/97:

> He used to come out to the club house and enjoy the *craic* on the morning before a Senior Cup game. He'd mix with everyone out there, kids, the whole lot. He enjoyed the *craic*. But when the fucking match was played, we fucking lost. He was a fucking Jonah. He was bad luck for us!

This was a common joke in Limerick rugby circles. Harris was considered to be jinxed. Whenever he showed up, the team underperformed. When Munster lost in the Heineken Cup Final in 2000 to Northampton, Harris was spotted walking out of Twickenham with his friend and fellow actor Peter O'Toole. One of the disgruntled Munster fans shouted at him: 'You're back? With a Man Called Horse and Lawrence of Arabia, we still couldn't fucking win.'

One of the actor's proudest moments came when he was made an honorary life member of Young Munster, at a ceremony before a game in 1990. He swore at the time that he would be cremated in the club jersey; a promise he fulfilled in 2002. And he was prepared to show his commitment in a more practical way, by digging into his pocket.

'He kept promising us money,' said Monahan:

> Then, in 1994, our centenary year, a fellow introduced me to him. And he said – the very words – he'd have it to me within two weeks. I had my doubts – there was a guy asking for ten years for that donation. But within two weeks I got a call to go down to Charlie St George's, that Richard Harris was down there looking for me.

Charlie St George's is a popular rugby pub on Parnell Street, and Harris's favourite watering hole when he was in Limerick. To this day one of the walls is festooned with memorabilia of the actor.

When it came to rugby, Harris was an anorak. He lived and breathed the game. He wrote in the *Telegraph*:

> The heroes of Limerick rugby are my heroes. Gladiators, square-jawed warriors who represent us on the battlefield. They are also heroes off the field – men who can drink, sing and talk of great deeds. I am intensely proud of individuals such as Peter Clohessy, Mick Galwey, Anthony Foley and all the boys. Keith Wood, whose father I used to play alongside, is another hero. He lives the rugby life we all dream of.
>
> I adore Thomond Park, which I could see and hear from my bedroom in our house on the Ennis Road. It is the citadel of Munster rugby; we have never lost a European Cup game there in seven years. If Ireland played there we would never lose.
>
> I would give up all the accolades of my showbiz career to play just once for the senior Munster team. I will never win an Oscar now, but even if I did I would swap it instantly for one sip of champagne from the Heineken Cup.

But living in London, he couldn't make every game. However, he had a plan B. One of his old schoolmates – who had played with him during the Schools Cup competition – was Vincent Finucane. After leaving school Finucane had gone into the electronics business, eventually setting up a very successful television and electronics shop on Upper William Street. When video technology became available, Harris asked Jack Donnelly to find someone to tape the games in Ireland and post them over to him at the Savoy Hotel in London. Finucane got the job:

Seventeen years I was sending him videos. Seventeen years – that's a long time. The girl in the post office would say to me, 'The usual?' From 1985 to his death. VHS was very big at the time. I would faithfully put the full match on the three-hour tape. I could only get one match to a tape. Then wrap it up, bring it to the post office, and off to Richard Harris, the Savoy Hotel.

I went over to the Savoy Hotel at least four or five times, and I met him there three times. First morning I remember, eleven o'clock, big tray came down, teas and coffees, all that kind of thing. Lunch there another time with him. He was so grateful; he was thrilled with the tapes. All the Munster finals and the international matches. He would bring friends of his into the Savoy Hotel, and they would all sit down, drinking and watching the tapes.

Any time he would come to Limerick he would call in to me, to thank me.

Finucane bumped into Harris once when he went to London for a rugby international. One of his old teachers from Crescent College, Fr Bates, asked to go with him. A third man, an elderly pharmacist, also travelled with them. The two men latched on to Finucane because they had never been abroad before or dealt with modern complexities such as the tube system. Finucane recalls:

The match was on at three o'clock. The two old men had me out to the field at a quarter to twelve, and we having three stand tickets! Luckily enough I had two English papers to kill the time. I sat down on the stands, and all I could see was Fr Bates and the chemist, no one else, only stewards tidying up the field. We had to wait until half two before any action happened, or anyone else arrived. Unbelievable.

They enjoyed the match. On the way out we met Harris. Ireland were after winning, and he just said hello to us. He had a great welcome for Fr Bates, because he had taught him.

'Rugby was his passion,' said Harris's brother Noel:

When Dick was an established actor, naturally he could be any place in the world making movies. He arranged to have every international match recorded and the tape to be sent out to him in the Bahamas, or at the Savoy. He built up a library of all these games, and he became an authority on matches. You couldn't argue with him. You daren't, because he was always right on rugby and those matches.

As has been mentioned, towards the end of his life Harris became great friends with Australian hellraiser Russell Crowe. On the set of *Gladiator* they struck up an instant rapport that developed into a deep friendship. While they were both clad in full armour Harris strode up to Crowe saying: 'Am I correct in saying you were born in New Zealand but chose to live in Australia?' When that fact was confirmed the Irish actor continued: 'Then you don't mind if I yell abuse at the Wallabies and talk in hushed tones about the All Blacks?' There followed many deep conversations on a range of topics, including rugby, and Harris expressed his undying love of Limerick and his passionate association with Kilkee. They bought tickets for the Ireland–Australia match scheduled for Lansdowne Road, Dublin, in 2003 but Harris died in the interim. When Crowe got a break from his film commitments he undertook a sentimental journey to Ireland in memory of his friend.

Crowe recalled his pilgrimage:

> I went to Limerick and had a pint of Guinness in Richard's local, Charlie St George's, and went on to sample pints in several others of his favourite pubs. Then I visited the Cliffs of Moher. I found myself in Dublin on the day of the match. The Australians couldn't do a thing right and the Irish ran rings around them. Tears flowed down my face at the final whistle and I was saying silently, Richard you are not dead. You're here to see what you have waited thirty-seven years for, you are here to see Ireland beat the Australians.

This was an incredibly touching tribute to the departed Irish acting giant from an international star who not only shared his passion for the game of rugby but also clearly appreciated an extraordinary man and artist in whom he recognised a kindred spirit.

In 2000 Crowe played a kidnapping expert in *Proof of Life* – and he also wore a Young Munster tie, in tribute to Harris. During his acceptance speech for the BAFTA award for Best Actor for *A Beautiful Mind*, he pinned the producer Malcolm Gerrie to the wall for cutting off his recitation of a Patrick Kavanagh poem in honour of the terminally ill Harris. He would get his opportunity to recite the poem after a memorial service in a hotel with the Harris family, and later to unveil a statue of Harris in Kilkee. A true celluloid soul brother and a recognition of one great actor by another.

EPILOGUE

W hat would make an actor in his declining years, knowing his health was failing, take on a role that would last a decade? All logic would have said that Richard Harris wouldn't walk away from playing Dumbledore in the Harry Potter franchise, he would run away as fast as his arthritic legs would carry him. Yet he chose to take on the eight-film project, knowing his chances of finishing the job were slim. Why? It was all down to a dream – and not even his dream at that. It was the dream of his granddaughter Ella that he play the wise old professor. To understand why, we need to look at how Harris spent his Christmases.

In his 60s he decided to come home for the festive season.

Few places honour their own, and Limerick is no exception. Local writer Frank McCourt discovered that when his book *Angela's Ashes* was a global bestseller – an achievement that got him nothing but derision Shannon-side. He couldn't walk the streets without protesters following him, venting their bile.

But Harris was different. There was something about him that neutralised the instinctive begrudgery of his countrymen. Perhaps it was his larger than life bonhomie, his natural wit, or the fact that he was a 'great *craic*'. But it probably had more to do with the fact that he had long arms and deep pockets.

The Irish drink in rounds. When three friends go to the bar, each one will buy a round of drinks for the others. So three friends means three drinks – or six drinks if they go to the second round; a good sociable night out. The problem creeps in when there are big crowds out on the town together.

Part of what made Harris special was that he did not shy away from the big rounds. He would buy drinks for everyone, and stay drinking until the last man fell or the last drop of Guinness spilled from the barrel. He was a legend in a country known for legendary drunks.

Guinness was his tipple of choice, chased by vodka. Sometimes he varied it with Scotch, and when necessity pressed he would drink anything so long as it was wet and alcoholic. Whenever he was home, his local watering hole was Charlie St George's on Parnell Street, and he would inevitably be still there at closing time.

In his honour, the pub runs a Harris tribute night every year, and they have invented a cocktail – a mix of Guinness, vodka, coca-cola and butterscotch liqueur – that they have called the Harris Hellraiser. The locals avoid it, but the American tourists lap it up. Harris, a decade after his death, is still a tourist draw.

In the 1990s Harris was financially secure and had his drinking fairly under control: no spirits and only a few pints of Guinness; once he had won his battle with the bottle he allowed himself the occasional beer. His children were grown, and the grandchildren were starting to arrive. He was at a stage in his life when he was ready to return to his roots and focus again on his family. He had had a happy childhood, and though his marriages had broken up, he remained on close terms with both exes, and with his children. So why not have a family get-together? In 1994 he decided to bring everyone home for Christmas. Not home to Limerick precisely, but home to a suitable venue for a king and his entourage. He chose Dromoland Castle.

The castle is the sort of gothic concoction that the idle rich loved to build during the height of the Empire. Dromoland had been the seat of the O'Brien's for centuries. The clan are descendants of Brian Boru, the last high king of Ireland. In 1835 they converted the fifteenth-century tower house into a rambling, turreted castle that could have graced one of the fairy tales of Hans Christian Andersen.

In 1962 the money ran out, and the 16th Baron Inchiquin sold the castle and grounds, retaining a small house on the estate. It has since served as a luxury hotel.

In 1994, when Harris decided to return home for Christmas, it seemed like the perfect place. He invited dozens of family members, and footed all the bills. It was an expensive Christmas. Once the decision was taken, Harris phoned the one person he knew could make it happen: his first wife, Elizabeth. Then on her third husband, she ran her own PR company in London, and she made all the arrangements.

As their son Jared said: 'One of the great things about my family is that no matter what's gone before, we've always managed to maintain a sense of togetherness. Mum and dad always got on, even after their divorce, and it was important to both of them that the family should be together at Christmas.'

Elizabeth got stuck in immediately, arranging travel for their three children, their partners, and their children. Family from Limerick were also invited, and she went to efforts to bring people from all over the world for the reunion. Relatives travelled from as far afield as Moscow, Los Angeles, Singapore and Sydney, and as near as 10 miles down the road. All the surviving siblings were there, but there were two notable absentees: his nephew and niece from his brother Dermot were not invited.

Dermot had been his manager, and they had been very close. They had worked together throughout their adult years and shared a passion for the stage. Dermot's marriage to Australian actress Cassandra Waites produced two children (Christopher and Charlotte) but ended in divorce. She went on to marry the Irish actor Pierce Brosnan and had a son with him. A generation younger than Richard, Brosnan achieved fame as James Bond, among other roles.

Three years after that marriage Dermot, aged just 47, died of a heart attack in Chicago. Richard took the death very hard. Brosnan, on the other hand, was pragmatic. He adopted Dermot's two children. Because of this, their name changed from Harris to Brosnan, and Richard took this as a personal affront. To the day he died he never got over his feud with Brosnan, and never spoke to his nephew and niece again. They were cut from his life. Cassandra died of ovarian cancer in 1991, but that was not enough to bring the family together. And they were the only ones not invited to the gathering.

'Richard adored Dermot, and was furious with Pierce for changing the children's names to Brosnan. They had no contact with the Harris family until after his death,' a source close to the family revealed. The two were eventually reconciled with the Harris family about three years after Richard's death in 2002.

But with fifty family members gathered, the two absentees were not missed. A range of activities were planned, including helicopter rides and clay-pigeon shooting. A clown was hired to entertain the children. This was Tony Baloney: 'I was also a reporter with the *Limerick Leader*. My colleague Eugene Phelan had warned me: "He [Harris] isn't a nice man to meet." I found him charming, modest and affable. And his hellraising was firmly behind him. He proved a very easy guest for the hotel.'

Dromoland managing director Mark Nolan remembers that Harris reunion, and the subsequent visits by the actor, fondly:

> Richard was a great character and we loved his visits. He spent a lot of time here and was pretty much part of the furniture. He always came over at Christmas time along with members of his family, and we would have anything from about seventeen to thirty of them staying here during the festive season.

Harris had given up drink in 1981, but like for many Irishmen, giving up the drink was an ambiguous concept. By 1991 Harris was back on the Guinness, and thoroughly enjoying it. Hard liquor was all that was off the menu. He spent much of that Christmas at the bar, holding court. But he was merry rather than drunk. The visit passed off without incident.

'He was a wonderful person, a real character who didn't like conforming,' Mr Nolan remembers. 'Richard always did things when he wanted to, but it was never any trouble for our staff to fix him a meal no matter what time of the day or night he chose to eat. We all loved having him stay here. We were very fond of him.'

The gathering was a great success, despite everything going wrong! 'He had all sorts of wonderful things planned for us – then the weather wrecked his plans,' laughed Noel Harris. The few days of the stay coincided with a storm, and the helicopters and outdoor activities all had to be scrapped. Everyone was confined to the gothic corridors of the castle. Only the children's entertainment was unaffected, as recalled by the clown, Tony Baloney:

I remember doing a magic show for the kids, with about twenty adults watching. It was while doing that show that I encountered Harris for the first time. It was Boxing Day. In Ireland, the day after Christmas is known as St Stephen's Day, or Wren Day. Traditionally, groups of young people walk from house to house carrying a stuffed wren and doing impromptu shows. They collect money and food for a big party that evening. Harris would have grown up with the tradition. He would have gone on the Wren as a child. He would have been home when the Wren Boys called. So it would have felt right to have sat in the hotel with his family while the strolling players staged their show.

Rather than use one of the big and soulless function rooms, I had set up my show in a wide corridor close to the hotel reception. There was plush red carpeting on the floor, and dark wood-panelled walls. The parents sat on chairs running down the walls, while the children sat on the floor. There were about a dozen children, including Harris's grandchildren, nephews and nieces. Near the front was one of the youngest, a lively dark-haired girl of around 5.

Ella was the daughter of Damian, Harris's eldest son, and his wife, actress Annabel Brooks. She was engrossed in the magic, shouting and cheering louder than the others. I was about twenty minutes into the show when Harris arrived, though 'made an entrance' would be more accurate.

The veteran actor swept into the room. He was no longer a handsome man. Too many hard years had etched their lessons on his face. He was weathered, and his long grey hair flowed dramatically around his shoulders. He was wearing a grey sports coat, and he could have passed for a farmer on a casual glance. But he carried a charge of charisma. Even if you had not seen him enter the room, you would have known that someone had come in. The atmosphere changed.

Immediately there was a silence, and all eyes turned to the new arrival. What I was doing was temporarily forgotten. Harris walked into the centre of the room, apparently oblivious to the stir he was causing. All the children turned towards him, warm smiles of welcome on their faces. He swept young Ella into his arms and began to dance her around him.

Then he noticed that he had stumbled into the middle of a show, and he stopped his little dance. Gently he deposited Ella on the floor from where he had plucked her. He straightened up, grinned at me, and nodded apologetically.

'Sorry about that,' he said, then walked over to the side, taking one of the chairs. I tried to resume the show, but after a few minutes he was still sucking the attention. Realising it, he stood up and tiptoed past me, then strode down the corridor and around the corner into the bar.

Afterwards he bought me a pint. I asked him had he tried the clay-pigeon shooting, but he just smiled. Christmas for him was eat, drink and be merry – indoors. It was more about being surrounded by the people he loved than anything else. The only effort he put in over the couple of days was when he dressed in red to play Father Christmas for the kids. Although he was enjoying his drink that evening, I saw no evidence of the legendary hellraiser. That was a role he would not be reprising.

The following year Harris returned to Dromoland. This time the hotel had a resident magician, illusionist Peter Blackthorn. He had been entertaining diners at the company parties in the build-up to Christmas, and the hotel called him in to entertain the actor's family. The event was far smaller – just a couple of the close family members joined Richard at the castle. For the next number of years that was the pattern. After the first gathering there were no more big productions. It was a smaller and more personal celebration of family and Christmas.

Blackthorn is an old-fashioned illusionist. He dresses in the tails and frills, while doing classic dove productions from balls of fire at his fingertips. His look perfectly gelled with the ancient castle. He carries himself with an aloof dignity, softened with a mischievous twinkle in his eye. The children loved him.

'Despite their money they were perfectly ordinary children,' Blackthorn said. 'They loved the show. I remember Ella well. She lapped it up.'

Harris didn't watch the show, but enjoyed some magic at the bar afterwards.

'He was a gentleman. I had been expecting an ogre, but he was charming and polite. He tried to buy me a drink, but I was working, so I said no,' said Blackthorn. 'He told me I was a fool, and I'd never get anyplace in showbusiness. All the great performers were great drinkers, he said. But he was laughing. I enjoyed his company.'

Unknown to Harris, he shared a tenuous connection with the illusionist. When he was a young man in Limerick, still playing rugby and working for his father's haulage firm, he had tried to date Blackthorn's mother.

'She often spoke about it,' said Blackthorn. 'He was a charmer, but he was a bit too rough for her back then, and she said no. He mentioned her once years later on a television show as one of the ones who got away, and she was delighted.'

Blackthorn performed for the Harris clan over a couple of years at Dromoland, and what struck him most was the close connection between the actor and his young grandchildren. 'They loved him – and he was mad about them,' he said.

With the family spread all over the world, it was those Christmas gatherings that kept them together. The few days in County Clare every year forged links that time did not erode. Those links were what finally drew Harris into the world of Harry Potter, and introduced him to a whole new generation of fans. They allowed him to end his career as he had begun, in a blaze of glory.

The Harry Potter franchise is one of the most successful in all of fiction. The seven books by J.K. Rowling, about a boy magician in a school of wizards, sold 450 million copies in sixty-seven different languages. In 1998 Rowling sold the rights of the first two books to Warner Brothers for a reputed $1 million. A notoriously controlling writer, she insisted that she have a say in the casting. She did not want any American stars; she wanted a British cast in order to preserve the feel of the books. She did relent, however, and allow other European actors to be considered.

Casting began in early 2000, and Richard Harris was approached to play the headmaster of Hogwarts, Albus Dumbledore. Already 69, and with his health failing, he declined the role. Other actors were considered, including fellow Irishman Peter O'Toole. But Harris was the man the director, Chris Columbus, wanted. He was asked a second time. Again he turned down the role.

'All I knew is that they kept offering me the part, and raising the salary every time they called,' he joked later that year.

He had not read the Potter books, but he knew all about them, and that several of his grandchildren were fans. Perhaps Hogwarts reminded them of watching magicians perform in the gothic surroundings of Dromoland.

'I've never read the books, of course, but I have a lot of respect for J.K. Rowling. She has an amazing mind,' he said.

But he knew that she was planning seven books, and if the movie was a success, there would be sequels. He could be committing to a decade of work on a single project. 'Anyone involved had to agree to be in the sequels, all of them, and that's not how I wanted to spend the last years of my life. So I said no, over and over again.'

The director asked a third time, with another hefty pay rise. Harris was all ready to say no. He had his legacy secured. He had more than enough money. Then his granddaughter Ella, by then 11, intervened. It was the final turn of the screw, and Harris was no longer able to resist the pressure.

'It was Ella, who's 11 years old, and whom I worship with all my life,' Harris smiled. 'She said, "Papa, I hear you're not going to be in the Harry Potter movie." And she said, "If you don't play Dumbledore, then I will never speak to you again."'

It was a fate worse than the cruciatus curse. Harris bowed to the inevitable and signed up to his final great role. But he turned down the big fee the producers were offering him. He took the role for free – and insisted instead on a percentage of the merchandising. He drove a hard bargain. In the end they gave in. None of the others did as well out of Harry Potter as Richard Harris. The shrewd business sense in his genetic make-up, inherited from his grandfather and great-grandfather, had not deserted him.

'I may have to do the whole lot of these Harry Potter movies. And I agreed to do them all for free,' he said. 'But I wanted 2½ per cent of the royalties from the merchandising. They're anticipating £700 million in profits. That's 2½ per cent of 700 million. And they told me, we'll pay you any money you like, but you're not getting any piece of the picture!'

They were wrong; he got his agreement. After his death, his replacement as Dumbledore, Michael Gambon, was back on a salary like every other actor.

Harris said at the time:

But the acting is perfect. It only lasts about ten weeks. Then I have the rest of the time to go to the pub, and have free time. Was it a good career move at my age? I don't know – I mean, I'm at the pinnacle of my decline!

It was an unfortunate truth, but Richard Harris had always the measure of himself and a far more accurate assessment than any other observer of his personal journey or his career. His intellect and his talent had always dwarfed the so-called experts. If he was in decline no one knew it better than himself. He was a giant and a maverick to the last.

APPENDIX

December 1987 Interview – *Hot Press*, Joe Jackson.

Jackson:

For here is a vastly underrated body of work which could be said to make a lie of his public image. There were those critically acclaimed concept albums (both written by Jim Webb) 'A Tramp Shining' and 'The Yard Went On Forever'. Also 'My Boy' (in part composed by Harris) which mercilessly captured almost all the pain caused by a broken marriage. And the book of his own poetry *I, In the Membership of My Days*, which though flawed contained at least two blindingly beautiful poems one about the death of his sister; the other about the death of his father.

The problem is of course, that Harris, like many Hollywood stars prefers to stage manage his own interviews. He is a master of leading interviewers through a merry dance of dazzling tales, anecdotes which though highly entertaining rarely reveal more than peripheral truths about the man. But then he was fond of saying the truth can be dull.

Harris on interviews:

You cut the cloth according to the suit. Jonathan Ross does not want anything in depth, nor do people like Johnny Carson. He'd always come into my dressing room before the airing and say: 'Keep it funny, keep it funny.' But although the old format of telling stories and jokes seems to be what the public wants, I have no fear of discussing my private life – at least those parts that should be made public. But I do not believe what you seem to be hinting at: because one makes one's living from the public does not mean that they are entitled to devour your private life. They are entitled to a good performance – that is all.

Jackson:

You don't think that the audience can get a stronger sense of the art if they know more about its creator?

Harris:

I think the very opposite, for example I know Peter O'Toole for more than twenty years and yet I don't know him at all. What is more important is that the mystery was preserved. I love to go and see him maybe because I don't know enough about him. Similarly the persona projected by Garbo has lasted right into her eighties – she is still a star because she was always an enigma. Whereas Bette Davis, same era, wonderful person, we have to admire her but more than that now she comes across as an old bitch.

Harris on films:

I haven't done a picture for four or five years because I get bored out of my skull doing them. I had made enough money so I stopped. I was offered *The Name of the Rose* and Shirley McLaine's last movie but I turned them down because I knew I would be bored. I was happier doing *Camelot* every night on stage for three years than doing any kind of movie. I loved working again in front of a live audience.

In the beginning I did try to do interesting movies but there comes a time when you are faced with obligations. You have a wife to support and children and want them to have what you didn't have. You can't support that on art films. I remember the day I made the choice. I am not making excuses, they were the realities. I had children and we were living in a flat in London, all of us sleeping together in two rooms and though there was no pressure from Elizabeth, I sat down and said: 'I have a choice between *The Luck of Ginger Coffey*, a fantastic piece but will only pay what I got for *Sporting Life* or I can get a fortune to do *Major Dundee* in Hollywood.' The latter is the choice I made. The right choice I still believe.

If I had my life to live over I would do the same things again. The only difference in terms of my career is that I wouldn't stay away from the stage so long. From 1964 to 1981 was a mistake which I have acknowledged but in the end I have done more than most.

Irish Times, Friday 31 December 1993

Joe Jackson asked people from the arts to choose their artistic highlight from the year.

Harris:

A definite highlight of 1993 was reading Marguerite Duras's book *Summer Rain*. What she does with her writing I wish I could do with my acting. All art has the same disciplines and here is a woman whose books like *Summer Rain*, *The Lover* and *Sailor From Gibraltar*, all show her to be a great artist because she writes and then subtracts and subtracts and keeps subtracting until you are down to the bare essence of what the book is about.

All art should be like that including acting. I have a tendency to give too much but the secret is to subtract like she does. A lesser writer would say something like: 'As I moved across the mountains the sun hit the edge of the sea, throwing sparkles of stars across the horizon that was moving at a feverish pace beyond a scope my eyes could grasp.'

She writes: 'Morning. Stars moving fast. I moved on.' That's all you need to know. Your imagination puts in the rest.

The actor's analysis is revealing in so far as his own art is concerned, the cliché goes that less is more and yet in his case, he admits that was not true. He was not a method actor and all within the ambit of his particular talent, all the better for it. His style was simply different. He had a very valid point but of course, acting and writing, by their very nature, are different disciplines, despite his protestation to the contrary.

And with a certain irony his version of the passage he offers to praise Duras is not half bad, in some ways redolent of that great writer F. Scott Fitzgerald. It is not to say that it diminishes his point but is some, if even thin proof that Harris could have exercised a talent for writing that would not have satisfied the tenet of his admiration for Duras but would have definitely been his own form of expression. Lesser, perhaps, but effective in its own fashion.

Monday 21 January 2013, *Daily Telegraph*

Michael Gambon received the Richard Harris award at the Moet British Independent Film awards in London. The 72-year-old actor was honoured for his long and distinguished career. The award was particularly poignant as Gambon had replaced Harris as Dumbledore in *Harry Potter* after the Irish actor's death. 'I knew him and he died and I took over his part in the Harry Potter films. He did only two and I did six films and all I did was copy Richard.'

Michael Winner, speaking after Harris's death

The lights have dimmed a lot with his passing. He was my neighbour for ten years and he was the most wonderful warm character. He was not only a great friend and wonderful person to be with he was one of our greatest actors and had this great charisma as a star which extended to his private life. He was the archetypal star, he was like an old Hollywood legend.

Michael Parkinson

'He was an extraordinary man, a great story teller, very intelligent.' Parkinson, who interviewed him three times, devoting one whole show to him on one occasion, added: 'He was a hellraiser – it's a cliché – but that is what he was and from the old school of stars like Peter O'Toole, strolling players, guys who love life.'

FILMOGRAPHY

ALIVE AND KICKING (1958)
Director: Cyril Frankel
Role: Lover
Cast: Sybil Thorndike, Kathleen Harrison, Liam Redmond, Stanley Holloway

SHAKE HANDS WITH THE DEVIL (1959)
Director: Michael Anderson
Role: Terence O'Brien
Cast: James Cagney, Don Murray, Dana Wynter, Cyril Cusack, Michael Redgrave, Glynis Johns, Sybil Thorndike, Niall McGinnis, Ray McAnally, Noel Purcell

THE WRECK OF THE MARY DEARE (1959)
Director: Michael Anderson
Role: Second Mate Higgins
Cast: Gary Cooper, Charlton Heston, Michael Redgrave, Emlyn Williams, Cecil Parker, Alexander Knox, Virginia McKenna

A TERRIBLE BEAUTY (1960)
Director: Tay Garnett
Role: Sean Reilly
Cast: Robert Mitchum, Anne Heywood, Dan O'Herlihy, Cyril Cusack, Marianne Benet

THE LONG AND THE SHORT AND THE TALL (1960)
Director: Leslie Norman
Role: Corporal Johnston
Cast: Laurence Harvey, Richard Todd, David McCallum, Ronald Fraser, John Meillon, John Rees, Kenji Takaki

THE GUNS OF NAVARONE (1961)
Director: J. Lee Thompson
Role: Squadron Leader Howard Barnsby
Cast: Gregory Peck, David Niven, Stanley Baker, Anthony Quayle, James Darren, Gia Scala, James Robertson Justice, Irene Papas, Bryan Forbes

MUTINY ON THE BOUNTY (1962)
Director: Lewis Milestone
Role: Seaman John Mills
Cast: Marlon Brando, Trevor Howard, Hugh Griffith, Tarita, Percy Herbert, Gordon Jackson, Chips Rafferty, Noel Purcell

THIS SPORTING LIFE (1963)
Director: Lindsay Anderson
Role: Frank Machin
Cast: Rachel Roberts, Colin Blakeley, Alan Badel, William Hartnett, Vanda Godsell, Arthur Lowe, Leonard Rossiter

RED DESERT (IL DESERTO ROSSO) (1964)
Director: Michelangelo Antonioni
Role: Corrado Zeller
Cast: Monica Vitti, Carlo Chionetti, Xenia Valderi, Rita Renoir, Lili Rheims

MAJOR DUNDEE (1965)
Director: Sam Peckinpah
Role: Captain Benjamin Tyreen
Cast: Charlton Heston, Jim Hutton, James Coburn, Michael Anderson Jnr, Warren Oates, Senta Berger, Slim Pickens

I TRE VOLTI (THE THREE FACES) (1965)
Directors: Michelangelo Antonioni, Mauro Bolognini, Franco Indovino
Role: Robert

THE HEROES OF TELEMARK (1965)
Director: Anthony Mann
Role: Knut Straud
Cast: Kirk Douglas, Ulla Jacobsson, Michael Redgrave, Roy Dotrice, Anton Diffring, David Weston, Eric Porter, Maurice Denham

LA BIBBIA (THE BIBLE) (1966)
Director: John Huston
Role: Cain
Cast: Ava Gardner, John Huston, Peter O'Toole, George C. Scott, Stephen Boyd

HAWAII (1966)
Director: George Roy Hill
Role: Rafer Hoxworth
Cast: Julie Andrews, Max von Sydow, Gene Hackman, Carroll O'Connor, Robert Oakley

CAPRICE (1967)
Director: Frank Tashlin
Role: Christoper White
Cast: Doris Day, Michael J. Pollard, Lilia Skala, Lisa Seagram

CAMELOT (1967)
Director: Joshua Logan
Role: King Arthur
Cast: Vanessa Redrgrave, Franco Nero, David Hemmings, Lionel Jeffries, Estelle Winwood, Gary Marshall, Anthony Rogers

CROMWELL (1970)
Director: Ken Hughes
Role: Cromwell
Cast: Alec Guinness, Dorothy Tutin, Frank Finlay, Patrick Wymark, Patrick Magee, Timothy Dalton

A MAN CALLED HORSE (1970)
Director: Elliot Silverstein
Role: John Morgan
Cast: Corinna Tsopei, Manu Tupou, Dame Judith Anderson, James Gammon, Lina Marin

THE MOLLY MAGUIRES (1970)
Director: Martin Ritt
Role: James McParlan/McKenna
Cast: Sean Connery, Samantha Eggar, Frank Finlay, Francis Heflin, John Alderson

THE SNOW GOOSE (1971, BBC)
Director: Patrick Garland
Role: Philip Rhayader

MAN IN THE WILDERNESS (1971)
Director: Richard C. Sarafian
Role: Zachary Bass
Cast: John Huston, Prunella Ransome, Percy Herbert, Denis Waterman, John Bindon

BLOOMFIELD (1971)
Director: Richard Harris, Uri Zohar
Role: Eitan
Cast: Romy Schneider, Kim Burfield, Maurice Kaufmann, David Heyman

THE DEADLY TRACKERS (1973)
Director: Barry Shear
Role: Sheriff Sean Kilpatrick
Cast: Rod Taylor, Al Lettieri, Neville Brand, Isela Vega

99 AND 44/100% DEAD (1974)
Director: John Frankenheimer
Role: Harry Crown
Cast: Edmond O'Brien, Ann Turkel, Constance Ford, Bradford Dillman, Jerry Summers

JUGGERNAUT (1974)
Director: Richard Lester
Role: Fallon
Cast: Omar Sharif, Anthony Hopkins, Freddie Jones, Roy Kinnear, Cyril Cusack, Shirley Knight

RANSOM (1975)
Director: Casper Wrede
Role: Gerald Palmer
Cast: Sean Connery, Ian McShane, Isabel Dean, William Fox, Richard Hampton

ECHOES OF A SUMMER (1975)
Director: Don Taylor

Role: Eugene Striden
Cast: Geraldine Fitzgerald, Jodie Foster, William Windom, Brad Savage

ROBIN AND MARIAN (1976)
Director: Richard Lester
Role: Richard the Lionheart
Cast: Sean Connery, Audrey Hepburn, Robert Shaw, Nicol Williamson, Ian Holm

THE RETURN OF A MAN CALLED HORSE (1976)
Director: Irvin Kershner
Role: John Morgan
Cast: Gale Sondergaard, Geoffrey Lewis, William Lucking, Pedro Damian

THE CASSANDRA CROSSING (1976)
Director: George Pan Cosmatos
Role: Dr Jonathan Chamberlain
Cast: Sophia Loren, Martin Sheen, Ava Gardner, Burt Lancaster, Ingrid Thulin, Lee Strasberg, Lionel Stander, Ann Turkel

GULLIVER'S TRAVELS (1976)
Director: Peter Hunt
Role: Gulliver
Cast: Michael Bates, Julian Glover, Catherine Schell, Bessie Love

GOLDEN RENDEZVOUS (1977)
Director: Ashley Lazarus
Role: John Carter
Cast: David Janssen, Burgess Meredith, Ann Turkel, Gordon Jackson, John Carradine

ORCA, THE KILLER WHALE (1977)
Director: Michael Anderson
Role: Captain Nolan
Cast: Charlotte Rampling, Will Sampson, Keenan Wynn

THE WILD GEESE (1978)
Director: Andrew V. McLaglen
Role: Captain Rafer Janders
Cast: Richard Burton, Roger Moore, Hardy Kruger, Barry Foster, Kenneth Griffith, Ronald Fraser, Percy Herbert, Jane Hylton

RAVAGERS (1979)
Director: Richard Compton
Role: Falk
Cast: Ernest Borgnine, Anthony James, Ann Turkel, Woody Strode, Alana Stewart

THE LAST WORD (1979)
Director: Roy Boulting
Role: Danny Travis
Cast: Karen Black, Martin Landau, Christopher Guest, Penelope Milford

GAME FOR VULTURES (1979)
Director: James Fargo
Role: David Swansey
Cast: Richard Roundtree, Denholm Elliott, Ray Milland, Mark Singleton, Sydney Chama

YOUR TICKET IS NO LONGER VALID (1981)
Director: George Kaczender
Role: Jason
Cast: George Peppard, Jean Moreau, Alexander Stewart, Michael Kane

TARZAN THE APE MAN (1981)
Director: John Derek
Role: James Parker
Cast: Bo Derek, Miles O'Keeffe, Phillip Law, Wilfred Hyde White

THE TRIUMPHS OF A MAN CALLED HORSE (1982)
Director: John Hough
Role: John Morgan
Cast: Michael Beck, Anna De Sade

HIGHPOINT (1984)
Director: Peter Carter
Role: Lewis Kinney
Cast: Christopher Plummer, Beverley D'Angelo, Saul Rubinek, Kate Reid

MARTIN'S DAY (1985)
Director: Alan Gibson
Role: Martin Steckert
Cast: Lindsay Wagner, James Coburn, Karen Black, John Ireland

WETHERBY (1985)
Director: David Hare
Role: Sir Thomas
Cast: Vanessa Redgrave, Ian Holm, Judi Dench, Suzanna Hamilton, Tom Wilkinson

STRIKE COMMANDO 2 (1989)
Director: Bruno Mattei
Role: (not established)
Cast: Brent Huff, Mary Stavin, Mel Davidson, Jim Gaines, Vic Diaz

MAIGRET (1988, TV)
Director: Paul Lynch
Role: Maigret

MACK THE KNIFE (1989)
Director: Menahem Golan
Role: Peachum
Cast: Roger Daltry, Miranda Garrison, Russell Gold, Julie Walters

KING OF THE WIND (1989)
Director: Peter Duffell
Role: King George II
Cast: Ian Richardson, Frank Finlay, Jenny Agutter, Glenda Jackson, Norman Rodway

THE FIELD (1990)
Director: Jim Sheridan
Role: Bull McCabe
Cast: John Hurt, Tom Berenger, Sean Bean, Frances Tomelty, Brenda Fricker, Joan Sheehy

PATRIOT GAMES (1992)
Director: Phillip Noyce
Role: Paddy O Neil
Cast: Harrison Ford, Anne Archer, Sean Bean, Patrick Bergin, James Fox, Samuel L. Jackson

UNFORGIVEN (1992)
Director: Clint Eastwood
Role: English Bob
Cast: Clint Eastwood, Morgan Freeman, Gene Hackman, Saul Rubinek

SILENT TONGUE (1993)
Director: Sam Shepard
Role: Prescott Roe
Cast: Alan Bates, River Phoenix, Dermot Mulroney, David Shiner, Bill Irwin

WRESTLING ERNEST HEMINGWAY (1993)
Director: Randa Haines
Role: Frank
Cast: Robert Duvall, Shirley MacLaine, Sandra Bullock, Piper Laurie

CRY, THE BELOVED COUNTRY (1995)
Director: Darrel Roodt
Role: James Jarvis
Cast: James Earl Jones, Jack Robinson, King Twala, John Whiteley, Vusi Kunene, Leleti Khumalo

THE GREAT KANDINSKY (1995, BBC)
Director: Terry Windsor
Role: Ernest Kandinsky

SAVAGE HEARTS (1996)
Director: Mark Ezra
Role: Sir Roger Foxley
Cast: Jamie Harris, Stephen Marcus, Angus Deayton, Jerry Hall, Julian Fellowes

THIS IS THE SEA (1996)
Director: Mary McGuckian
Role: Old Man Jacobs
Cast: Gabriel Byrne, John Lynch, Dearbhla Molloy, Ian McElhinney

THE HUNCHBACK (1997)
Director: Peter Medak
Role: Dom Frollo

TROJAN EDDIE (1997)
Director: Gillies MacKinnon
Role: John Power
Cast: Stephen Rea, Brendan Gleeson, Angeline Ball, Brid Brennan, Sean McGinley, Maria McDermottroe

SMILLA'S SENSE OF SNOW (1997)
Director: Billie August
Role: Dr Andreas Tork
Cast: Gabriel Byrne, Julia Ormond, Vanessa Redgrave, Jim Broadbent, Bob Peck

GRIZZLY FALLS (1999)
Director: Stewart Raffill
Role: Old Harry
Cast: Bryan Brown, Oliver Tobias, Trevor Lowden, Chantel Dick.

TO WALK WITH LIONS (1999)
Director: Carl Schultz
Role: George Adamson
Cast: John Michie, Ian Bannen, Kerry Fox, Honor Blackman, Omar Godana, Geraldine Chaplin

THE BARBER OF SIBERIA (1999)
Director: Nikita Miklhalkov
Role: Makkreken
Cast: Julia Ormond, Isabelle Renauld, Oleg Menshikov, Vladimir Ilyin, Mac McDonald, Alexander Yakovlev

GLADIATOR (2000)
Director: Ridley Scott
Role: Marcus Aurelius
Cast: Russell Crowe, Joaquin Phoenix, Connie Nielson, Oliver Reed, Derek Jacobi, David Hemmings

THE PEARL (2001)
Director: Alfredo Zacharias
Role: Dr Karl
Cast: Lukas Haas, Jorge Rivero, Ryan James

HARRY POTTER AND THE PHILOSOPHER'S STONE (2001)
Director: Chris Columbus
Role: Albus Dumbledore
Cast: Daniel Radcliffe, Rupert Grint, Emma Watson, Gary Oldman, Alan Rickman, Robbie Coltrane, Maggie Smith, Emma Thompson, Julie Christie

THE APOCALYPSE (2002)
Director: Raffaele Mertes
Role: St John/Thephilius
Cast: Vittoria Belvedere, Benjamin Sadler, Erol Sander, Ian Duncan Bruce Payne, Luca Ward

THE COUNT OF MONTE CRISTO (2002)
Director: Kevin Reynolds
Role: Abbé Faria
Cast: Jim Caviezel, Guy Pearce, Luis Guzmán, Alex Norton, Freddie Jones

HARRY POTTER AND THE CHAMBER OF SECRETS (2002)
Director: Chris Columbus
Role: Albus Dumbledore
Cast: Daniel Radcliffe, Rupert Grint, Emma Watson, Kenneth Branagh, John Cleese, Robbie Coltrane, Warwick Davis, Alan Rickman, Richard Griffiths, Jason Isaacs, Fiona Shaw, Maggie Smith

JULIUS CAESAR (2002, US TV)
Director: Udi Edel
Role: Lucius Sulla

MY KINGDOM (2002)
Director: Don Boyd
Role: Sandeman
Cast: Lynn Redgrave, Jimi Mistry, Tom Bell, Aidan Gillen, Paul McGann

KAENA: THE PROPHECY (2002)
Director: Chris Delaporte, Pascal Pinon.
Role: Opaz
Cast: Kirsten Dunst, Angelica Huston, Keith David, Michael McShane, Greg Proops

BIBLIOGRAPHY

Anderson, Lindsay. *Never Apologise* (London, Plexus, 2003)

Brando, Marlon. *Brando: Songs My Mother Taught Me* (London, Century, 1994)

Callan, M.F. *Richard Harris: Sex, Death and the Movies* (London, Robson Books, 2003)

Doyle, Mick. *Doyler* (Dublin, Gill and MacMillan, 1991)

Doyle, Mick. *Zero Point One Six* (Edinburgh, Mainstream, 2001)

Goodwin, C. *Behaving Badly: The Life of Richard Harris* (London, Virgin, 2003)

Halliwell, Leslie. *Film and Video Guide* (London, Harper Collins, 2005)

Harris, Richard. *I, In The Membership of My Days*

Harrison, Elizabeth. *Love, Honour and Dismay* (London, Weidenfeld and Nicolson, 1976)

Hillier, Jim. *The New Hollywood* (London, Studio Vista, 1993)

Jackson, Carlton. *Picking Up the Tab: The Life and Movies of Martin Ritt* (Ohio, Bowling Green, 1994)

Prendergast T. and S. (eds). *International Dictionary of Film and Filmmakers*, fourth edition (London, St James's Press, 2000)

Smith, G. *Richard Harris: Actor By Accident* (London, Robert Hale, 1990)

Storey, David. *This Sporting Life* (London, Vintage, 2000)

Thomson, David. *The New Biographical Dictionary of Film* (London, Little Brown, 2002)

Walker, Alexander. *Hollywood England: The British Film Industry of the Sixties* (Michael Joseph, 1974)

Wogan, Terry. *Is It Me* (BBC Worldwide, 2000)

Newspapers and journals

The Irish Times, The Times, New York Times, Guardian, Irish Press, Limerick Leader, Limerick Chronicle, Daily Mirror, Daily Mail, The Sun, Hollywood Reporter, Variety

Hot Press interview by Joe Jackson, 1987

ACKNOWLEDGEMENTS

A number of people were very generous with their time and expertise during the preparation of this book. In no particular order we would like to thank the following people.

Richard Harris's only surviving sibling, Noel Harris. Lifelong friend Manuel Di Lucia and Dickie's other friends who spoke to us, including Vincent Finucane and Kevin O'Connor. Editor Alan English and news editor Eugene Phelan of the *Limerick Leader*. The patrons of Quinlan's Bar and Charlie St George's in Limerick. Tommy Monahan of Young Munster Rugby Club. Illusionist Peter Blackthorn and magician Tony Baloney. Ronan O'Leary for his time and invaluable expertise. And all the Limerick people who shared their stories of the great man.

We thank them, but the opinions in the book are our own. Any errors that may have crept in are entirely our fault!

INDEX

f you enjoyed this book, you may also be interested in…

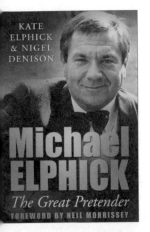

Michael Elphick

KATE ELPHICK WITH NIGEL DENISON

Discovered by Laurence Olivier as a young electrician, Michael Elphick's most famous role was in one of the most popular British films of all time: *Withnail and I.* Elphick's illustrious career also included major supporting roles in films such as *Quadrophenia* and *The Elephant Man.* He appeared on television in much-loved soaps *Coronation Street* and *Eastenders,* as well as in *Schultz* and *Boon.* However, Elphick's private life was every bit as varied as his career. Racked by alcoholism and devastated by the early death of his partner, Elphick died at the age of 55. Join Kate Elphick and Nigel Denison as they present the first comprehensive biography of the renowned character actor.

978 0 7524 9147 9

Harry H. Corbett

SUSANNAH CORBETT

Harry H. Corbett rose from the slums of Manchester to become one of the best-known television stars of the twentieth century. Widely respected as a classical stage actor, his life was changed forever by his part in *Steptoe and Son.* However, the show business couldn't hide the scars he bore from his time in the Royal Marines during the Second World War, when he saw first hand the devastation wrought by the Hiroshima bomb. Naturally shy and a committed socialist, fame and fortune didn't sit easily on his shoulders until his untimely death at the age of only 57. Written by his daughter, this is the first biography of Harry H. Corbett, the man who was once described as 'the English Marlon Brando'.

978 0 7524 7682 7

Alastair Sim

MARK SIMPSON

Supported by extensive research and an interview with playwright Christopher Fry, Simpson examines Alastair's roles in the Quota Quickie films of the 1930s/40s before he became established as the most idiosyncratic star of screen in such famous British comedies as *The Happiest Days of Your Life* and *The Belles of St Trinians.* He goes on to explain why his popularity suddenly waned as the cinemagoers taste for the risque evolved during the latter part of the 1950s. Alastair's life outside of films, including his marriage to Naomi Sim whom he first met when she was 12, his extensive work on stage, his championing of the 'youth' and his stalwart refusal to sign autographs are also explored.

978 0 7509 4966 8

Visit our website and discover thousands of other History Press books.

www.thehistorypress.co.uk